GIVE WORK

Give Work

REVERSING POVERTY
ONE JOB AT A TIME

Leila Janah

PORTFOLIO/PENGUIN

Portfolio/Penguin
An imprint of Penguin Random House LLC
375 Hudson Street
New York, New York 10014

Most Portfolio books are available at a discount when purchased in quantity for sales promotions or corporate use. Special editions, which include personalized covers, excerpts, and corporate imprints, can be created when purchased in large quantities. For more information, please call (212) 572-2232 or e-mail specialmarkets@penguinrandomhouse.com. Your local bookstore can also assist with discounted bulk purchases using the Penguin Random House corporate Business-to-Business program. For assistance in locating a participating retailer, e-mail B2B@penguinrandomhouse.com.

ISBN 9780735211896 (hardcover)
ISBN 9780735211902 (e-book)

Printed in the United States of America
1 3 5 7 9 10 8 6 4 2

Book design by Daniel Lagin

For SAC and ATJ, who remind me of my better angels

CONTENTS

GIVE WORK

INTRODUCTION

I N DECEMBER 2015, I WAS RACING AROUND, TRYING NOT TO SLIP ON the high-gloss floor of a Mission District tech incubator that had allowed me to use its gleaming contemporary space to host my very first "un-gala." For years my nonprofit, Samasource, had thrown big, fancy black-tie parties to entertain and impress wealthy philanthropists so that they would support our mission to give living-wage work to the poorest people in the world via impact sourcing—a company practice of intentionally hiring the destitute and marginalized. But we had finally decided there was something a little unseemly about spending three hundred thousand dollars to throw a party so people could get dressed up to talk about solutions to poverty. So we decided to scale back and hold an un-gala to raise money, inviting only our core hundred or so donors who we knew cared deeply about our cause. It would be free, casual, a lot less work for our staff, and, we hoped, still a lot of fun. The theme was "Your First Job," and I was dressed as a 1990s legal secretary, which was how I earned my first paycheck back in high school. Hence the heels and the danger of slipping.

After dashing around, checking on the only decorations in the industrial, red-accented room—small, white floral centerpieces placed in the middle of a few cloth-covered bar tables—I went over to a group of my staff who were reviewing the guest list. As I leaned over their shoulders to see, I heard one of them say, "Hey, does anyone know who this person is? Vanessa Kanyi?"

I could not believe it.

Vanessa Lucky Kanyi was one of Samasource's very first employees, a data-entry operator in Nairobi who had done transcription work for one of our early contracts for bestselling author Tim Ferriss. Prior to working with us, she had been slowly trying to earn a psychology degree at Mount Kenya University, living in a Nairobi slum while earning less than a dollar a day in a dead-end job. "It was rough," she would say later. "It's not money you can live on." At eighteen, she was, in fact, lucky to have a job at all—youth unemployment in Kenya hovers around 35 percent. Unofficially, it's 70 percent—in a place like Kenya where so many work in the informal economy, it's hard to get concrete numbers.

It didn't take long for us to notice Vanessa at Samasource; she was a quick learner and did her job with speed and precision. When the Tim Ferriss job was done, Samasource connected her to a Canadian client who hired her as a virtual assistant. Over the three years she worked with Samasource, Vanessa was involved in increasingly complex projects, eventually moving into quality control, then becoming a supervisor and finally a manager overseeing a job that took her to West Africa. By then she was earning enough to complete her university degree, but she had reevaluated her priorities. "It was kind of a funny conversation with myself," she says. "School? I had a chance to go to West Africa!" And now, unbelievably, she was in California on the guest list to our un-gala.

I was so excited I quickly grabbed my phone and called the number next to her name. She answered and good-naturedly answered my hundred questions. It turns out that in 2013, she was invited to speak at the fourth annual international Social Good Summit about how impact sourcing could help turn around youth unemployment rates in Africa. The Social Good Summit is a yearly three-day conference held during

UN week in New York City where the likes of Malala Yousafzai, Melinda Gates, and more than two hundred of the world's leading innovators and thinkers get together to discuss how technology can solve global problems. There, Vanessa explained to hundreds how the skills and opportunity she'd gained through impact sourcing had changed her life and that of many others.

Inspired by her few days in New York City—"I looked around and thought, 'Cool!'"—she decided to apply for a scholarship at Santa Monica Community College in California, where she had a distant relative. She got it, and now she was living in Los Angeles working part time as a nursing assistant and getting a degree in engineering, which she had decided would serve her better in the short term than a degree in psychology. She had taken the day off from work and headed to the airport as soon as she was done with her morning class to be with us that night.

I confess that I put her on the spot that evening by asking her to do a short Q&A in front of our guests. She graciously agreed. Poised and elegant in her black suit, her hair pulled neatly back from her high, round forehead, she spoke slowly and softly about everything she had accomplished since she'd left that first job that promised nothing but a hardscrabble day-to-day existence. She explained the difference impact sourcing made to slum dwellers, and how it gave them what they desperately needed—a chance to make enough money to go to school, support their families, and even create a business. She revealed that she had developed a strong interest in philanthropy. "I can't just sit around and watch everything crumble when I can do something about it."

It was an incredibly moving moment. Standing before us was a perfect example of what kind of talent is being wasted every day because of our tendency to dismiss the poor, and what they can achieve when given a fighting chance. Vanessa represented the culmination of everything we were trying to do at Samasource. In fact, she showed us our efforts had paid off beyond anything we could have imagined. Our original goal was to give people a chance to be productive, to escape their misery and move above the poverty line, but I don't think any of us anticipated the extent of what could happen once they'd crossed it. I looked over to see our board chair, Olana Khan, sobbing. I was crying, too, but not nearly as much as I would a few hours later, when I found out that Vanessa had made a $250 donation.

In 1964, Martin Luther King Jr. accepted the Nobel Peace Prize with the following words: "I have the audacity to believe that peoples everywhere can have three meals a day for their bodies, education and culture for their minds, and dignity, equality, and freedom for their spirits." He gave that speech more than fifty years ago, and yet we are still a long way from achieving that goal. How can that be? There's been no lack of effort; in that time the world's richest countries have given more than $2 trillion in foreign aid to the world's poorest. In 2015, the United States alone donated approximately $373 billion to charities, with 80 percent coming from individuals, not foundations or corporations, and a little more than $15 billion of that money going to international charities. If you ever needed proof that we do not live in an indifferent world, there it is. Still, despite the West's best efforts and goodwill, around 10 percent of the global population struggles to survive on less than $2 per day (adjusted for purchasing power). That's more than 2.8 billion people. Three hundred thousand women die annually in childbirth (the World Health Organization estimates that 99 percent of these deaths are preventable and due to poverty). Millions of children suffer brain stunting due to malnutrition (in India alone, this number is 54 million for children under five years of age); 783 million people live without clean water, and 2.5 billion don't have adequate sanitation.

We've been at this a long time. Is it possible that poverty is an intractable problem, something we can hope only to alleviate, not solve?

Only if we keep doing what we're doing.

Historically, we have responded to our citizens in need—global and local—by developing federal and state government services to help them. But after decades of experience, we know that the programs in place to reduce poverty don't always work. The need is too great, and the large bureaucracies required to manage these programs result too easily in tremendous inefficiency, administrative sluggishness, and sometimes even corruption. While many nonprofits and nongovernmental organizations (NGOs) do noble work, such as helping communities build wells for clean water or distributing insecticide-treated mosquito netting, they are too often treating the symptoms of poverty rather than the causes. Another potential fix for people in need is the microfinance system, the idea pioneered by Nobel Peace Prize laureate Muhammad Yunus of giving small loans to poor people so they can grow their businesses and escape the cycle of debt created by money lenders. This sector continues to grow, providing a lifeline to many of the world's poor. But its benefits often bypass women in conservative countries, and it allows entrepreneurs to sell only a few more goods or services, like tomatoes or cleaning services, to their local markets, thus limiting them to other poor consumers, not the richer ones they could reach if they could transcend barriers to global markets. The informal economy of bartering plays a large role in developing countries, but it, too, relies on an exchange of goods and services made by poor people for poor people; selling produce or handicrafts and doing odd jobs for other people living on less than two dollars per day will not catapult anyone out of poverty. It certainly increases people's incomes, but not enough to make a catalytic difference. And while giving to traditional charities certainly makes donors in the United States and other developed nations feel good, many of these organizations don't actually have much lasting impact on the people they are supposed to be helping. Traditional charity models rely upon donations to provide access to goods and services, access to food, access to education, access to health care, access to clean water and other life-saving interventions. But what people really need and desperately want isn't access—it's income.

When you ask people living in desperately poor regions whether they would prefer to receive aid or work, they choose work, because work gives them access to the necessities listed above *and* the long-term ability to procure them without outside help. In addition, work gives them what we in the West prize so highly: agency—the means with which to make their own decisions and chart their own lives. This realization is why I started Samasource, a nonprofit founded with the express purpose of giving dignified work opportunities to the world's poorest people.

Vanessa Kanyi is proof that the world's most destitute citizens are not poor because they are hopeless. They are not poor because they lack smarts, talent, motivation, or will. They are poor because they lost the income birth lottery, born in countries where but for those lucky few with resources and connections, the chances of finding work that pays more than three dollars a day are slim to none. Even in developing countries, that's barely enough to survive.

They are people like Ken, an orphan who graduated from one of the top high schools in Nairobi only to discover that in a society where getting a job is all about whom you know, a slum kid with no connections has little choice but to go back to the slums.

Like Martha, a Kenyan student on the verge of aging out of the orphanage that had given her shelter and at risk of becoming homeless if she couldn't find work to help pay for housing while she attended school.

Like Luc Emmanuel in Haiti, an engineering graduate who compared the effort to find work in his country with crossing the Sahara.

And like Fatem, a Syrian refugee who lost everything before finding safe harbor in Lebanon and was anxious to rebuild a life for himself and his family.

They are also people living in our own country, in disenfranchised American communities where the promise of global trade and tech has proven empty. People like Gary, a veteran laid off from a factory that was supposed to reopen but didn't, living in an area of the Deep South where any job is scarce, and Robinette, a mother trying to finish her bachelor's degree on a part-time teacher's salary of seven dollars per hour.

It's lack of opportunity, not character or potential, that undermines the billions of people at the lowest end of the economic spectrum. In the 1970s, the great design thinker E. F. Schumacher wrote a little-known book called *Good Work*, in which he postulated that the biggest problem in the future would be the surplus of educated people, what he termed a "moron shortage." Sure enough, education rates are soaring. As of 2006, the UN reported that more people would receive a formal education in the next thirty years than in our entire human history. But to what end, when in Africa surging population growth, weak economic conditions, and poor labor markets mean low-income secondary school graduates in developing countries can't find work that pays enough to buy more than one meal per day, much less tuition for the university degree that gives middle- and upper-class youth a leg up? When the jobs that *are* available, such as breaking rocks, hauling coal, or collecting metal scraps, offer zero opportunity for advancement? Or in the States, where it's possible that the best job you can find is two hours away and barely pays enough for gas in the car? Forget a career ladder; these jobs keep people locked in the basement with the lights out. And after too much time in that darkness, the soul starts to die.

Solving this problem is not simply a moral imperative—it's critical for our survival as a species. At the root of almost all the world's worst scourges, from terrorism to domestic violence, from piracy to prostitution to poaching, are unemployment, poverty, and lack of opportunity. Erase these three culprits, and you remove the impetus for all the world's ills except for climate change. Many well-meaning people will insist that eradicating poverty is impossible. Perhaps that was once true, but thanks to technology, it's not anymore. Traditional charity, however, is not the answer. Work is.

Much has been written about how our foreign aid programs, anti-poverty strategies, and nonprofits consistently undermine the people they are supposed to help, and we'll outline these arguments in the following chapters. This book, however, takes up where most of them leave off. It is about viable solutions. The massive changes in the labor market of the last few decades have created an unparalleled opportunity for formerly marginalized people to participate in the global economy. We'll examine those changes, as well as how a new generation of social entrepreneurs is capitalizing on the massive shifts in access to broadband Internet and powerful social and professional networks by starting to chip away at poverty and other global problems from the ground up. Some of us run nonprofits and some don't. Regardless, we are just some of the organizations and businesses employing people in places where no one expected people could do good work. It is a prejudiced, discriminatory assumption that poor people, whether in developing countries or living in our own rural or financially hard-hit urban communities, are incapable of adapting to and being useful in the new digital economy. When given the chance and the right training, they reveal that this presumption is patently false.

Our goals are not pie-in-the-sky—we have the metrics to prove that we are making steady progress. The success stories you'll read about will shatter the notion that nonprofits can't fund themselves or deliver innovation the way "real" companies can. We can and we do every day, doing all the same things it takes for-profits to succeed, like solving customer problems and delivering on promises, despite drawing from a disadvantaged labor force and despite facing higher social and environmental standards than many profit-maximizing businesses. In fact, we do this enough that there is ample reason to foresee a day when the boundaries between the for-profit and nonprofit sectors will dissolve, and social impact and profitability will be closely interconnected and equally valuable. We are the future of business.

My own company is the product of an epiphany I had in 2005 on the floor of a massive call center in the middle of Mumbai. I was twenty-three years old, and my experience with various NGOs and even the

World Bank had already left me cynical and frustrated with the limitations of our foreign aid strategies and the traditional antipoverty movement. I realized that in general, aid organizations had designed their programs to help passive, fundamentally needy consumers. What would happen if instead we brought a start-up mentality to the problem and recognized these people's potential as producers? What could we accomplish if we tapped into the tremendous brainpower of the 4 billion people living at the bottom of the economic pyramid? I set out on a quest to find out.

Today, Samasource workers have tagged images for the world's largest image database, transcribed video lectures for major American universities, and digitized handwritten records from national archives, completing a range of work worth millions of dollars in contracts from more than one hundred companies, including Walmart.com and eBay. Through impact sourcing, these companies hire us to do content generation, moderation, or review, as well as other discrete tasks that can be done with some training and demand a high level of quality. Much of the new data processing coming out of Silicon Valley is a result of new tech that uses machine-learning algorithms. Humans have to teach computers to drive cars, recognize objects within images, and detect human motion for the next smart devices, from self-driving cars to virtual sports games. This is new work that didn't exist before, and Samasource supplies the data. To date we've paid out more than $10 million to people the world had written off. That's not $10 million of one-time donations that we need to request again and again. That's $10 million in direct income that has been reinvested in communities and actually moved people out of poverty, changing the trajectory of their lives.

The Samasource success story is also my own. I am a first-generation immigrant born to parents whose lives in the United States were charted by work. I got through Harvard by cleaning toilets, serving cocktails, and tutoring wealthy kids, and then worked my butt off to build a company that measures its success in lives transformed, not just lives touched. And always I was aware of how fortunate I was to be born in a time and place where I could act on my passion and purpose, because everywhere I went I met people who were hungry for the chance to do the same. This book will take you to some of the poorest places in the world, like the fetid streets of the Dharavi slum in Mumbai, a center for mothers suffering horrific childbirth injuries in Sierra Leone, the ruins of post-earthquake Haiti, and forgotten communities in the United States. And it will also reveal that talent, courage, and ambition are in ample supply everywhere. So the question facing our generation isn't "What can you do to help the less fortunate?" but "What can you do to unlock all that untapped potential?"

It will require rethinking the roles of business and charity in society. We have long believed that business—traditional business—fuels human progress. If you took Economics 101, you learned about Adam Smith and his concept of the "invisible hand"—that if everyone individually optimizes for his or her own gain, market forces will create the best outcomes for all. (It is strange that, even after the financial crisis in the late aughts, we still think this way.)

The mantra of American business is that we have to focus on maximizing profit to move the world forward and keep the engine of economic growth churning.

Meanwhile, we seek to balance this focus on profit with heart, with the effort we pour into charity, family, and friends. We feed our souls when we volunteer at the local animal shelter, or mentor a neighborhood kid, or take care of an aging parent. This work, we're taught, is motivated more by emotions than by rational thinking. It also exists on the periphery, relegated to nights and weekends or the second half of our lives.

So we've created a society in which our head—the business-oriented, profit-maximizing part of our psyche—is fundamentally disconnected from our socially conscious, compassionate heart.

The future is integration.

If you are an entrepreneur and just starting out, you have a golden opportunity to think deeply about the influence you want to have on the world. This book will highlight all the reasons why it will be in your best interests to incorporate social impact, and specifically giving work, into your company right from the start. If you're already in business, you'll learn how other companies have secured their futures, boosted customer satisfaction, and transformed employee happiness by adjusting their hiring practices and purchasing decisions to increase their impact on the poor and the marginalized. As you'll see, social impact and profitability are not mutually exclusive. In addition, this book will show how we as consumers can vote with our dollars and pick which products and services go beyond charity to give work and empower people.

Hugely successful entrepreneurs and heads of companies will approach me at events to congratulate me on Samasource's success, often adding, "I'm so glad you do what you do. We need more people like you." But they're wrong. We don't need more people like me. We need more people like *you*. We need more creative, determined, and compassionate entrepreneurs to build organizations that don't just act as a revolving door between donors and communities but actually bring new opportunities that negate the need for donations in the first place. We need people to choose products that give work. It's wonderful when anyone does anything for someone they don't know, especially on the other side of the world, but raising money to build a school is not enough; charity should be merely a temporary stopgap to ease people's suffering until they've built up the resources to invest in their own lives and communities. (Charities, too, will find some inspiring new ideas in this book.) Those resources can materialize only through work. And not just any work. Not work that pays slave wages, or foreign direct investment that might one day "trickle down" to the neediest, but living-wage work that specifically targets the poor. Entrepreneurs and businesspeople are all about job creation; my hope is that by the time you finish reading this book, you'll be inspired to look closely to see where you can weave social impact more tightly into the fabric of your company or organization.

It is also my hope that those dedicated people working at the government level and within international agencies will see in this book an exciting new foreign aid model, one that could overhaul the role of organizations like the World Bank and the International Monetary Fund (IMF), as well as improve transparency and outcomes, and thus the public's confidence in aid. Imagine if instead of allocating funds to foreign contractors and governments we directed money straight to the people, funding only those enterprises that directly moved them out of poverty by hiring from marginalized communities and paying living wages. We'd create a new kind of job market, one that incentivized direct, measurable social impact for the most vulnerable people. We wouldn't have to wait for trickle-down economics or trickle-down aid to have an effect. And imagine if a version of this model could also help address some of the issues causing the grief and insecurity that have roiled our own country. I think the stories you'll read here will give you reason to be optimistic.

Finally, we'll also explore the future of work. How can we provide opportunities in a world where even an education, once the great equalizer, offers little protection against an increasingly automated workplace? How will work change? How will society absorb so many educated human beings? What will any of us do if work becomes irrelevant, and how will we encourage productivity and innovation? The possibilities are intriguing and exciting.

This is not a book for wishful thinkers. I wrote it for anyone radical enough to agree with another line in Dr. King's acceptance speech: "I refuse to accept the idea that man is mere flotsam and jetsam in the river of life, unable to influence the unfolding events which surround him." His belief in a world where no one goes hungry, and where everyone has access to education, dignity, equality, and freedom, does not seem too audacious to me. Vanessa Kanyi may be an outlier today, but

I don't believe she will be forever. In my parents' lifetime, we've ended apartheid and put a man on the moon. We can end extreme poverty. And the best way is to give people economic agency through work. Work, for so many of us, means independence; it is the triumph of the human body and mind over all that is within our power to control.

Work transcends every other issue by shifting the balance of power and giving people a choice in how to spend their resources. We know more than anyone else what makes us happy. Give work—dignified, steady, fair-wage work—and you give the poorest people on the planet a chance at happiness. Give work, and you give people the freedom to choose how to develop their own communities. Give work, and you create infinite possibilities.

Chapter One

FROM THE GROUND UP

WHEN MY BROTHER AND I WERE YOUNG AND WE'D ASK MY FATHER for an allowance or spending money, he would raise his voice to oratorical heights and recite a line by the Roman poet Juvenal: "My children, 'luxury is more ruthless than war.'" It was his way of teaching us the concept of *jugaad,* which is a Hindi word that means "resourcefulness." He wanted us to be strong and scrappy. It might also have been his way of avoiding having to spell out the truth, which was that he probably had little money to give.

The first stepping-stones in my path to Samasource and this book were laid long ago, before I was even born. My parents emigrated from Bombay to Buffalo, New York, in 1978. The Rust Belt city was a brutal adjustment for this artistic, worldly couple; my mother's ancestral home in Kolkata was such a hub for the Indian literati it had been dubbed "an incubator of souls." And then there was the weather. In the winter of 1981–82, nine months before I was born, Buffalo recorded 112 inches of snow. A few years later, desperate to escape the region's frigid winters, my tropical parents followed the sun to Arizona, moving multiple times before finally settling the four of us—by this time my brother, Ved, had been born—in Southern California. Although we were never poor by most standards, my family was incredibly money-conscious. We shopped exclusively at discount and thrift stores, we rarely ate out, and our tightly budgeted vacations took place in campgrounds and national parks. Our biggest expense was our home, which my parents rented in a neighborhood beyond what they could comfortably afford to ensure that their children attended good public schools. As little as we had, we made do. My only inkling of what true poverty might look like came from an anecdote my mother shared when her children didn't finish their plates, the one about the time she threw a piece of bread onto her Kolkata street for the local stray dog, and a street kid rushed over, pushed the animal away, and gobbled it up.

That story often made me wonder, why was I so lucky when there were so many children in the world who were not? Along with the words of Roman poets, my father also passed down to his children a deep sense of social justice, a legacy, perhaps, of his Jesuit education in the Catholic schools of Jamshedpur, about 140 miles west of Kolkata. We were expected to notice the inequities in the world and try to make things better. I took the lessons to heart and did what I could. In middle school I joined my local chapter of the American Civil Liberties Union (ACLU). When I was about fifteen I won first place at the state science fair for a marine microbiology project that addressed the issue of world hunger by testing the possibility of growing food from chemosynthetic bacteria (bacteria that don't need sunlight to create energy). I started my high school's chapter of Amnesty International. As I got older, however, I came to the conclusion that merely making things better was not sufficient. There was an underlying problem fueling most of the injustices these organizations were created to address, a root cause that needed to be fixed. Fortunately, I come from a long line of passionate, determined people who showed me through example that every individual has the power to instigate change. In fact, if my maternal great-grandfather hadn't believed it, that street child could easily have been me.

A FAMILY RISES

My great-grandfather's name was Sharat Chandra Janah, and he did something exceedingly rare for a boy from a low-caste Indian family: he rose. Born in a poor fishing village in West Bengal, his intelligence attracted the attention of the nuns in his Catholic school. With their encouragement he went on to university and law school, becoming one of the top trial lawyers of Kolkata. Yet he never forgot how he had been forced to sit at a separate table from his schoolmates because of his low caste, and he always chafed against any system that barred people from opportunity by virtue of their station in life. He made it a point to take pro bono cases of tribal people who were being discriminated against and had no prayer of finding representation. My mother had memories of strangers staying at the family compound for days while they waited for their court appointments.

Her parents met because, like my great-grandfather, my grandmother Christiane, a beautiful Belgian redhead, took an opportunity to change her destiny. I know this story because Christiane documented her amazing journey in a book called *Le tour du monde avec cinq dollars*, which translates to *Around the World with Five Dollars*. Her family, the Zeebroeks, fled Belgium in 1940 to escape the Nazi occupation. When she was twenty-five years old, craving adventure and fed up with the stifling secretarial job she had landed in Paris after finishing university, Christiane joined a group of friends planning to travel the world spreading a postwar message of peace. They called themselves Les Messagers (The Messengers). Starting out with nothing more than five dollars, some packs, and a few tents, the four boys and two girls hitchhiked across Europe down to Italy. From there, the merry band crossed the Mediterranean to North Africa and continued across the Middle East, until finally arriving in Kolkata.

My great-uncle Sunil, my grandfather's brother, was a prominent Bengali photographer who was known for his coverage of the Indian independence movement and the human rights abuses committed by the British during that period. He happened to attend one of Christiane's lectures at the University of Kolkata, and, intrigued by the group's story, he invited them to stay at the family home. And so Les Messagers trooped over to 57 Rashbehari Avenue, which was also the headquarters for Chandra Janah's law practice, and set up their tents on the terrace. That evening, as legend has it, my grandfather, Ashis, was coming up to see what all the fun was about as my grandmother was coming down the stairs. He saw her standing above him with the moonlight illuminating her red hair. He fell madly in love. She wasn't so sure. Shortly afterward she continued on her journey, crisscrossing Asia and traveling by boat to the United States before returning to Europe. Hearing that she was back in Paris, my grandfather tracked Christiane down and enrolled at the Sorbonne, taking the last option they had left, a ceramics course, just so he could be near her. She must have come around because they married in Paris within the year, and my mother was born a few years later at her mother's family home in Nice.

Unsurprisingly, Christiane did not settle into typical domestic married life. Instead, she and my grandfather returned to Kolkata and opened India's first art ceramics studio. Though she lived in a city famous in the West for Mother Teresa and child prostitutes, my mother was educated at private schools and raised in a rare sliver of Indian society, middle-class intellectuals who were neither poor nor particularly rich. She grew up steeped in an incredible melting pot of artists and cultural leaders whom her parents frequently socialized with and entertained. She was also often left alone to fend for herself.

Awkward and isolated at school as well—biracial students were still unusual, and the strange stories she told of things she'd seen in France as a child alienated her from her classmates—she turned inward, finding solace in caring for animals. In a city plagued with acute poverty, strays and injured creatures were the lowest priority. Even as a young girl my mother, who never studied anatomy or medicine, became known for her uncanny healing powers. With no animal shelters in Kolkata, people would leave wounded animals on the doorstep of 57 Rashbehari. She mended a squirrel's broken bone, and after that he never left her side, happily riding around in her pocket on the bus.

My mother found it hard to warm up to people, but she was incredible with animals. My brother and I would groan every time she'd pull over to see if she could resuscitate what looked to us like roadkill, chalking up her behavior as just one more reason our odd family would never fit into the Southern California suburbs. Yet through her grace toward wounded creatures she gave us a powerful connection to nature and a sense of duty toward the suffering. In her own way, too, she showed me that individuals can make a difference even when situations appear hopeless.

My father, Sahadev Chirayath, grew up in a middle-class family from Kerala, where generations of men in his family had worked for Tata Steel in Jamshedpur, the Pittsburgh of South Asia. Around the age of nineteen, my dad transferred to Bombay to finish his studies at that branch of the Indian Institute for Technology after narrowly escaping expulsion from the IIT Kanpur campus for staging a play in the nude on a rooftop (it was after all the 1970s). A polymath who loved poetry, spoke multiple Indian languages, played classical Indian music, and loved James Joyce, he was not your typical structural engineer. It was in Bombay where he met my mother, who was pursuing a degree in English literature. She was eighteen.

Like thousands of other young, educated Indian graduates in the mid-1970s, my father realized his future was abroad. In the 1970s and 1980s, India's economy was still mostly agricultural, and there just weren't enough jobs around to absorb the waves of newly minted technical talent. So my father moved to the United States after finding work as a civil engineer in Buffalo, New York. A few months later, he proposed to my mother in a letter. She accepted with a two-word telegram—"I will." They were married shortly afterward in a civil ceremony in Cleveland, Ohio, where my father's brother was a professor.

Like most immigrants, they came to the United States with little more than the clothes on their backs and the skills in their heads and hands, which, in my father's case, were in great demand. My mother was less lucky. An English literature degree from India would not be particularly marketable in the United States now, much less in 1977 Buffalo. She was so talented and smart—she could recite long passages from *Macbeth* from memory—yet the only job she could get was chopping onions at the local Wendy's near their apartment in Grand Island, a suburb just south of Niagara Falls. To this day, I see her in the many immigrant cabdrivers, restaurant workers, and other low-wage employees I encounter who were doctors, lawyers, and white-collar job holders in other countries, but whose educational or professional credentials aren't recognized to allow them to practice here in the States. As if that weren't demoralizing enough, neighbors would remark in amazement, "Wow, you speak such good English!" and she would have to explain again and again that English was the official language of India and that she had been speaking it, along with several other languages, since she could talk. Some people said uglier things, like "Go back to India," or asked her, "Did you live with monkeys?" They had no concept of an intellectual class in India. This is the core challenge that Nigerian writer Chimamanda Adichie refers to in her TED Talk on the "danger of a single story"—so often, immigrants in America are given a single narrative: they're either desperate and poor, or lazy and ungrateful. Life was not easy, and the financial pressure and social isolation were hard on my parents' marriage. But they did their best. I was born four years after they arrived.

After we moved to Arizona my mother started fresh, enrolling at Pima Community College in Tucson and taking computer science courses, which she thought would be more bankable than her English degree. She also ran a plant nursery and later got a job at United Airlines as a contractor. As she was able to excel, my mother's confidence and sense of self returned. Upon receiving her computer degree she started working in IT and learned how to write BASIC software. My father continued his engineering career.

When I was seven, my dad got a job in Southern California. My parents scraped together everything they had to move us into a neighborhood zoned to one of the highest-ranked schools in the area. Bookish and passionate about science—one of my favorite experiments was setting fire to things in the backyard to see which items would burn the fastest—I started school with enthusiasm. But by the third grade it became clear that there were rules for survival and fitting in, and I didn't know them. The school was affluent, and the kids were merciless. This was long before the days of Mindy Kaling and *Quantico*'s Priyanka Chopra, and South Asians were invisible in mainstream culture. I was the only person of color in my grade and I felt it. My ashy skin and hairy legs, not to mention my clothes, handmade by my mother or bought at the Pic 'n Save, made me an easy target for the mean girls in the Guess sweater sets. When I'd get on my bike to go home, they would surround me, blocking my way and jeering at me in their own form of pig Latin. I retreated into books. Things got marginally better once I moved to a less affluent school, but still, I'd have done anything to trade in my straight black hair for a cascade of blond permed curls and rename myself Rebecca.

I was pretty miserable until high school, when I was accepted into a math and science magnet program called CAMS, the California Academy of Math and Science. Drawing from ten different school districts around the L.A. area, its mission is to expose more women and minorities to the STEM fields. Finally, I had found all the other Southern California nerdy misfits from lower-income backgrounds. The universe opened up for me.

AN INTRODUCTION TO WORK

Around this time my home life became extremely difficult as my parents' marriage, frayed since the beginning, began to seriously unravel. School and work became my escapes. I joined every extracurricular activity I could, falling in love with dance, and did odd jobs around the neighborhood. I launched a babysitting business. Fanned by my father's emphasis on *jugaad*, I learned early that if I wanted something badly enough, I was going to have to figure out how to earn it myself. But work also helped me understand what I was good at. And unlike school, I got paid on the basis of how well I overcame challenges. That was a real revelation, that I brought value to the world that was worth someone else's money. It gave me confidence, which I sorely needed when things were so unstable at home.

I did everything I could to stay out of the house, even participating in extracurricular activities that I hated, like water polo. And I worked. The summer between my freshman and sophomore years, I took a job as a junior legal secretary, commuting from San Pedro to a downtown law firm located in one of the big skyscrapers that spiked the skyline. The bus left once an hour, and I had to transfer to the Red Line in Inglewood, so I had to get up at 5:00 a.m. to be in the office by 8:30. It was eye-opening to see how full those buses were so early in the morning. I felt privileged. Though I was only fourteen, I was going to a white-collar office job, while most of the people around me were on their way to clean houses or cook food. Everyone was tired and quiet. Some people would fall asleep. Many carried their lunch in their hands.

That job revved my self-esteem. Even though I'd purchased my clothes from thrift stores, I felt a profound sense of pride when I dressed up in my suits and pantyhose every morning. I was a working woman, and I took myself a little too seriously. I even wore little scarves around my neck.

The head legal secretary, a woman named Liz Dempsey, who seemed like she came straight out of the movie *Working Girl*, with her coiffed hair and perfect acrylic nails, was a master at creating order from chaos. She taught me how to use Outlook and Excel, manage the calendars of half a dozen lawyers, and graciously greet the weirdos who'd come into the office to be deposed.

I made about a thousand dollars that summer, which was a fortune compared to the money I'd previously earned from babysitting and the other odd jobs I'd found. I knew I was low on the totem pole, but I loved the feeling of being absorbed in something bigger than myself. Whatever concerns I had about my family life or school fell away when I was at the office. Even then, it was clear that work brought out my best self.

I also started to think deeply about what people needed from work. My mother was active in picket lines and protesting for workers' rights in the factories of L.A., and sometimes I'd go with her to see what they were fighting for. The experience always left a bad taste in my mouth. So often the protests were completely disconnected from action or results of any kind; the protesters themselves were disorganized and didn't know what they wanted. I felt like our time would have been much better spent in a courtroom fighting for their rights or, better yet, building a business that paid them living wages and gave them access to training and other job benefits, and showed consumers a real alternative.

I resolved to try to align my form of protest with real results, measurable improvement that combined the scientific method I'd studied in high school with the social justice orientation I learned from my parents.

With this new view, the world seemed limitless. With a year and a half's worth of college credit already complete (my school was on a Cal State campus, which meant I could take college classes for free), and eager to get away from home, where my parents were embroiled in a bitter divorce, I started making plans to graduate early. I applied for every scholarship I could. Shortly after my sixteenth birthday, I won a ten-thousand-dollar "Teen Helping Influence People" award for community service. What I hadn't noticed when applying was that the award was sponsored by the Lorillard Tobacco Company. Now I was caught in an ethical dilemma. I had little interest in supporting or promoting Big Tobacco, and I was relatively sure that neither of the two progressive organizations to which I had given my heart and soul would approve. What was I going to do? I had a very patient guidance counselor who had already spent many hours talking to me about my options for leaving home. With his help, I came up with a plan: instead of using the money for my education, I would use the money to do something educational. Preferably someplace far, far away. I wanted to serve, I wanted to escape the havoc at home, and, like my grandmother Christiane when she was young, I craved adventure and wanted to see the world. There had to be something bigger out there for a teenager than worrying about SAT scores and college applications. I was disappointed to learn that I was too young to join the Peace Corps, but an online search led me to another program, the American Field Service (AFS), which managed study abroad programs for high school kids and had just launched a service program in Ghana.

And that's how in January 2000, three months after my seventeenth birthday, during what would have been my second semester of high school, I left suburban Los Angeles and moved to Apirede, a village in the southern part of rural Ghana. My friends' parents were horrified that I'd been allowed to leave home at such a young age to live in what surely had to be a dangerous country. But my parents gave me their blessing. They understood that freedom was a powerful teacher, and were sure I would be fine. As it turned out, rural Africa is probably a hundred times safer than most big American cities, provided you avoid mosquito bites and have access to healthy food.

AFS didn't offer any formal teaching training; they simply arranged the trip and teaching position, and paid my host family a stipend to cover my room and board. After that I was pretty much on my own. My assignment was to teach English to blind kids. I had no teaching experience and no knowledge of Braille (I started studying it as soon as I arrived). The village, home to about 250 people, was in a remote part of the country about thirty miles north of the capital city of Accra. There was only sporadic electricity and no phone; to make a long-distance call I'd have to walk to the neighboring village.

My host family's son had left Africa to find work and fulfill his ambitions. He had made it as a doctor in the United States and periodically sent them money, but they had chosen to stay in Apirede. Their home, the only house in the village, was small but had several comfortably furnished rooms, a veranda, and a solid tin roof. During the monsoon the fattest drops of rain I've ever seen would drum to a deafening crescendo on that roof. An immaculate Toyota Camry sat parked out in front, a gift their son had somehow shipped to them from the States. To my knowledge no one ever drove it; it didn't budge the entire time I lived there. The family was extremely warm and kind. My host mother made it her mission to fatten me up and marry me off before I left Ghana.

Like many Americans volunteering abroad, I assumed my destitute charges at the West African School for the Blind, where I was assigned, would speak terrible English and depend on me to get them through the basics. A small part of me assumed something else: that I'd help my students—and, by extension, their families—become less poor by teaching them to value education and giving them the confidence to work hard. Somewhere along the way, despite my involvement with poor and marginalized communities in California, even I had internalized the somewhat racist myth I'd commonly heard in the media and would continue to hear, even in the halls of Harvard—that people without means might be in their predicament because they were not willing to work hard enough or had not developed the right personal or family values, or that certain regions had become poor because they were not "culturally oriented" toward working hard and creating wealth.

It was a shock, then, when I realized that no one could have worked harder than my new neighbors. The people I met in my village in Ghana would leave early in the morning for their fields, where they would cultivate several staple crops, like maize, bananas, plantains, cassava, beans, and pumpkins. If the villagers were lucky they would bring home enough food to feed their families. If they were unlucky, they might be forced to watch their children and loved ones suffer from malnutrition or illness.

It's difficult for people who live in relative wealth to fathom what it is like to try to survive on the other end of the spectrum. I thought my extensive reading, my volunteer work, and my experiences in the United States had given me a greater-than-average understanding of what poverty looked like, but I could not conceive of the deprivation I saw in Ghana. In the United States, poverty is defined as a family of four living on less than about $23,000 a year. This is a very low number, and not nearly enough to make ends meet in the richest country in the world. But extreme poverty is on a different level. Extreme poverty is currently defined as living under $1.90 a day, and half the population of sub-Saharan Africa lives there. You might think that in a country like Ghana, that amount would buy you plenty more food and basic goods than here in the United States. But what most people don't understand is that these figures, when reported by the World Bank, are already adjusted for purchasing power. We're not talking about actually living on about $2 a day, but on what about $2 would buy you in a day in an average American city in 2011.

Think about that.

There were mangoes and avocados everywhere, but protein was expensive and hard to get. The first week I arrived, a tiny little girl came running to our house carrying a plastic cup the size of one of the 7-Eleven Big Gulps my friends and I would buy in high school, handling it as though the contents were liquid gold. She proudly presented me with the cup. Inside were three eggs, two with a crusty feather still stuck to their sides. She grinned. I didn't get it. My host mother patiently explained that the little girl was from one of Apirede's poorer families, and as a gesture of hospitality, her parents had sent her over with their most precious gift—three eggs from a chicken that didn't lay many—to greet the new Obruni. *Obruni* means "white man" or "foreigner" in Twi, the language of the Ashanti people of southern Ghana. One of the great things about travel is getting out of your comfort zone and being forced to feel like an "other," especially if that's not your default mode. Still, it felt extraordinarily strange for this brown girl to be lumped into the same category as the white men who also colonized her parents' homeland. One of the things I learned in Ghana is how fluid ethnic identity can be—one country's "white man" is another's "brown girl." It's all relative, which means the lines that divide us can't be that significant.

Lives were often cut short savagely by avoidable causes. Families in Apirede were so poor that they couldn't afford the most basic health care. One young boy died during the time I was there because his parents couldn't afford a four-dollar malaria medication. This was just after I recovered from a bout of malaria myself, after suspending my Lariam tablets because they were giving me vivid, hallucinatory nightmares that made me too afraid to sleep. I quickly contracted the disease, developed high fever, and felt like I was going to die. My Obruni friends in Ghana chuckled and told me to go to the clinic and get a package of Fansidar. I bought it for four dollars, and quickly got better. The idea that a child in my village could die so easily was deeply upsetting. I cried for days wishing I'd known he was ill so I could have done something. This kind of avoidable tragedy was a daily fact of life in Ghana. People died because they didn't have the money to give birth in a hospital, from hemorrhaging because they couldn't afford to get stitches after an auto accident, from infections because they couldn't pay for antibiotics. The kids in my classes were often blind from causes that could have been addressed in their infancy or in utero, had they been detected and treated early enough. That fate had led me to be born in a hospital in upstate New York, with the facilities to stop my mother from hemorrhaging during a very difficult twenty-four-hour labor, and led other kids in Ghana to lose mothers under the same circumstances, made me sick. I became deeply depressed, despite the many joyful aspects of life in Ashanti land: a rich tradition of fashion and sculpture, dance, music, and close families and communities.

Everywhere in Ghana I saw people working at the limits of their physical capacity, but not earning enough to live decent lives. How could they still be so poor? It didn't add up. I had grown up in the States and believed in meritocracy because it had worked for my parents. I knew not all schools were equal—as an intern with the ACLU I'd worked on a case against the California State Board of Education on behalf of a school where students were demanding access to at least one Advanced Placement class, even as their more affluent peers in the neighboring school district could choose from almost fifty. I had also read Jonathan Kozol's book *Savage Inequalities*, about how inequality is perpetuated in the American public school system because of the way schools are funded through local property taxes, which favors wealthy districts with higher property values. But still I believed that if you could get a basic education and worked diligently, you should be able to earn enough money to live with dignity. My understanding of *jugaad* was based on the underlying assumption that hard work inevitably reaps rewards.

After I had spent two months in Ghana, a young boy named Femi Abass shattered this way of thinking. My students ranged in age from nine to twenty-five. Many were just getting their primary education. In this country with few resources for people with disabilities, some families, ashamed of the stigma, hid their children until they could send them away to this school, the Akropong School for the Blind. Established in 1945, it was the oldest school for the blind in West Africa. The one-room library was filled with moldy books. The materials I had to use to teach my young charges were laughably bad and boring, Braille texts donated by Queen Elizabeth to support a 1950s curriculum developed for Western schoolchildren whose life experiences allowed them to comprehend sentences like "Penny wore her red cloak to the market when it snowed." I was appalled. I'd learn that the colonial educational system in developing countries enforced a sort of inferiority complex on students. Even in the year 2000, the materials still drew from Western countries that had little bearing on life in a place like West Africa, rather than drawing from the children's own cultures. Ghanaian kids learned more about life in England than about their own rich traditions. It seemed like much of the colonial education system had been set up to build a sense of loyalty to the mother country, not to the colony.

Later, in college, I would study the political movement behind the repatriation of art that was taken during colonial times from sub-Saharan Africa and remained housed in European museums. Unlike art owned by Jews and stolen by the Nazis, much of which had been returned, this plundered art remained in the hands of those who took it. And that meant that millions of African schoolchildren were deprived of the chance to see what their ancestors had created. For too long, schoolchildren in developing countries have been taught, explicitly or implicitly, to deny their own heritage. In addition, historians like Samuel Huntington, who posited that poor regions were poor because they "lack the Protestant work ethic," would point to the complex artistic works in places like Rome and Alexandria as evidence of Western superiority. But just as being poor does not correlate with a lack of work ethic—one only has to spend a little time with someone earning less than two dollars a day to see that she works harder than any person behind a desk receiving benefits—the amount of art developed by a civilization does not correlate with greatness. Besides, poor countries in Africa *did* produce complex artistic works; they had just been plundered by colonialists. The two largest collections of Nigerian art are housed outside Nigeria, in Europe. (I wrote my senior paper on the movement to bring back two iconic ivory hip masks depicting a famous Benin Empire queen, Idia, from the Met and the British Museum, where they are part of the permanent collections.) How could a young historian in Africa grow up feeling pride in his culture's contributions when so much of the evidence of those contributions remained on another continent?

Yet Femi Abass was proud. Femi was a ten-year-old student whose eyes had acquired a milky-white coating in early childhood from a preventable condition his mother could not afford to treat, which I'd later realize was probably cataracts. His single mother had fled fighting in her Nigerian hometown to find refuge in Ghana, where she had wanted her son to go to the best school she could find. He'd stay after school almost every day and loved to talk about the books he was reading, especially Nigerian author Chinua Achebe's *Things Fall Apart*. Femi had the kind of raw talent that can evolve into genius under the right mentors. It was Femi who inspired me to trash the standard rote curriculum in favor of Harlem Renaissance poems I picked up from the American embassy library in Accra, one of the crown jewels of our presence in West Africa, a library I'd heard about from a friend and then visited in weekly pilgrimages to collect new reading and writing material. I transcribed the poems into Braille using a stylus that punched little holes into paper, then used a Braille printer called a Thermaform machine to make copies. Shamelessly stealing my high school teachers' lesson plans, I led the students through riveting discussions about the works of Langston Hughes, Claude McKay, and Countee Cullen. And so their rhythmic verses, influenced by the African roots of blues and jazz music, flowed through the school hallways and captivated kids who, I felt, had an extradeveloped sense of sound and rhythm owing to their underdeveloped eyesight. My students reveled in the idea that learning could be fun, pursued just for the sheer joy of it. They were fascinated to learn about the African diaspora and to discover that they shared common ancestors with African Americans. In fact, for more than a century, Ghana was the hub of the European slave trade, and it was fewer than a hundred miles away that millions of slaves were warehoused in the dungeons of the infamous Cape Coast slave castle before being loaded onto ships that would transport them to the Americas, unless they died at sea during the Middle Passage.

I launched a creative writing program, and the work my students produced was poignant, insightful, and wise. I had stumbled into a pool of incredible talent. These were smart kids who listened to Voice of America and BBC, who could name U.S. senators and had opinions on Bill Clinton's last speech. Led by Femi, a handful of students stayed after class each afternoon to pepper me with questions about poetry, life in America, and their future in Ghana. One wanted to be a doctor, another a teacher, a third a journalist. They were so hungry for knowledge. All asked me to help them move to the United States because they thought our country was a place of opportunity.

It was not hard to see that I had landed in America and they'd landed in Apirede by an accident of birth, and that our fates were, statistically speaking, tied tightly to this accident. Femi would have smoked me in fourth grade had he not been born to a single mother in a country where the average daily income was equivalent to two American dollars in 2005. The disparity made me sick. At least once a week, I wept alone in my room and tried to imagine what I could do to make Femi's life better. In retrospect, it's clear that Femi planted the small seed of frustration that forced me, years later, to become a social entrepreneur. His talent made plain the fact that any success I enjoyed had less to do with my work ethic than with my birthplace in the richest country in the world.

It's so easy when you're living in a middle-class suburb with good schools and enough food on your plate to think that there's some reason why some people make it and others don't, that our fate is entirely dictated by how hard we work. I had subconsciously bought into the myth that poor people are poor because they didn't want to better themselves, because they squandered opportunities and wasted their talents. It had never occurred to me before that there were places where there simply were no opportunities. Over the years I would learn more about how that lack of opportunity is internalized and affects the human psyche. In their book *Scarcity,* professors Sendhil Mullainathan and Eldar Shafir explain how the brain changes when operating under conditions of extreme scarcity, shifting its focus to short-term survival. Through a series of novel experiments, the authors found this to be true even for people who were once wealthy. Deprive a successful CEO of food for long enough, and her ability to make long-term plans, concentrate on abstract tasks or higher-level projects, and avoid obsessive thinking about food falls dramatically. This is the predicament that more than 2 billion people find themselves in daily, and it severely curtails their ability to enjoy the fruits of being human—making plans for the future, learning, or playing games or sports, for example. If we think about extreme poverty as akin to enforced scarcity, we start to see its debilitating impacts on the brain and on communities and entire societies. How can a country "develop" if more than a quarter of its citizens' brains are obsessed with thoughts of food almost constantly?

My blind students had the same big dreams as anyone else, but the likelihood that they would achieve them was slim. There just weren't enough jobs to go around to everyone who wanted one, and certainly not for a blind child with no connections. The realization was heartbreaking. If you truly believe that all humans are created equal, then you can't sit back and watch people live lives of utter desperation and suffering for no reason but the circumstances of their birth and do nothing about it.

One thing that did help me feel like I was making an immediate difference was the work I did conducting reproductive-health surveys for Planned Parenthood. At the time, Ghana had one of the lowest rates of HIV/AIDS in Africa, which many people attributed to the high adoption of condom use. This was Planned Parenthood's central program, and it was remarkable. They had only local staff and ran a lean operation: peer educators strapped boxes of condoms marked "USAID" to the backs of motorcycles to take into villages that were inaccessible by road.

I learned that part of the program's success was that it was set up as a social enterprise. Rather than give the condoms away, peer educators would sell them at a very low price, a few cents in U.S. dollars, and thus make a bit of money to incentivize them to distribute more condoms. At the same time, the population that bought condoms valued them more than if they'd been given out for free. I was fascinated by how this kind of hybrid thinking had resulted in an improved outcome. It seemed counter to most of what I saw in the NGO world, where goods and services were doled out for free, often with devastating consequences for the local economy. I would confirm the reasons behind the program's success over the following years as I studied the causes of poverty and the often counterproductive effects of aid and charity: even health interventions are most powerful when they are market driven—when local people have enough money to purchase the services they need (or to be taxed, and thus contribute to funding services at the government level).

Eventually my time in Apirede came to an end. Ultimately, the only "danger" I encountered during my entire seven months in Ghana, other than contracting malaria, was getting my camera stolen during a visit to Akropong's main craft market. While haggling with a sculptor in one of the stalls, I had put my Nikon down, and left without it, not realizing my mistake until a few hours later. I went back to the vendor, who denied that I left it until I started lecturing him about being a good Christian. Sheepishly, he retreated to the back of his shop and pulled my camera out from below a pile of wood shavings. He apologized profusely and offered to give me a refund for what I had bought from him. Overall, I had extraordinarily positive experiences. Taxi drivers in Accra, the capital city, would often refuse to let me pay my fare once they heard I was volunteering in a school for blind kids. Shopkeepers would give me and my two Obruni friends, Coralie and Manuela, from Belgium and Switzerland, respectively, free Fantas in exchange for our stories and to show us their gratitude for volunteering in Ghana. When I'd ride the *tro-tros*—packed minibuses similar to the modes of transportation seemingly found everywhere in the developing world, from Jeepneys in Manila to *matatus* in Nairobi—and tell people I was American, passengers would eagerly talk about Bill Clinton, still excited about his visit two years earlier, when he'd been the first U.S. president to visit their country. I felt welcomed everywhere I went.

When the semester was over I backpacked around the country with Coralie and Manuela. We talked endlessly about the differences between our respective countries, and I learned a great deal about European social policy from them. For example, in their native Belgium and Switzerland, it was unthinkable that someone would go without health care because they couldn't afford it, and it was accepted that a portion of people's tax dollars should be allotted to international relief efforts. By contrast, in the United States, where we pay significantly lower taxes than Europeans do, many people believe we should reduce our aid spending to less than 1 percent of the budget, wholly unaware that, in fact, we already spend less than a tenth of that.

We all agreed that our time in Ghana had been transformative. The idea of a gap year to volunteer overseas is very common in Europe, but mostly still foreign in the United States. And yet it's one of the best things a young person can do for herself. A friend of mine even started an organization to promote a new version of the concept—Global Citizen Year— after seeing the data that shows that people who do service learning trips at a young age, especially when they are on their own and not in a highly structured group environment, improve their job prospects and tend to make more compassionate choices as they get older and progress in their careers. Indeed, in my surveys of people in "do-good"–type careers like mine, I found that most could point to some sort of catalytic moment they experienced when they were working in a poor community that made it impossible for them to ignore social issues in their future careers. After the injustice I'd seen, it would have been impossible for me to go home and not devote my life to trying to fix it. Samasource is a direct result of the time I spent with the families of Apirede.

Most people think that you have to have a trust fund to volunteer in Africa. That's bullshit. Anyone can find a way, whether by saving money from a summer job or by convincing local businesses to sponsor you. And you aren't limited to international service or the Peace Corps. The proposed 2017 federal budget threatens its funding, but as of the writing of this book we have our very own domestic version in Ameri-Corps, which could match you with any number of projects in focus areas like disaster services, economic opportunity, or education, to name a few.

There's been a backlash against Western volunteers abroad in recent years. In early 2016, Courtney Martin wrote a brilliant essay decrying the white, Western savior mentality that leads so many well-meaning young people to travel abroad to volunteer. Ignorant of the complexities surrounding the social problems in non-Western countries, they think it will be easier to make a difference there than in their home countries, a trend Martin calls "the reductive seduction of other people's problems." But in criticizing white—or any—young people for trying to help the poor in developing countries, authors of this new wave of anti-NGO press commit the very sin they're trying to avoid: they "otherize" the brown and black people with whom they want to stand in solidarity. There are better targets for our vitriol than would-be do-gooders just getting started in life. Only by learning just how complicated the world's problems are will they be inspired to come up with real solutions.

Six months after I'd arrived in Ghana, I boarded a plane to return to the States. My experience had left me ecstatic, but also a little overwhelmed and depressed. Colors were a bit less vivid and music less joyful when I thought about the masses of people sharing the planet with me who couldn't enjoy the same things I could. It was a burden that I'd carry forever, one that I know I share with many who have had similarly eye-opening experiences and have devoted themselves, even for a short time, to focusing on the problems of poverty and social injustice. I now knew I wanted to address the issue of global poverty, but I had no idea how. I arrived home, however, to something that would give me a shot of optimism: boxes of pale blue aerograms. My former students had asked for my address so we could remain pen pals, and their friends and relatives had sent me letters asking for help. "Dear Sister Leila, please send me a box of crayons." "Dear Madam Leila, I would be grateful for drinking water." One actually said, "Show me the money."

Someone else might have been offended or disappointed. Six months studying creative writing together, and all I get are requests for handouts from my students' relatives? But I saw something else. It takes a lot of effort to write a letter in rural Ghana. You have to find a pen, which isn't a cheap item there. You have to buy the paper. And then there was the fact that these were long letters that had taken quite a bit of time and effort to write. Anyone willing to go to such effort to compose a letter asking for something that costs less than $2.50 is doing it because it's the only thing he can do. In an environment where high school and college graduates face 70 percent unemployment, asking for handouts is the best use of their resources. If they or their parents could have worked to earn those crayons or bottles of water, they would have. I had talked at length to my students and their families to better understand their economic situations. Most people in countries like Ghana make their living in the informal economy, doing jobs like selling snacks by the side of the road, bringing produce to the weekly market, or tailoring. These jobs are unregulated and don't pay living wages. People usually have to work several of them at once to make enough money to get by (taking what's called a "portfolio approach" to income). What my students really wanted more than anything else was good work, and the chance to earn enough money to experience the kind of freedom, adventure, and independence that I took for granted. If these tough, smart kids were given a fair shot to make a living, how far could they go? They had skills and they had potential. All they needed were jobs.

I never saw Femi again, and I don't know what happened to him. We exchanged a few letters after I left Ghana, but in those pre-Facebook days, when connectivity could be found only in a few Internet cafés in downtown Accra, it was tough to keep in touch with people in rural Africa. But I think about him every time I meet people whose lives have been transformed by work—not because they are more intelligent, or more determined, or have more hustle, than anyone else, but because they got a shot at the kind of opportunity that Femi and his classmates so desperately wanted.

For example, Janet, a worker in the Samasource Super Center at Gulu University in Uganda, used her income to support her sister and cover her school tuition, clear her father's medical bills, and pay off some of her own school fees. A stunning woman, Janet has a quiet, dignified presence and speaks in low, soothing tones. Since joining in 2012, she has proven to be one of Samasource's most capable workers, rising from data-entry agent to quality analyst to team leader. When asked to describe the impact employment has had on her community, she replied, "It has helped us develop ourselves and develop our families." She added that she especially appreciated the new skills she learned, in particular effective communication. "I was a shy person, but now I'm confident and I can speak in front of everyone without fear."

Martha lives in Nairobi, Kenya, but shares a similarly triumphant story. Abandoned by her mother at a young age, she was raised by her grandmother and then sent to live in a slum with her aunt and uncle. Her uncle often came home drunk and abused her, making enough of a ruckus to alert the neighbors. "It was emotionally tormenting. It was a very hard life." After her aunt died, her uncle kicked her out of the house. Eventually she was sent to live in an orphanage, but when she graduated from high school and aged out, she was faced with desperate uncertainty: though the nuns running the rescue center would help her pay for college, where she planned to get a marketing degree, she had no way to support herself and nowhere to live. Then Martha heard from a trainer at her college that Samasource was hiring. She dressed up and went for an interview, assuming she would never get a callback. But several days later she was offered a job—her first job ever. "That was my happiest day." She started working the shift that runs from 2:00 p.m. to midnight so she could attend school in the mornings. With her earnings, Martha was able to rent, for the first time, her own tiny room. The door is broken, but it has a secure lock. In a small kitchen hang a few pots; her bedroom holds only a bed and a tidy pile of clothes. But it's all hers. Finally, she is realizing her dream "to have my own place, pay for my rent, buy my own food, [and] be independent." She still pays visits to the orphanage; her salary allows her to bring sweets and toys for the children.

Janet and Martha came from environments as equally challenging as that of my students in Ghana. But by the time I met these young women, I no longer felt helpless and inadequate. By then I had developed the tools to connect people to meaningful work, and the women's success proved that our strategy could make all the difference.

GETTING READY

The tools were not the ones I originally thought I'd use. A generous scholarship allowed me to spend the next few years after Ghana at Harvard, where I initially majored in government because I thought that would best prepare me to tackle the issue of poverty, before switching to a major I designed myself that combined international economic development with a focus on Africa. I studied French and Portuguese, the continent's two other major colonial languages. And I took a class with Kiaran Honderich, a visiting professor who exposed us to what were, in 2003, pretty heretical teachings that ran counter to those of Samuel Huntington and so many of the old white men who peddled economics and history orthodoxy. Honderich and a professor named Caroline Elkins, who went on to win a Pulitzer Prize for her work on the Mau Mau rebellion in Kenya, showed me a new way of thinking about Africa from the perspective of Africans, rather than that of the colonial powers. I learned how Caroline tirelessly interviewed hundreds of octogenarian Kenyans, asking them detailed questions about the colonial period and the Mau Mau rebellion, a resistance movement against the British in the 1950s. It's this kind of listening that's so rare in the world of foreign aid and development. True listening requires a sense of solidarity with the speaker, a belief in the other person's inherent worth and dignity. And true listening is what turned me on to the idea of giving work.

It was in Honderich's class that I read ethics professor Thomas Pogge's most famous book, *World Poverty and Human Rights*. This book would be one of the greatest influences on my thinking about development and aid, and crystallized why I should care about poor people on the other side of the world. Then a professor of ethics at Yale, Pogge linked the basic ideas that moral and political philosopher John Rawls popularized in his seminal theory about social justice—the idea that in a truly just society, policy makers would make laws and design institutions behind a "veil of ignorance" about where they might land in the hierarchy, so they'd be motivated to design a system they'd be happy with regardless of whether they were born into a poor family or a rich one. Rawls's theory of justice became a staple of moral philosophy, but Pogge argued that it was wrong in one key way: it applied only to citizens of one country. Pogge deftly summarized the main problem with globalization: that because capital and goods move easily across borders, but people can't, global consumers are complicit in a system that keeps some people poor and allows others to grow rich. Social policy isn't designed from behind a veil of ignorance locally, and even less so globally, since there is no global governance. Thus, Pogge argued, we have a "positive moral duty" to help the poor. A positive moral duty is a duty not just to avoid harming someone (this is what philosophers call a "negative moral duty")—it's a duty to help. And this duty is a consequence of our involvement in a system that oppresses people.

Anytime I put gas in my car, buy something made with parts, minerals, or labor from overseas, or otherwise participate in the global economic system, I'm part of it. And as a part of it, I'm therefore responsible in some way for the other people in the system. This is the cornerstone of the school of global justice in moral philosophy. For the first time, Pogge gave legitimacy to something I'd felt in my heart but had never been able to rationalize in my head: that I had a moral duty to help people who were far away from me physically, yet victimized by a system in which I was complicit.

Despite a full course load and a custom major, I worked, because even with a scholarship, life in Cambridge was expensive. At one point I held three part-time jobs: barmaid at the local theater, tutor to a child with mild autism from a wealthy family, and research assistant at a firm in Waltham. One summer I saved money for another trip to Africa by joining dorm crew, Harvard's euphemistically named janitorial service. This involved literally cleaning the shit off the wealthier students' toilets. I found the work bizarrely satisfying. I began to calculate purchases by the number of toilets it took to afford them, and honed my discount shopping skills. I bonded with my crewmates and discovered one of them had a father who taught in the neuroscience department. Mine weren't the only parents who believed that hard work was character building.

I raised enough money in grants to allow me to spend many summers and a full semester working for nongovernmental organizations, doing field research, and traveling to developing countries like Rwanda, Mozambique, and Senegal so I could understand the root causes of poverty. In 2002, I worked in India for the social entrepreneur network and incubator Ashoka on their nascent Law for All Initiative.

My efforts scored me a research gig at the mecca of international development and a leader in the fight against poverty, the World Bank.

I took a semester off so I could work there under two different professors, Michael Woolcock, whose class I'd taken at the Kennedy School at Harvard, and senior economist Varun Gauri. They didn't have roles for undergraduates, but I weaseled my way in by offering to work for a very meager contractor salary, an option because a friend offered me a free place to stay in D.C. It should have been a dream job. Though still an undergrad, I worked with the Development Research Group, a bit like a mini think tank, and did research to support the 2006 *World Development Report on Equity,* as well as a paper on social and economic rights. For a while I thought I might go for an academic or policy career and travel the world studying these kinds of macro issues. But though the World Bank was populated by incredible, committed people, it was also bogged down with red tape and complicated hierarchies. And I thought the bank's approach to addressing poverty at the time was misguided. We were focused on job creation via foreign investment in big infrastructure projects and large companies, the kind of trickle-down policy that ended up helping wealthy entrepreneurs in developing countries, but not the worst-off, lowest-income people. For all these reasons, I feared innovation might be difficult within this setting, and I had begun to realize that only innovative entrepreneurial thinking was going to get to the heart of the problem I wanted to solve. Which was why after graduating from Harvard I made a calculated move: rather than head back to another NGO or set my sights on getting a Ph.D., I took a job offer at Katzenbach Partners LLC (which we all called KPL then; now it's Booz & Company), a consulting firm in New York City. I was recruited by the firm's cofounder, Niko Canner, who asked me the first time I met him what I would do to reduce global poverty if I had a billion dollars. I loved his way of thinking about big hairy problems, and thought that working for KPL would prepare me to make better contributions afterward in the international development sector, which badly needed the kind of business thinking in which consulting firms specialized. I also needed to pay off my school debt. I took the job knowing I would leave it. It would be a stepping-stone, a place where I could acquire the business skills I'd need to one day launch my own company that would create jobs for poor people.

It was an emotionally difficult time. I felt like I was working for The Man in my client work for big companies, which was uninspiring for someone who had figured out that her purpose was to fight poverty. Yet KPL was a great, progressive company that sponsored many social initiatives. I loved much of my time there, and I was given a lot of autonomy to work on interesting projects outside of day-to-day work. I hosted Susan Davis, a leader at Ashoka, for a discussion at the firm. I signed up to consult to KIPP, the award-winning charter school network that was making waves by proving that with access to the right kind of schools, poor inner-city kids could make it into Ivy League colleges and successful careers. It was also during that time that I read *Banker to the Poor*, a memoir by economist and Nobel Peace Prize laureate Muhammad Yunus, about how he founded Grameen Bank, which did what no other bank would do: offer small loans—microcredit—to the rural poor of Bangladesh. As of December 2015, Grameen has disbursed $18 billion worth of collateral-free loans to about 9 million borrowers, 97 percent of them women, giving them the capital they need to start businesses or finish their education and build a future.

Professor Yunus structured Grameen as "a non-loss, non-dividend" company. The structure of this social business, as he would call it, was intended to blend the best of both the for-profit and nonprofit worlds. Profit was encouraged, but not at the expense of the social mission and always reinvested back into the company. Eliminating the private profit motive would protect the mission of the business should it come under pressure to put profit ahead of social impact, as so often happens. There may be some new exceptions to this rule with novel company structures, but a nonloss, nondividend company is a self-sustaining enterprise that's not dependent on donations, with leadership that retains pride of ownership yet has no incentive to profit from the labor of the end beneficiary.

I was utterly inspired, and began to think about possible models for my own business. When I hosted David Bornstein, the *New York Times* writer who'd authored a book on social entrepreneurs, for a KPL lunch-

and-learn event, he told me about a number of other companies using the same model, such as VisionSpring (then led by Neil Blumenthal, now a cofounder of Warby Parker). I wanted to spend my time on this kind of work, not what I was then doing, which was driven by KPL's business needs to help our clients become more successful and increase their profit margins.

On my first project, Katzenbach Partners sent me to Mumbai to help take a large Indian outsourcing company public. Their call center was housed in a sleek, modern building, where young people answered phones and handled customer service transactions for airlines and credit card companies in an enormous room lined with tables divided by hundreds of three-sided cubicles. Humming with voices, this call center represented just one of the thousands across Asia that were contributing to the tremendous outsourcing market. At the time I was reading a book about globalization that heavily featured this industry— *The World Is Flat*, by Pulitzer Prize–winning journalist Thomas Friedman. The title refers to his assertion that the rise in cheap access to connectivity and hardware in developing countries was flattening the global playing field, making it possible for them to compete for the knowledge work that had previously been the exclusive domain of a few wealthy countries, namely, the United States. He explains how outsourcing was transforming poverty in countries like India, where more than 2 million young people worked in call centers or business process outsourcing firms (BPOs) completing back-office work for multinational corporations. The book marked a turning point in Americans' perceptions of India; people had begun to see the subcontinent as an economic powerhouse and, more contentiously, as a competitor for white-collar jobs, and no longer exclusively as a country racked by extreme poverty.

The extreme poverty still existed, of course. When I first traveled to Mumbai in 2003, through my student work at Ashoka, I'd seen it up close. Now, as a management consultant, I could have avoided it. My comfortable corporate housing and the call center were both located in the pastoral suburbs of the city, and my corporate American Express card allowed me to travel by private car or cab. Elites never traveled by train. But I was loath to remove myself completely from the reality of daily living in an Indian city, and I was still searching for meaning and a way to connect the work I had done in Ghana with what I was doing now. So I traveled by auto rickshaw instead of by cab to visit the company's call centers, and I traveled on the train, jammed shoulder to shoulder among the rest of the city's lower-income residents. The train meandered through some of the nicest and the poorest neighborhoods in Mumbai. That's India—the best and the worst of everything exists side by side. It was the same inside the train. Maybe there have been some upgrades since, but at the time there were no doors on the train cars, so inside the women's-only compartment, the smell of talcum powder and tuberoses braided through the women's hair mingled with the stench of open sewers that announced our arrival near the slums. Those train rides were uncomfortable, but they allowed me to see the country, especially its crushing poverty. And they gave me ample opportunity to ponder the turns of fate that had led to my being born in the United States to a life that was now filled with every luxury imaginable, even as so many young women in India were confined to lives of relative misery. I thought about my roots as a Bengali, known for our rebellious streak and argumentative nature, and how those traits had manifested themselves in a family dedicated to social justice, from my great-grandfather defending peasants pro bono to my photographer great-uncle Sunil documenting India's struggle for independence and the horrific 1943 Bengal famine and to my mother, who protested for factory workers' rights in Los Angeles. And here I was, a member of the global elite, in a position to really do something to help the poor, yet not quite sure where to begin.

In addition to steeping myself in daily Indian life, I did my best to talk to as many people as I could. It was while talking to some company employees that I discovered that though most came from the educated, middle-class Indian families that typically staffed these kinds of businesses, a few did not. In fact, I found out that one worker traveled to the call center every day from Dharavi, one of South Asia's biggest slums. I'd seen it from a distance. The slum was only about three miles from Bandra, a trendy neighborhood full of cafés and restaurants, and impossible to miss during my treks on the trains. You might be familiar with Dharavi—it served as the setting for the movie *Slumdog Millionaire*. It is a desperate place, filled with refuse and raw sewage, a place where children die far too young from preventable diseases. And when I heard about this worker, I immediately saw the starting point I'd been searching for.

The World Is Flat didn't tell me anything I didn't already know—it was describing a trend that had existed in India for quite some time already. But Friedman made it click for me. He connected the dots between what was happening with technology infrastructure, the rise of cheap broadband, and the fact that millions of educated young people in the developing world now spoke English and could do work via computers. The biggest barrier to economic development is the fact that masses of people are constrained by geography due to a lack of resources, and yet capital can move freely across borders. Digital work circumvents this. It frees workers to find jobs in the richest countries, even if they can't ever physically leave their slum. And this direct connection between a poor person and a job that pays well was completely unprecedented at that time.

With the book fresh in my head, my work at the outsourcing company revealed to me a whole new possibility. Friedman had concentrated his analysis on how outsourcing was affecting job creation for middle-class and low-income countries. But I thought what Muhammad Yunus did for microfinance, I could do with outsourcing. The drawback to microfinance, however, is that the customer base is the same as the entrepreneur base. When everyone is making less than two

dollars per day, there is no wealth transfer. I envisioned a marriage between Muhammad Yunus's social business concept and a totally new
model for creating work for the poor, one that didn't rely on a local
customer base of people who were also poor. In this case, customers
could be anywhere. Through global trade, real wealth transfers occur
when poor people exchange with rich people. I thought of all the dis-
posable income of my Harvard classmates who came from wealthy
families. Imagine if they could easily hire a tutor for their kids from
Senegal or Ghana, someone who could work remotely and earn twenty
times the local wage doing satisfying work that was skill building and
leveraged their education. What if low-income people could participate
virtually in the supply chains of the future? At that time, I was often
thinking about how technology was widening our circles of empathy.
Facebook launched on my college campus while I was a senior. I was
among the first two thousand people to join before it expanded rapidly
around the country. It was clear even back then that the connective
tissue that bound communities together would soon bind people across
nations and continents, even as massive inequality in rich countries
would drive internal political divisions and threaten the global compact
(a temporary reaction that will ease as soon as we're able to find better
solutions to job losses that result from automation—more on that later).

This employee and his cousin came from one of the most destitute
places in the world. Upon learning where these men lived, most upper-
class people would have dismissed them out of hand as surely too un-
educated or too ignorant of basic office protocols to be able to handle
desk work. And yet because they were lucky enough to work for a meritocratic firm that rewarded hardworking, ambitious employees with a
lot of opportunities for advancement no matter where they were from,
these men—who had likely started out as entry-level workers like tea
servers (*chai-wallahs*) or janitors—were now answering calls on behalf
of a major airline company. I was seeing with my own eyes the embod-
iment of what Thomas Friedman had documented in his book. The In-

ternet was not just a way to share information; it could be a work superhighway connecting the poorest people in the world to the global economy. It had given rise to companies and platforms that necessitated the creation of digital jobs to handle work that had never existed before, like image tagging, data entry, and content creation. Large companies needed this work done, and there was no reason why young, literate poor people, people like Femi Abass in Ghana or the slum dwellers of Dharavi, couldn't do it as long as we could get them connected to the Internet. I returned to New York and to my management consultant job, but I started working nights and weekends researching and developing my idea for a start-up that would hire only people like them. Outsourcing was a billion-dollar industry, and I was going to find a way for the poor to get a piece of it.

In his book *The Hypomanic Edge,* psychologist John Gartner posits the theory that the reason America produces such a high number of entrepreneurs is because so many of us are descended from immigrants. The thinking goes that anyone willing to leave behind everything they've ever known to build a new life in a strange, foreign country might be genetically programmed with a higher-than-average tolerance for risk. Perhaps it's true. I'm the great-granddaughter of a man who defied the limits of his caste, the granddaughter of a woman who would not settle, the daughter of a mother who could heal what had been left to die, and a father willing to sacrifice everything for a better future. I'm shaped by the legacy of three generations of people who would not be constrained by circumstances. I took my fancy New York City job because it was the practical thing to do, but in the end it brought me full circle to the country of my ancestors, where I confirmed what I had discovered in Ghana, which is that where there is opportunity there is the potential for every human being to do as my family members did— and as most immigrants and marginalized people dream of doing: to rise, and to decide for themselves what is possible.

Chapter Two

AID: WHAT WORKS, WHAT DOESN'T, AND WHY

I ARRIVED IN MATHARE IN THE SUMMER OF 2014. HOME TO APPROXI-mately six hundred thousand people, the three square miles that make up the second-largest slum in Nairobi, Kenya's capital city, is one of the most destitute places I have ever been. From above, the flat roofs are crammed so close together it looks like a sea of corrugated metal, the flimsily constructed hovels beneath so fragile it would likely take only a gentle push to send them tumbling like dominoes to the cracked, dung-colored, trash-strewn ground. It is an intense, cholera-infested place notorious for carjackings and violent crime, so perhaps I should not have been surprised when my cabdriver refused to take me there after I slid into his backseat and announced my destination. He told me I was crazy to want to go there, and no amount of pleading would make him budge. Finally, I called the person I was traveling to meet and explained my predicament. He suggested that we meet him in a nearby hospital parking lot.

We pulled in and a smiling, handsome, neatly dressed young man in a light, short-sleeve button-down waved at us to stop. He leaned into the driver's open window and, speaking in Kikuyu, one of the local languages, assured him that he would get him through Mathare safely. Reassured by the newcomer's easy manner and warmth, the driver finally relented. As he settled into the passenger side next to the cab-driver, the man turned around and leaned between the seats to shake my hand. "Hello. I'm Ken Kihara," he said, throwing me a big, peppy smile. I noticed he had no front teeth. Assuming the role of local operative, Ken guided our cabdriver through the narrow streets of Nairobi leading to Mathare. Along the way, he told me his story.

But for a brief interlude, Mathare had always been his home. Orphaned around the age of eleven, Ken moved in with his uncle until a priest at the local school noticed his intelligence and maneuvered to get him a full scholarship plus room and board at one of the top high schools in Nairobi. He did well academically but was almost kicked out for stealing toothpaste and toilet paper from his classmates. Unable to afford these basic necessities, he had been too ashamed and embarrassed to ask for them. Fortunately, the dean of the high school took pity on him and agreed to let him finish the term. Upon graduation, however, he had no job, no money, and no connections to help him get either. So he started doing what he had done to survive throughout his childhood and adolescence, scavenging along the banks of the Mathare River—a revolting, stinking stream of raw sewage that flows through the middle of the slum—to find food as well as bits of metal to sell to the local recycler. That income plus a little money picked up by doing other odd jobs allowed him to scrape by on about $1.50 per day, which even in the slums was barely enough to buy something to eat. Eventually he found more lucrative work brewing a local moonshine called *chang'aa*. The word literally translates to "kill me quickly," and many have died drinking the foul mix of distilled corn and untreated water drawn from the Mathare River. It's referred to as "jet fuel" because it is often sold spiked with kerosene to make it more potent. That's how Ken lost his front teeth—they rotted away when he started drinking *chang'aa*, and he could never afford to see a dentist.

Ken was just one of many slum residents on the hustle treadmill—working unbelievably hard just to stay in the same place—when he heard about a computer training center located right on the edge of the slum. He had always loved technology and been curious about the computers he saw in various Internet cafés around Nairobi, but he had never had the opportunity to work with them. So he decided to check things out. The center was managed by a nonprofit that ran a work program that recruited people from the slums. Ken was intrigued enough to apply. That program was a feeder for Samasource. After doing well in an initial class for basic computer skills, he was referred for a job at one of our Samasource centers in Nairobi to do image tagging for Getty Images, where he earned more than three times the local wage. By the time I met him, Ken had been working for Samasource for about a year.

We left the cab and he escorted me through the narrow streets. Before arriving I had seen the movie *Elysium*, which takes place in a future in which all the wealthy citizens of Earth have decamped for a luxury space station, leaving behind the rest of humanity to die in squalor on the ruined planet. The scenes set on Earth were filmed in a real slum in Mexico City, a site so contaminated the actors were told to destroy the clothes they wore to work each day. But the movie might as well have been filmed here. Mathare is a postapocalyptic landscape. There is nothing green. Breathing is difficult because every inhalation fills your lungs with soot, smoke, and other pollutants. In fact, multidrug-resistant tuberculosis, a particularly virulent strain that thrives in prisons, slums, and other densely populated dirty areas with poor ventilation and air quality, is rampant. Ken lost his mother and seven of his eight aunts and uncles to the disease.

Finally, we arrived at a mud-walled one-room shack. Inside, everything was neatly organized: a small cooking station, a bed, a television. There was no running water, and the home was backed by a river of deep brown raw sewage. Pay-per-use public squat toilets were located a five-minute walk away, but Ken confided that he was always afraid of being attacked on his way to the bathroom at night. So were many other

Mathare residents. To avoid the danger, at night many would just go to the bathroom wherever they could. The stench permeating the house was almost unbearable. I met Ken's daughter, Roselyn Nyambura, a beautiful little girl dressed in pink, pristine clothes, utterly incongruous given the environment she lived in. Ken invited me in to continue our conversation, proudly showing off his few books, which he had read and reread numerous times. We talked for a long time about his youth, his family, and his country. With his Samasource salary he had bought a laptop and a modem, and at night he was teaching himself how to program. HTML, CSS, Java—he would dial up on his home modem, paying per minute, to take free online coding classes as his wife and daughter slept.

Ken told me his greatest fear was continuing to live in Mathare, because it was so violent and full of disease. He wanted to get out so Roselyn wouldn't get sick. It would take a little longer, though, because while saving to move into a cleaner, safer neighborhood, Ken was also using his earnings to invest in his and his daughter's education. With his job he could pay her tuition at one of Nairobi's best private schools, as well as her health-care costs. He dreamed that one day they would both go to college. He told me he was filled with hope.

Ken Kihara was on his way to becoming another casualty of poverty, but opportunity—in the shape of a job in the formal economy, one that didn't put him in physical danger, that was regulated by formal labor laws, and that offered chances for advancement—gave him a way out. Why opportunity was in such short supply for a man as intelligent and motivated as Ken is a complicated story that goes back centuries.

WHY IS MUCH OF AFRICA SO POOR?

The first challenge to economic growth in Africa might have been geographic. The theory of geographic determinism, discussed in depth in Jared Diamond's book *Guns, Germs, and Steel,* essentially posits that regions that have large contiguous landmasses can easily share technologies across many groups of people, thus advancing progress and prosperity. Africa's geography, like that of other so-called primitive societies, such as Polynesia, put it at a global technological disadvantage. Its massive, impenetrable jungles and major deserts locked in communities, and until very recently deprived them of the kind of knowledge sharing possible throughout Europe and Asia, which are part of one contiguous, traversable landmass. For example, the technology and cultures that developed in Egypt and North Africa couldn't spread south because of the Sahara, and those that developed in other areas, like Mali or Ethiopia, couldn't breach the dense forest zones of central Africa.

Second, like most of the developing nations of the world, Kenya is a former European colony. It was managed by the British to extract the country's natural raw resources and bring them back to the seat of the empire. In Kenya and elsewhere, when colonial powers established institutions or services, they often didn't keep the best interests of the native populace in mind. In fact, locals were sometimes prohibited from holding government offices or even studying civil service, as in Mozambique, where before achieving independence from the Portuguese in 1975, educational opportunities for black Mozambicans were so limited, 93 percent of the black population was illiterate. It's important to recognize that this colonial past wasn't that long ago. Kenya achieved independence from British rule in 1963.

But other postcolonial countries, especially in parts of Asia, are now prospering. Why hasn't Africa been able to catch up? Because of the third challenge: no other postcolonial countries experienced the kind of institutionalized slavery and brutality that marked sub-Saharan Africa. Even where the slave trade was less organized, such as in the Congo, the prevailing ideas of race that put black Africans at the bottom of the spectrum of humanity made it possible for people like King Leopold II of Belgium to murder upward of 8 million Congolese in his thirst for rubber, the precious export that paid for the gold-leafed monuments that decorate Brussels today. Much as some expect African Americans in the United States to consistently have the same educational and financial outcomes as whites just a few decades after the end of centuries of the most violent, institutionalized deprivation and abuse, so, too, do some expect the former colonies of sub-Saharan Africa to "get with the program." This thinking denies basic tenets of modern psychology, which hold that trauma begets trauma unless major therapeutic interventions take place. On a national scale, such an intervention might resemble Germany's official apologies for perpetuating the Holocaust, or South Africa's Truth and Reconciliation Commission, convened after the end of apartheid to bear witness to the human rights crimes that had been committed during that era. Without such an intervention, the trauma cycle continues, even across generations.

A BRIEF HISTORY OF AID

Given the role of the West in creating the deep poverty rampant in African countries and other former colonies, some say that foreign aid should actually be considered a form of reparations. Making these amends, however, was not the motivating factor in the founding of the first and biggest official organizations that today tackle global poverty. Our current era of international aid started with the Marshall Plan, conceived to help rebuild Europe after World War II. Over four years, $13 billion was poured into war-ravaged European countries. It was intended to be a quick fix, and it worked; some would say spectacularly well. European industrial production started up again, destabilized countries rebounded, and growth not only resumed but also sustained its momentum. Once the relief effort subsided, organizations like the World Bank and the IMF—founded to help finance postwar reconstruction and stabilize the global economy—were now wealthy with allocations from Congress, and so began expanding to other regions, like postcolonial Africa and Asia. Over the last few decades, together with other organizations, like the international relief agency CARE (where I served on the board from 2012 to 2016), Oxfam International, and USAID, they have successfully lowered the number of people living in abject misery. In fact, in 2010 the World Bank announced that it had met one of the first of the Millennium Development Goals (MDG)— cutting the 1990 poverty rate in half—five years ahead of schedule.

However, much of this was due not to aid but to globalization, which spurred job growth in Asia by increasing manufacturing and, to a much smaller extent, new fields like IT-enabled outsourcing, which employs millions of people as workers and in ancillary services, such as cooks and drivers. Globalization seems to have allowed some poor people—but not the poorest—to use new opportunities in the industrial economy to climb up to the middle class. But for people living in extreme poverty, this good news didn't register. It left 2.8 billion people still struggling to survive on less than two dollars per day, with more than half of them living in sub-Saharan Africa. They are often rural subsistence farmers or indigenous groups dependent on fishing and foraging who have been disproportionately affected by dramatic and unpredictable weather patterns due to climate change and natural resource degradation, or people like Ken Kihara, unable to connect to new infrastructure and opportunity. These people are bypassed for the jobs in the formal economy that come with a steady wage, job security, and health insurance, and that fall under local labor laws. They end up cobbling together a few jobs in the informal economy, which doesn't move them out of poverty. More than $1 trillion has been invested in sub-Saharan Africa over the last sixty years, with few gains for those living in extreme poverty. For them, trickle-down economics has not worked, because wealth drips down too slowly.

IS AID REALLY DEAD?

Carved into a wall near the entrance of the World Bank headquarters in Washington, D.C., is the bank's motto: "Our dream is a world free of poverty." We are clearly not there yet. Prominent economists have offered many explanations, but few practical solutions. Jeffrey Sachs, famous for his influence and partnerships with celebrity activists like Bono, Angelina Jolie, and Madonna, has expressed confidence that we can eliminate poverty in our generation by increasing the amount of aid we offer developing countries. Paul Collier is more cautiously hopeful, believing that aid needs to be redirected in the form of Western interventions that can neutralize the four "traps"—conflict (the link among wars, coups, and poverty), natural resources, being landlocked with bad neighbors, and bad governance in a small country—that hurt these countries' growth. William Easterly asserts that the industry's lack of interest in seeking feedback and accountability means things are unlikely to get better, because too little is invested in the scientific evaluations necessary to know which programs actually work, and then expand on them.

I agree. We don't think of low-income people as customers of aid "products"; we think of them as passive recipients of handouts. Therein lies the problem. How can aid be accountable to the poor if we don't treat them as the primary stakeholders? We should take a page from the consumer tech industry, which uses the Net Promoter Score to measure how likely a user is to recommend a product or service to someone else. Imagine the difference it would make in gauging the efficacy of aid programs if we asked poor people directly whether they were seeing the promised benefits.

Finally, Dambisa Moyo, the only thinker on the circuit actually born and raised in Africa, makes her position quite clear with her book's scathing title: *Dead Aid*. Her point is that aid takes the place of capitalism, and capitalism is the main driving force behind poverty reduction.

I don't agree with Moyo's argument entirely, because there are many instances when capitalist market failures result in disastrous consequences for the poor, as in the case of public housing (an industry in which traditional market forces drive prices beyond the point of affordability for many people, creating a downward spiral that can lead to homelessness). In these instances, a social business approach is needed, but Moyo doesn't discuss that option much, nor does she explore the power of using aid as a kind of venture capital for social enterprises solving critical social or environmental problems.

Here's where I stand: Aid in and of itself is not dead. Few, including Moyo, would argue that there is no need for charity and humanitarian aid. The emergency or charitable aid agencies that provide food, medicine, clothing, and other goods or services to alleviate immediate suffering, often in the aftermath of a disaster, are vital (although cash might still be more effective, as we'll see). But aid as we have traditionally known it—large chunks of money flowing to governments? It must be laid to rest. It was flawed from the beginning, modeled after what was meant to be a stopgap solution. For too long we have been trying to reproduce the success of the Marshall Plan and failing. There are many reasons why what worked so well in Europe simply cannot work in Africa.

THREE OBSTACLES TO MAKING AID WORK

First, corruption is an undeniable problem. Following the dismantling of colonization, most newly independent countries were left in a leadership vacuum, with few people trained or experienced in governance ready to take over. Many colonial borders still in place were drawn up by European politicians (read: old, wealthy white guys) with no regard to a population's language or ethnic groups, or any sort of shared affinity, leaving many different groups vying for control. At the dawn of independence, some nations did have enlightened leadership, like Ghana's

Kwame Nkrumah, or Léopold Senghor in Senegal. But in other countries, colonialism left behind deep wounds that did not heal after independence. For example, prior to European colonization, the region of what is present-day Rwanda had a history of peaceful interaction and intermarriage between the two dominant ethnic groups, the Hutus and the Tutsis. But forty-three years of Belgian rule (and thirty-five years of German rule before that), which supported "divide and rule" policies that pitted one group against the other—going so far as to issue national ethnic ID cards and favoring the tall, long-nosed, light-skinned Tutsis over the darker-skinned Hutus—fueled ethnic rivalries that lasted long after the country achieved independence and ultimately led to civil war and genocide. When I traveled through Mozambique as a writer for *Let's Go,* I landed in the town of Beira. It stank, and when I asked people why, they told me something I couldn't believe: that on the eve of independence in 1975, local Portuguese shopkeepers poured cement down the sewers, just to spite the Mozambicans. With such violent, tension-filled histories and a legacy of active and often legislated racism, is it any wonder that across the continent new regimes were plagued by corruption, abuse of power, and mismanagement?

Yet even in countries where development money is applied toward, say, infrastructure projects, the local economy doesn't seem to benefit. Why?

The second reason traditional aid hasn't worked is that when the formal colonial era ended, the outgoing government structures were replaced by corporate structures whose feet were planted squarely in the West. There's a lot of money to be made in development, and the tax incentives alone make these projects extremely attractive to foreign companies. To benefit the poor, any administration or company receiving loans and other forms of development aid funds would need to promise that it would hire primarily local people from low-income populations (not just elites) to complete projects. Aid recipients could bring in foreign experts to help with local training, but no money would be exchanged without proof that the poorest citizens would benefit first and foremost. That's not what happens, however. Countries that receive development loans from the IMF, for example, generally use them to pay foreign firms, most of them for-profit companies with no clear social or environmental mission, to complete infrastructure projects. Even assuming that the expertise to complete a project must initially come from elsewhere, there is no incentive to promote local job creation. Citing time and training expenses, these foreign companies generally import Western labor. And so once again, wealth is shipped elsewhere. The formal colonial era might have ended, but in its current incarnation foreign aid abets a new kind of economic colonialism. This is not to say that global trade is bad, but it can work for poor countries only when their residents have the capacity to participate as equals. They can't do that when everything from labor to materials is imported, and they are refused the experience and training necessary to eventually produce for themselves.

Colonialism is also why a solution similar to the Marshall Plan did not meet with the same success in Africa as it did in Europe. Europe was never colonized—its nation-states were formed organically. In Africa, colonialism meant that aid was layered on top of flawed governance models—government there was set up to extract resources, not represent the people. When Europe received aid under the Marshall Plan, it went to governments that were, flawed as they might have been, much more representative of the populations they governed.

Finally, foreign aid warps the relationship between a people and their government. In a modern democratic system, work creates income, income is taxed, and those taxes are used for the benefit of the people, creating a healthy social contract between a government and its citizenry. When the majority of a country's money comes from tax revenue, the government is necessarily more accountable to the people paying those taxes. When it does not follow through, the people have leverage to rise up and demand change. But in many developing countries, massive flows of foreign aid eclipse the revenue coming from the people and rob them of the ability to hold their governments accountable for providing services like health care, education, and infrastructure; there is no incentive for the government to serve its people first. When a country receives $500 million in aid, that does not mean $500 million makes it to the pockets of the people—priorities are set by whoever provides the most cash flow. For example, in the interest of fostering international relations, a host country might choose to funnel funds toward counterterrorism efforts—the donor country's priority— instead of to local entrepreneurs (despite the fact that encouraging local businesses is also an antiterrorism effort). Accepting foreign aid puts recipient governments in the position of having to build relationships with donors instead of upholding their social contract with their citizens and responding to local needs. It essentially usurps a country's self-determination and ability to come up with its own solutions and plans. It also doesn't help when the majority of the World Bank's private investments in sub-Saharan Africa go to companies that use tax havens, thus further starving poor countries of tax revenue they could use to combat poverty, as Oxfam reported in 2016.

QUESTIONING THE STATUS QUO

At the time that I started working at the World Bank, investment bankers and financiers had been leading it for decades. On my first day, I walked past the etched marble in the lobby and felt a surge of pride. That is, until I walked farther and saw a signboard advertising an employee seminar that read HOW TO FINANCE YOUR SECOND HOME. I was shocked. How could an institution whose mandate was to fight poverty encourage employees to worry about financing their second home? The message seemed off. I imagined that when you want to recruit people from the banking sector, who are used to huge bonuses and perks, you have to maintain some level of this kind of aspiration or you won't have any staff. But why, I thought, did the bank need to be staffed by bankers? It was their influence that had led to the strict economics-only approach to development that was in vogue. But I was studying development through a much wider lens than that. In addition to economist Kiaran Honderich, I studied under political economist Robert Bates, who championed the idea that the decisions made by the rural poor in Africa are a rational response to uncertainty, even if Western economists might not always recognize it as such. I had also taken courses with historian Caroline Elkins, art historian Suzanne Blier, and anthropologist Pauline Peters. This diverse set of perspectives showed me that reversing poverty couldn't be a matter of merely imposing financial reforms.

Today the World Bank is more directly accountable to the poor than it was when I was there, and its culture has changed dramatically. It underwent a sea change in focus from economic development to broader, boundaryless issues like climate change and refugees following the 2012 appointment of Jim Yong Kim, a social entrepreneur and co-founder of the award-winning NGO Partners In Health and a former president of Dartmouth College. He was the first president to announce clear targets for extreme poverty eradication: getting rid of it entirely by 2030. This made so much sense to me. Any organization with "Bank" in its title and the ostensible goal of a world free of poverty should be measuring progress against that goal with hard numbers and outcomes.

But Jim Yong Kim had not started his tenure when I arrived, and though the two professors I had come to work for at the World Bank were deeply committed to helping poor people, I was dismayed by the corporate culture there, which I felt was disconnected from the grassroots work I'd seen at places like Ashoka and Planned Parenthood. The World Bank and the International Monetary Fund had been promoting foreign direct investments for a long time, believing in the power of trade. But the kind of trade those institutions encouraged relied on trickle-down economics to reach the poor. Where was the evidence that this strategy was working?

In all my time on the ground, any progress I had seen was almost always a result of direct income increases to poor people. I had seen one of the best examples of this in 2001, when I spent the summer working for an NGO called CRESP, run by Marilyn Zeitlin. Her mission was to preserve the griot culture of indigenous oral storytelling (a West African version of Aesop's fables, with elaborate myths and stories that contain moral and practical teachings) by creating French language learning textbooks from the stories. Young people were losing them, preferring TV and radio to memorizing long fables by the fire at night, as their ancestors did. But Marilyn realized that this well-meaning effort would mean nothing if she didn't create jobs for local youth, who graduated from the same schools where her storybooks were used. So she started a cyber café, staffed by young people she trained, where locals could use the Internet for a modest fee. The café also did digital projects—brochures and signs for local merchants, for example—and ran computer classes. I thought her model made so much sense: the community in Yoff, a fishing village close to Senegal's capital, Dakar, wanted to preserve its identity, but not at the cost of accessing new kinds of jobs. Young people were so eager to learn about technology, thanks to former president Abdoulaye Wade's emphasis on fiber-optic capacity. So many young Senegalese spoke beautiful French, owing to Senghor's emphasis on La Francophonie and the country's rich cultural legacy; some were now tutoring kids in French remotely, demonstrating a totally new kind of job. I didn't see it so clearly then, but this helped sow the seeds for Samasource many years later.

A year later, in 2002, while working for Ashoka in India, I had the chance to meet a woman who helped me understand how powerful work can be to change lives. Sister Jeanne Devos had moved to India decades before and became sickened by the rampant abuse of domestic workers, including girls as young as six or seven. In a country with enormous disparities of wealth, families in rural areas often have no choice but to send one of their children to work in the city. Earning less than a dollar a day is common, and the girls, working under the table outside the bounds of the law, are vulnerable to physical and sexual abuse. Jeanne wanted to do something about this—she felt that being a Catholic meant taking action on behalf of the poor. So she decided to organize domestic workers, using the church as her base of operations. India, because of its incredible religious diversity, has very progressive laws allowing people to practice their faith. Jeanne started inviting all the domestic workers she could find to church on Sunday. But rather than proselytizing, she focused on educating her mostly female charges about their rights. Under India's labor laws, workers are entitled to time off, sick days, and other basic workers' rights. Domestic workers, often kept at home and frequently illiterate and unable to access education, are some of the most mistreated workers on the planet.

By the time I'd met her, Sister Jeanne had organized more than ten thousand of them and lobbied to change India's laws to officially recognize domestic workers and give them the chance to pursue legal action if they were denied basic protections. She understood that the solution to curbing mistreatment wasn't stopping domestic work altogether, or making it impossible for teens to work—that would put further financial pressure on workers' families, driving them even deeper into the poverty that led them to this situation in the first place. Jeanne realized instead that the solution was to ensure that her girls were paid decent wages and empowered to stand up against abuse. And thanks to her work, tens of thousands of the most downtrodden women in India were able to earn more money and live better lives. This is the kind of social action that inspired me: working together with people who might otherwise be written off as "victims" to achieve measurable results. Jeanne was anything but top-down: she was in the trenches, meeting with domestic workers every day, connecting them with legal, emotional, and financial support wherever she could, and, most of all, taking them seriously as peers, not as charity cases.

Her example stuck with me over the years, especially when Mother

Teresa, another India-based Western nun, was canonized. Mother Teresa has been heralded as a champion of compassion and an advocate for the poor, but, though I admired her ability to build awareness about poverty, I thought her approach to fixing it was flat-out wrong. Through her network of hospice centers, she provided kindness, food, and compassion to people no one else wanted to care for. But she never ventured to address the deep sociopolitical injustices that had condemned her charges to their fates, nor took steps to ease their pain and suffering in the long run. And she refused to track the impact metrics for any of her hospice centers, believing that the hard work of God didn't require a hard-nosed approach to measuring outcomes. As a result, many contend that her facilities actually exacerbated conditions of poverty, perhaps most famously in Christopher Hitchens's blistering critique of her work in *The Missionary Position*.

The impulse to give from the heart and to help people is noble and beautiful. But to make a difference—a real difference—we can't just throw money at a cause or do what feels good for our own psyche. Moral philosopher Peter Singer wrote about "effective altruism" in his book *The Life You Can Save* and in the *Boston Review:* "Effective altruism is about making a difference in the world. . . . So [effective altruists] don't give to whatever cause tugs strongest at their heartstrings. They give to the cause that will do the most good, given the abilities, time, and money they have." He then goes on to explain that while effective altruists will have different definitions for "the most good," most of those definitions will revolve around some shared values, namely, a preference toward a world with less suffering and longer life spans (a perspective not shared by Mother Teresa, who once said, "I think it is very beautiful for the poor to accept their lot. . . . I think the world is being much helped by the suffering of the poor people").

All the data tells us that reducing poverty is the best way to achieve that goal. According to Singer, effective altruists, therefore, have a duty to ensure that their donations or humanitarianism actually result in material advances for poor people. That doesn't mean we have to necessarily increase our donations—spending is not a proxy for effectiveness. It means we have to do our homework. And for aid agencies and charities, it means they have to make it easy for us, through transparency and impact measurement. Lengthy reports stuffed with academic jargon appeal only to a niche within the world of development economics. When we don't make it easy for laypeople to understand poverty reduction, it makes them susceptible to believing that we spend more than we do to fund international aid. If on top of that they don't think aid works, they're likely to think their money is being wasted.

But here's the reality: each government agency calculates U.S. foreign aid spending differently, which is what leads to discrepancies in spending reports; yet even when including military aid or "nontraditional assistance," like research, America spends less than 1 percent of the federal budget on international aid. And though there are many reasons why traditional charity doesn't work, there are many aid programs that do. We have the tools to prove it using randomized testing, like the method pioneered by the Poverty Action Lab at MIT. More than eight hundred studies in seventy-seven countries have been conducted to understand the real impact of aid programs and guide better allocation of public money. In areas like basic health care, primary schooling, and drug research, public funding is critical—these are areas in which the market typically fails to provide adequate services to people living in poverty. We also have organizations like GiveWell, which were founded to evaluate charities based on impact, not just financials. In addition to the financial audits required by law, nonprofits can now opt to undergo an external "impact audit" from ImpactMatters—an independent group of development economists led by Yale professor and poverty measurement expert Dean Karlan—which provides rigorous, objective research and data to help these groups validate their evidence, offers recommendations to improve performance, and educates donors (Samasource completed its first impact audit in early 2017, receiving eight out of nine stars). The effectiveness of nonprofits shouldn't be based on how little they spend on overhead; that keeps their benchmarks too low. No one cares how much money it takes to develop a lifesaving drug. All they care about is that the drug works, that it offers a competitive return on investment, and that it gets into the hands of those who need it. The same efficacy standard should be used for nonprofits. Donors should ask themselves one key question: is this the most cost-effective use of my capital to solve a given problem based on the social return created per donor dollar? These new measurement tools allow donors and the taxpayers who fund foreign aid to see the objective impact results, making it easier for nonprofits to use their funds the way for-profits are allowed to—to hire top talent, advertise, fund-raise, and experiment.

Aid dollars can absolutely have a positive impact, but they have to be directed to the right programs. In my view, these programs are best run by social entrepreneurs who produce real, measurable results, rather than by bureaucrats. There was a time when measuring how many people were lifted out of poverty through aid was impossible, so instead we tracked progress by the number of people we reached—for example, the number of people we fed. We doled out food aid by the ton, and in the process undermined local farmers' ability to supply their countries with affordable food. Who really benefited? American agribusinesses, which won enormous contracts producing cheap grain for countries overseas, subsidized by the American taxpayer.

This is the inherent challenge with giving away stuff in poor countries. Western good intentions have destroyed local markets for the very goods and services people need most: clothes, shoes, water, and basic sanitation. And we call it charity. Locals have felt the pain of this acutely, and many are frustrated that the same model, which started with food aid back in the 1960s, continues today. Now that we have the tools to track impact and measure outcomes, giving money or clothes or food just for the sake of giving, and not in a manner that attempts to solve the reason for these shortages, is unacceptable. The charity industry has become too wrapped up in making donors feel good about giving—to keep donations coming in—rather than concentrating on treating marginalized people as equals who want the same prosperity and security that we have.

THE PROBLEM WITH FREE STUFF

Whenever I have asked foreign aid recipients whether they would prefer aid or work, they almost always choose work. When I was a travel writer in Mozambique, Malawi, Brazil, the Philippines, and Borneo during the summers of 2002 to 2004, I spent a lot of time with locals, living on the cheap (I often went days spending no more than two or three dollars on food and camping on the beach or in the cheapest flea-ridden hostels I could find). I'd ask them what they thought of the NGOs, whose four-by-fours would often line the parking lots of the nicest hotels. People had very mixed reactions. It seemed the biggest value many of these agencies provided was job creation—nonprofits like CARE and Save the Children worked hard to hire mostly local staff. Most of the service workers I encountered had experience working for NGOs as cooks, drivers, translators, or administrative assistants on contracts. They were plum gigs, akin to getting a "government job"—basically a stable source of income, and one of the only industries that had decent jobs. Why was this? Why did the aid industry dominate? It seemed so broken that instead of getting a job at a local, say, shoe shop, people were more likely to get a job at an NGO that gave away free shoes.

Something else I found interesting: when pressed to discuss politics, most poor people would tell me that agitating for justice came second to feeding their families. The first time I encountered this was in 2002, when I traveled to Rwanda with five Harvard classmates to spend two months studying the Gacaca tribunals. Gacaca refers to Rwanda's traditional grassroots community justice system, where elders would hear disputes at the village level and mediate, bringing reconciliation to fighting individuals and families. As it tried to heal from the 1994 Rwandan genocide, in which hundreds of thousands of people—most of them minority Tutsis—were tortured, murdered, and raped, Rwanda decided to bring back Gacaca at the national level, moving low-level prisoners to community courts where their crimes would be heard out in the open and community members could weigh in. The hope was that this would significantly reduce the long wait (estimated to be 120 years) to get all the prisoners flooding Rwandan jails to trial. Our research team had learned about the courts in a class called African Political Economy, and we wanted to know whether they would satisfy international legal norms, or actually promote reconciliation. Our professor, Robert Bates, took note of our interest and suggested that if we really wanted to understand this system, we couldn't do it from an ivory tower; we needed to travel to Rwanda and talk to people. So we did, each of us raising money from every grant-giving institution we could find to fund our trip, and recruiting a young professor to come along with us to add legitimacy to the project.

It was an unbelievable opportunity for us to do serious field research in Africa. We interviewed several high-profile government officials, including the head of the Supreme Court and Paul Kagame, Rwanda's president. But the most enlightening meetings were with victims and perpetrators of the genocide. The perpetrators we met were average Rwandans who were often forced to commit atrocities, like murdering their neighbors. Many of them were stuck in prison for years without trial because the courts were so overcrowded. I thought the Gacaca court was a noble project, but was surprised to discover that the victims and perpetrators we talked to didn't seem to care much. I remember meeting with the head of one victims' rights group. She was a single mother, and through her short-cropped hair you could see the scar of a machete wound. Her husband and one of her children had been murdered, and another had survived. When I asked her whether she thought Gacaca would serve to create justice for average Rwandans, she schooled me. She looked at me warily and said, "Only you foreigners care about these questions. We struggle to eat, to feed our children. My worry is to find a job so I can afford to buy necessities." Countless Rwandans told me the same thing. Every day people asked, "Hire me as your driver? Do you need a guide?" They were far more consumed with day-to-day concerns like affording food, housing, and health care than with the kinds of projects most academics were working on, which didn't make a direct impact on their daily lives.

Don't get me wrong: it's important to study new legal systems and understand whether they're working. But my concern then was the same concern I have now, which is that much of the aid establishment is focused on initiatives and projects that don't have a fast, direct, measurable impact on the world's poorest people. The only thing that will truly solve the problem of poverty is to put more money directly in the hands of the world's poor. The most sustainable, cost-efficient, and socially beneficial way to do this is to give work via direct job creation to connect these poor populations directly with employers. Impact sourcing can move massive amounts of capital from the coffers of large companies that have enormous procurement budgets, currently not used to fight poverty, directly to poor people.

Direct is key. It's not enough to encourage investment in poor countries. That money too often goes to elites, who create firms that might employ locals, but might not pay living wages or create good jobs, and often concentrate wealth at the very top. To ensure job creation benefits the poor, the incentive can't just be for investment, it has to be for job creation specifically among the poorest. Only then will we see firms competing to employ the worst off in ways that provide living wages and decent working conditions. This kind of incentive for direct job creation should be financed by aid programs. If instead of shelling out billions of dollars to giant beltway bandits, USAID financed firms that proved they were hiring people making less than two or three dollars a day and lifting them up to a living-wage level in their countries, that would have a huge impact. Money would go to where it actually makes a measurable dent in poverty. Businesses would have incentives to create more employment among previously untapped resources. And poor people would earn income, invest in their own infrastructure, pay taxes, and demand more from their governments, which could start collecting more money from tax revenue than from aid transfers. So the problem isn't with aid. The problem is with the large sums of money that go from one government to another government or company with little accountability, either to the people funding the aid or to those it's supposed to help.

THE SOLUTION

The idea that sprang into my head on the floor of the call center in Mumbai would put money into people's hands. As I stood there, realizing that a slum worker was eminently capable of performing the same kind of work as his middle-class counterparts, everything I'd read by Thomas Friedman and Muhammad Yunus, along with everything I'd absorbed over the years from Sachs, Easterly, Collier, and all my professors, and everything I'd learned through my conversations with the people we all wanted to help, converged. I suddenly saw the key to creativity, a direct model where I could have a measurable, immediate impact. This was how I could fulfill my positive moral duty. The outsourcing industry had generated billions of dollars for a few wealthy businessmen. What if I started a company that inverted the outsourcing concept and used it to generate a few more dollars for the billions of people at the bottom of the pyramid? The World Bank and many other NGOs I'd observed on the ground took an indirect approach to job creation by focusing on infrastructure and investments whose benefits were expected to trickle down to reach the poor. I wanted to start with the poor and watch the benefits trickle up.

I spent a year and a half refining my idea until finally, using a series of online templates to guide me, I conceived a business plan for a company I named Market for Change. A two-sided marketplace that would benefit clients and workers, it would hinge on a brand-new concept, which at the time I called ethical outsourcing. I would eventually work with the Rockefeller Foundation to come up with a label that would do for local outsourcing what the term "fair trade" had done for agriculture and manufacturing. And thus the term "impact sourcing" was born.

Today impact sourcing is a global phenomenon, taking up $4.5 billion of the roughly $200 billion outsourcing market, but at the time few people were talking about it, and only a few progressive companies, like Digital Divide Data, with a presence in Cambodia, Laos, and Kenya, were even touching it. Impact sourcing is a subset of outsourcing that focuses specifically on giving work opportunities to the poorest of the poor—women and youth living in rural areas, slums, or anywhere of high unemployment. Market for Change would be a new type of outsourcing company, a social business, one initially grounded in seven principles Muhammad Yunus would later outline in his 2010 book, *Building Social Business:*

1. The business objective is to overcome poverty, or one or more problems (such as education, health, technology access, and environment) that threaten people and society—not to maximize profit.
2. The company will attain financial and economic sustainability.
3. Investors get back only their investment amount. No dividend is given beyond the return of the original investment.
4. When the investment amount is paid back, profit stays with the company for expansion and improvement.
5. The company will be environmentally conscious.
6. The workforce gets market wage with better-than-standard working conditions.
7. Do it with joy!!!

It would recycle profits into recruiting and training very low-income people to do digital work like data processing, rather than hiring middle-class, skilled workers who would quickly generate profits for investors. Raising the profile and skill levels of the poor would move everyone up the value chain.

All the technology trends had aligned to make this idea feasible. Traditionally, outsourcing companies took on high-touch jobs such as customer calls that required a relatively high level of language and computer skills. But increasingly much of the work companies were outsourcing was digital, any work that could be done via the Internet. A lot of it was coming out of Silicon Valley. And much of what made the tech industry's innovations viable and desirable depended on relatively low-skill data-processing tasks like image tagging, address verification, or content moderation. This kind of digital work, though necessary, was worth too little to interest either traditional outsourcing companies or the middle-class employees they usually hired. It would, however, pay enough to make a tremendous difference in the life of someone living in a slum. That's where my company could fill in the gap.

We wouldn't teach people to code. Coding jobs are often discussed as a solution to poverty, but coding jobs are fewer and farther between than the most basic digital jobs done by computer that are typically found in the outsourcing market, and I was interested in the lowest-hanging fruit. I envisioned securing computer centers where we could teach workers to do basic tasks on inexpensive machines, connecting them with clients in the States through project management. We'd work with local partners like entrepreneurs, schools, or NGOs to establish or use existing computer centers and Internet cafés and recruit and train local employees. And not just in the big cities, either. One of the main obstacles to job creation among poor people is that while capital can move freely, labor often cannot. As a result, poor people are often stuck in rural zones cut off from modern infrastructure. If I wanted to make it easier for more poor people to earn a living without having to

leave their communities and families, I would have to figure out how to
get connectivity to rural areas. Once upon a time, that challenge alone
might have squashed my plans, but the costs of technology and infrastructure were plummeting. Whereas in 1858 there had been only one
transatlantic cable in existence, by 2007 there were many more snaking
their way across the bottom of the sea, and we knew that fiber-optic
cable, which would enable high-speed global telecommunications, was
on its way to East Africa. The excitement over this was palpable—the
impending arrival of cable was a constant topic of conversation. It was
the holy grail of progress.

Even without cable, satellite-based Internet and 3G data had spread
across East Africa. The age of the one-hundred-dollar laptop was upon
us, and low-cost netbooks made in China were sold at markets in Nairobi and Kampala. Cheap computers couldn't compete with higher-end
models for graphic displays and memory, but they would be more than
sufficient to handle the kind of digital work I wanted to procure.

Until now, there had been few ways for individuals or small companies in developing countries to reach out to big global players and compete for a piece of their business, but already some people were proving
that applying a few modern business strategies and concepts to the aid
industry could increase the amount of money that actually made it to a
developing nation's people. In 2006, the Peace Dividend Trust (now
Building Markets) conducted a study tracking the finances of ten UN
peacekeeping missions to postconflict countries and war zones and
found that only 5 percent of their budgets actually made it into those
countries' economies. The U.S. Department of Defense, for example,
was allocating most of its contracts in Afghanistan to foreign firms and
bringing in its own talent to build infrastructure even though there was
plenty of local labor available. To correct this, the organization, founded
in 2004 by a Canadian named Scott Gilmore, created a database of verified local firms as a resource for procurement officers at the Pentagon
and foreign aid agencies, and trained the local businesses to bid for

those agencies' contracts. Since then, Building Markets has facilitated more than $1 billion in contracts to Afghanistan, representing about sixty-five thousand new full-time jobs.

I wanted to redirect procurement funds, but I saw great opportunity in targeting the private sector, not just foreign-aid nonprofits and government entities. Multinational companies had masses of money to spend, including deep outsourcing budgets and even money set aside for social initiatives. Local entrepreneurs needed a liaison who could convince these companies to take a sliver of their budget and commit it to hiring a vendor in a poor region—specifically one that had committed to creating work opportunities for the poor and the marginalized—to handle some of their outsourcing work. This new model would put cash directly in the hands of poor people, the only way to move them out of poverty and keep them out. We'd give aid in the form of jobs in which people would learn skills that they could continue to use as they built careers.

SPOILER ALERT: IT WORKED

In the decade since we launched we've been able to show progress and traction toward an outcome. We have the impact data to prove that our employment methods work and produce the same or better end results than foreign aid in the best case (when it works), such as raising incomes, stabilizing families, and promoting civic engagement. On average, in their first four months at Samasource our workers move from two to more than eight dollars per day. And they stay out of poverty over time. There's no backslide. Three years after leaving us, the average worker is earning up to 3.7 times more per year than before they started working at Sama, and many are earning more. In the centers we manage ourselves, like our main center in Nairobi, we have moved workers to 16 times their baseline income!

Workers learn skills that make them relevant in the new economy and increase their marketability. In fact, they often stay only a little more than a year. Unlike more traditional companies, we see high turnover as a great marker of success, because when our workers move on, they move on to higher-paying work, and often to higher education. After leaving Samasource, 85 percent of workers continue to work or pursue their education. Of those who continue working, 98 percent remain in the formal sector, mostly sticking to information and communications technology (ICT) and customer service, but with a number going into finance and accounting or starting their own businesses. Lately, the trend is that many are choosing to stay longer to work on higher-value projects for us, presenting us with a new challenge: choosing between keeping them in a seat that could go to someone else or losing the skilled worker we have invested in training for so long. We're trying to find the right balance. This is the kind of struggle that social enterprises always navigate—the line between profitability and social impact.

That progress translates into improvements in a worker's overall health, too. As in the States, poor people in developing countries often subsist on cheap carbs, especially sugar. But as soon as our workers start earning more, they change the way they eat. They start buying more protein, vegetables, and healthy food, and then they invest in health care and education for their children. Within about six months, they move out of the slums. That's what happened to Ken Kihara, the former bootlegger and slum resident of Mathare. Not long after I first met him, he moved himself and his family out of the slums and into safe housing. He wasn't far from Mathare, but he was living in a real apartment building with indoor plumbing and toilets, away from the violence and grime of the informal settlement. When I saw him again about a year later, he had been promoted to a training position and was earning about four times what he'd made before joining Samasource (over the course of three years his pay would rise to about sixteen dollars per day, putting him squarely in the Kenyan middle class). Something else had changed, too. His smile, always wide and full, now showed off a perfect set of brand-new teeth.

WORK LIFTS WOMEN

A chilling global reality is that wherever men have a hard time finding work, women have an even harder time. The one thing that remains constant no matter where Samasource goes is that when we target women, we see total transformations for all. Women make up 60 percent of the world's chronically hungry. Their labor force participation is only at 55 percent, with participation as low as 25 percent in the Middle East and North Africa. When they do work, women continue to earn, on average, 10 to 30 percent less than men for paid labor, yet they are the sole breadwinners in one in three households around the world. In many countries, women are discouraged or forbidden from pursuing an education; in fact, women make up the majority of the world's illiterate adults. Women in the United States were 35 percent more likely to live in poverty than men in 2015. But as of 2011, only 7 percent of all philanthropic donations were given to organizations that addressed the specific needs of women and girls, and the Foundation Center estimates that less than 10 percent of total foundation giving goes toward this group. Yet women are likely to reinvest an average of 90 percent of their income back into their families, whereas men are more likely to reinvest only 30 to 40 percent. What does that mean? If you really want to lift all boats, raise the women's boats.

Generally, when women have paychecks, they spend them on family expenses, specifically on health care and education. Multiple studies have shown that when women do better, their babies and children do better, reaping the benefits of improved maternal health, better nutrition, safer housing, and early education. Those good head starts in life can add up to exponential improvements in a family's overall health and income over the course of generations, the benefits of which can spread out over an entire community. Research and impact reports that Sama-source has published bear out the same conclusion. One study we con-ducted with a researcher from the London School of Economics and Political Science in a center in the village of Rukka, in the Jharkhand state of India, revealed that while access to employment and the devel-opment of new computer skills raised the "confidence, dignity, and self-respect" of all the participants in the program, the women (who worked in all-female centers) reported that they had actually gained status in their homes as a result of their employment. They experienced other shifts as well:

- They felt they could have a say in making purchasing decisions.

- In a region where women are often sold into brothels, families treated them with more respect. In fact, one worker's father-in-law offered to watch her children so she could keep working.

- They were able to help their children with their studies.

- They "found a voice to express their thoughts, ideas, and concerns" and believed they were now considered "valuable members of their family, community, and the workplace. . . . They have also started recognizing and participating in various political situations affect-ing their lives, such as speaking up when they believe they are being unfairly treated." At times they seemed astonished at how much their lives had changed: "I thought empowerment was only in the books. A job really empowers you."

There are plenty of women's empowerment programs, but the best kind of empowerment is cold, hard cash given directly to low-income women. These organizations are doing important work to support women, but many of the problems they aim to fix, from gender-based violence to inequality to a lack of access to education, are rooted in cultural and religious beliefs about women and their worth. Those beliefs are exceedingly hard to change. Imagine that you were a member of one of these cultures—would you want to listen to anyone who tried to persuade you, even in the most respectful way, to rethink your entire worldview because they consider it backward and self-defeating? Trying to change social mores from the outside hardly ever works. Change has to come from within the community. And when women get jobs and gain economic agency, that change starts to happen. The world starts to look dramatically different and the barriers that traditionally hold women back, from the threat of violence to social structures to legal obstacles, fade when women earn as much as men (or, for that matter, any money at all). Digital work is a hammer that can hit many different nails. Give a woman the tools to raise her economic position, and she raises her value to her family and community. Money transcends religious and cultural barriers. We have found this holds true even in the most conservative areas where we have introduced our program.

The women of Metiabruz, a devoutly Muslim neighborhood located on the outskirts of Kolkata, are not allowed to walk outside uncovered or unaccompanied by a male family member. Nor are they allowed to work in mixed company outside the home. While their husbands can travel to the city to pursue all kinds of work opportunities, women are limited to teaching small children—provided a family member is available to chaperone them to and from school every day—or working from home sewing and doing beadwork for local factories. This is work that is paid by the piece and earns them about ten cents per hour.

We were careful. Antipoverty work in a community can backfire when you show up with a missionary philosophy or agenda. The Play-Pump, for example, was supposed to be the answer to water deprivation in Africa. It was a merry-go-round water pump that would be powered by children at play. Maintenance costs would be paid for by selling advertising space on the side of the water storage towers. The idea was so obvious and so appealing that the U.S. government, the Case Foundation, celebrities, and other donors together pledged more than $16 million in 2006 to fund a rollout of PlayPumps across southern Africa. But just a few years later, many PlayPumps lay abandoned and still. The pumps, which cost $14,000 apiece, were expensive to maintain, and it was hard to get parts delivered to the rural areas where they were located. Ad sales hadn't produced much revenue. In some areas, there weren't enough children around to power the pump, so adults, usually women, had to do the work. They sometimes found it embarrassing to rotate the "merry-go-round" when they knew people were watching who did not know what it was for. Of those interviewed during a UN evaluation, not one woman in Zambia liked operating the pumps, and in one community adults actually paid children to "play." Women said they found their original hand pumps much easier to manage. Tellingly, no one associated with PlayPump ever asked them if they wanted to make the exchange. "The pumps just arrived."

You have a far higher chance of making a real difference in a community when you are invited in. So when a local organization that was considering opening an all-women's center in Metiabruz asked if Samasource would like to partner up, we jumped. Careful not to make waves or challenge the area's deeply held beliefs about gender roles, hard as this was for a feminist like me, we approached the local imam to ask his approval to open the center. We knew we would need his blessing before parents or husbands would give their daughters or wives permission to participate. Predictably, he was reluctant, concerned that the center would bring in bad values and corrupt the community. We begged him to let us open for one month, during which he could get a sense of how we operated and what we were asking of his female community members. We promised that if he didn't like what he saw we would shut the center down.

What happened? The women quadrupled their income, and any resistance they might have met from their families faded away as soon as their households felt the dramatic effects of their paychecks. In fact, we were quickly asked how fast we could ramp up the program. The imam became a big supporter, and at our peak we were able to supply work to about 120 women at one time. Eventually the local partner grew enough that it didn't need us to supply jobs anymore and we moved on, but they are still in operation. Arfana, a young woman who used to work in her father's embroidery business earning five to ten dollars per month before joining Sama, which allowed her to bring home ten times that amount, testified to the dramatic change in her community's attitude toward women: "Earlier the thinking was that women should lead a normal life, cook at home, be a housewife," she told us. "Now all families want their women to work. The whole community is changing the way they think."

In West Bengal, on the border of Bangladesh, the women living in one of the largest minority Muslim communities in the world are also some of the most marginalized. Neha Parveen, a doe-eyed twenty-year-old with a huge smile, is the only girl in her community with a job. Her parents were skeptical about allowing her to accept a position at Sama. Among other concerns, how would she pay for her school fare? But once she started working, she was not only able to pay her tuition, she started contributing to the family income, supporting her father, mother, and brother. Her parents are proud of her, she says, not only for helping them but also for helping to change society. When asked about her dreams, she confesses that she wants to be a pilot, though she knows it's unlikely in her present circumstances. But she adds, "When I am not in [my town], after the time will pass, I will achieve my dream." The mere fact that she can envision a life elsewhere indicates that work has done more than enrich her life—it has broadened her horizons and sense of possibility.

To be clear, I am generally appalled at the way women in India are treated, and it still shocks me that we have to ride in a "women only" compartment in the train in order not to be grabbed or ogled. But the pragmatist in me realized that the fastest path to change is through understanding and shifting economic incentives. Few people ever change unless they have a reason to. By putting money in the hands of women, Samasource provided that reason. This isn't to say that we don't need to pursue legal reform and other kinds of systematic change. Increasing income alone is not enough to move the needle as far as it needs to go. But it doesn't make any sense to run NGO programs that, say, educate the population about women's rights while ignoring the income issue. On a trip with CARE to Benin in 2012, for example, I learned that the biggest cause of gender-based violence wasn't cultural attitudes but women's lack of economic agency. Families often sent their girls, some as young as five or six, to work as housemaids and servants in wealthier households in Nigeria, which shares a fairly porous border with Benin. Abuse was rampant, with reports of rape, physical and emotional abuse, and generational trauma. CARE's response was to run educational programming in Benin encouraging women not to send their daughters away. Yet when I spoke to many local women about labor trafficking, they'd respond, "I went away, too. We had to. She has to. How else can I feed my other children?" The U.S. ambassador to Benin at the time told me that he thought the only way to stop the practice locally was to give rural women another option to increase their income, such as building a major export industry, the way other West African countries had done with shea butter. CARE's other flagship program, Village Savings and Loan Associations, shows more promise: these revolving savings groups have helped millions of women access credit for critical expenses.

The only way to solve poverty is by creating economic agency, which also shifts the balance of power. That plays out in a tremendous way in communities where women have traditionally been repressed, but it also reveals itself at the micro level. For example, I once spoke on the phone with a worker who was indignant that his government, with little notice, had made plans to demolish a swath of the slum where he lived to build a road. He believed that as a tax-paying citizen, he had a right to weigh in on a decision that would adversely affect members of his community. That's what happens when people start earning money—they start questioning the decisions made by local leaders and representatives. In Jharkand, most workers already voted, but they didn't participate in other political activity. After working at our center, they expressed more willingness to engage politically and stand up for their rights. It's the same reason women in Metiabruz became interested in voting for the first time. I suspect this shift happens because when you're not terrified of today, you have more time and energy to think about the future and the broader questions that will affect it. I've heard from many of our workers that you're not a full-fledged person in modern society until you've had the chance to open a bank account or do the other kinds of official things that most people without income just can't do, like apply for a passport, or regularly vote. Working, earning money, providing for yourself and your loved ones, and believing you can affect those who represent you in government make you feel like a true citizen.

WORK LIFTS DISASTER VICTIMS

We've seen the Give Work model successfully operate as a form of emergency aid, too, but one that carries people forward once the immediate crisis is over. For example, in 2009, at a talk in Palo Alto, I met Dr. Paul Farmer, a physician, medical anthropologist, and cofounder of Partners In Health, an NGO dedicated to bringing advanced health care to developing countries, including Rwanda, Lesotho, and Haiti (and a man who, in my estimation, should have long ago won the Nobel Peace Prize). Once covered in lush forests and a major source of the world's mahogany, sugar, and tobacco, more than two centuries ago Haiti's economy took a terrible hit from which it still hasn't recovered: an international boycott, in which the United States participated, meant to punish the slave rebellion that led to the country's freedom from France. In exchange for lifting the boycott, France demanded an "independence debt" to repay slave and plantation owners for their losses, a debt satisfied only in 1947. That setback combined with severe deforestation that increased the likelihood of mudslides—the ravages of the region's frequent tropical storms and hurricanes—and decades of political corruption has led to Haiti's rank as the poorest country in the Western Hemisphere. Dr. Farmer explained to me that often, in addition to asking for healing, his patients ask if he can help them find work. That got me thinking. With 53 percent of the population literate in French and English, and located only a short plane ride from the States, wouldn't Haitians be great candidates for digital work?

Six months later, Dr. Farmer introduced me to the director of 1000 Jobs Haiti, an organization committed to developing sustainable jobs based in Mirebalais, a small town in Haiti's central plateau, and we decided to look into partnering up. On January 12, 2010, our program director e-mailed the team to share the news that 1000 Jobs had been accepted into the next phase of our training program and that we would prepare to open our first Haitian work center. Twenty minutes later, we got word that a catastrophic earthquake had struck just west of Port-au-Prince.

The quake left more than one tenth of the population homeless overnight. The city was leveled. I called the center manager and asked if we should divert our focus to something more immediate, like sending food or water. He said, "Of course not! Tens of thousands of people have lost their livelihoods—their small shops, merchandise, or kitchens. What Haiti needs most right now are jobs." The areas around Port-au-Prince, including Mirebalais, had seen a huge influx of refugees in the earthquake's aftermath. They needed relief, but they would also need to rebuild. I decided to expedite the opening of the center and fly there myself to launch it, taking the first commercial flight after the earthquake from Santo Domingo, in the Dominican Republic, to Haiti's devastated international airport on a Sunday afternoon. Though my flight was eight hours late, I arrived in Mirebalais to see fifty people waiting outside our new computer center. A few minutes into my presentation the power shut off. Our recruits used the light from their cell phones to continue poring over the course packet, staying late into the night.

Aid agencies had of course rushed to the scene as soon as they got news of the earthquake, but there was no national 911 number for people to call and tell these agencies where to find them and what kind of assistance they needed. In response, a group of for-profits and nonprofits banded together to quickly create an SMS-based 911 number to connect emergency responders from the International Red Cross with Haitians who needed help. Called Mission 4636, it allowed anyone within the country to send a free text to the number 4636. Through a special Give Work app we created with a San Francisco–based crowdsourcing company called CrowdFlower, we translated the tens of thousands of texts that poured in. Unfortunately, most aid workers arriving in Haiti didn't speak or read Haitian Creole, the language spoken by most of the survivors, and the translation software wasn't up to the job. The U.S. State Department offered funding to outsource the translation and geolocation work necessary to make the emergency number effective. While many volunteers from across the Haitian diaspora stepped up to provide services, we, along with several other organizations, worked together to make sure that Haitians, and not an international outsourcing company, got those translation and geotagging jobs.

One thing we needed was laptops, and in my quest to find them, I bumped up against the frustrating strictures of traditional aid. On my way to Haiti, I'd stopped in Cambridge, Massachusetts, to meet with a few friends in the MIT Media Lab who I thought could help; they put me in touch with Guy Serge Pompilus, director of One Laptop per Child, in Port-au-Prince. OLPC was a program created by MIT professor Nicolas Negroponte to improve the education of poor children around the world by giving everyone their very own laptop. The machines, designed in a child-friendly bright green and white, ran on free open-source Linux software and were supposed to give the children a chance to play, explore, and learn on a computer like any other child in the digitally connected world. When I arrived on that first commercial flight to Port-au-Prince from Santo Domingo, on a tiny airline called Tortug'Air that gave me my ticket on a handwritten carbon-copy form, the first person I met was Guy Serge.

Guy was super friendly when I asked him for laptops. I needed fifty, for the fifty people I was about to train in Mirebalais. Guy said, "I have a whole warehouse full of OLPCs sitting in Port-au-Prince, but I can't give them to you."

"What?" I said. "You have laptops collecting dust. I have a way to get them to the neediest people, who will use them to earn money and feed their entire communities, and you can't give them to me?"

He shook his head, obviously extremely disappointed. OLPC has a policy, he said. The laptops could be used only for "educational purposes, and for kids." This was a mandate from the top.

I thought about this for a long time. Here we had a program, financed by many well-intentioned donors, that had the absurd and, frankly, paternalistic mandate that children be the only ones to use their laptops. The core idea was well meaning—to ensure that the computers weren't taken by adults in the children's households and used for purposes other than education. But how could we dictate terms like this in countries where parents are struggling to earn two dollars a day to feed their families? How absurd must this kind of policy seem to the average person in a country like Haiti? I was livid.

We ended up buying laptops, while the OLPC machines sat unused.

The program has since received many critiques for this kind of top-down approach to development. The design was torn apart for being the brainchild of idealistic academics who didn't seem to grasp that what poor people wanted was to use the same tools that we do in the West, so they could compete in the same markets and communicate on the same platforms. Some people I talked to in Africa felt that the green-and-white design was a "giant poverty banner" that made poor kids feel conspicuous. They would have rather just used normal laptops like everyone else.

OLPC's downfall was adhering so closely to a strict ideology and orthodoxy that it could not, or would not, hear the feedback it was getting from its users and adjust so that it truly served them well. Start-ups don't have that luxury. Samasource and the other organizations we collaborated with in Haiti, born and raised in Silicon Valley, which has a borderline unhealthy obsession with avoiding bureaucracy and "disrupting" things, are forced to pivot when needed. It's why we were able to work together quickly to come up with solutions to the immediate aid challenges posed by the earthquake, and help long term by getting cash directly to people in need, not through a series of one-time donations but through work projects.

Ultimately, Samasource was able to hire fifty people for about eight months of steady work assisting in transcriptions and other necessary recovery work. Today we still have about twenty-five workers in Haiti doing a range of services for clients based in Montreal, and also for 360 Incentives, a marketing services firm in Ontario. When they needed French-speaking workers to serve their customers, they turned to us. Jason Atkins, founder and CEO of 360 Incentives, who was so moved by the Give Work model that he later married in Haiti, said they "were looking around the world [for] how we could fulfill the third commitment of making a difference. . . . I believe that if you give a man charity, you help him for a day, or maybe a month . . . but if you give him work you change his life forever." And they did change lives. "We were hopeless," says Luc Emmanuel, the engineering graduate who found work with Samasource's Team Haiti, "but now we've got hope that our lives will change in the future. Now I am studying chemistry and would like to be a biochemist. I would like to help my country by testing the food we are eating." Work, not aid, transforms how people think of themselves and their place in the world.

WORK LIFTS REFUGEES

We've found that the power of work holds true even in the most desperate circumstances. I'm not sure there is anywhere worse off than Dadaab, a huge refugee camp with more than 450,000 inhabitants on the border of Kenya and Somalia. For more than twenty years, Somali refugees fleeing horrific violence and war in their native country have taken shelter there, stuck in a no-man's-land supported by the Kenyan government, humanitarian nonprofits, and international donors. Recently, as the refugee crisis in Europe has worsened, many of those donations have been diverted or decreased. In 2015, the United Nations High Commissioner for Refugees (UNHCR), which runs the camps, received pledges of only $110 million of the $500 million it requested to keep up the humanitarian standards of its refugee programs in Kenya and Somalia. As of mid-2016, it had received only $7.2 million, or 1.4 percent of its original request. The thing is, the $500 million would still provide only the bare minimum of nutrition, health care, sanitation, and security for close to a million people. And, of course, that money isn't destined to go directly to the refugees, where it might have a direct impact; rather, it would fund the management of the camps. The ultimate goal should be to give the refugees a life outside the camp, and for that they need jobs, training, and income. It was to provide that opportunity that Samasource set up a center in Dadaab, a story I'll share in greater detail in the next chapter. For reasons outside our control we could stay for only a few months, but we saw so much potential that we made it a priority to get back into the camps as soon as we could.

We almost didn't get the chance. In May 2016, the Kenyan Ministry of the Interior announced that it would move forward with plans to shut down the camps within a year, citing "pressing national security" concerns, such as a terrorist attack at Garissa University College that killed almost 150 people the year before, and the strain on a country trying to cope with a refugee population that has swelled to more than 600,000. The ministry added its assurance that the "AU [African Union] has also confirmed that Somalia is now safe, ready, and willing to receive her citizens." The following February, Kenya's High Court proclaimed the government's order "illegal and discriminatory," and as of this writing, the camps remain open. The Kenyan government has said it will appeal. The threat of expulsion adds just another layer of stress onto a population that has borne more than their fair share. Even though it would seem that foreign aid has not sufficiently curbed the desperation and frustration that are often at the root of religious terrorism, there are other ways to ease the burden of Kenya's refugee problem and prevent terrorism from spreading than tearing down the only home some refugees have ever known.

There are causes of terrorism that we still don't know how to address, such as mental illness, religious fanaticism, and gun access. And then there are some that encourage what I call opportunity terrorism. These acts of violence are not inspired by a desire to force a religious agenda, fantasies of heroism, or even revenge or hatred, but because they pay. In many communities, terrorism is the only job you can get that earns enough to survive, support a family, and garner respect, so even if you don't espouse the dangerous views of militia leaders, for example, you might follow the dollars. In an article for *Wired* about the economics of Somali piracy, written right around the time Samasource was first in Dadaab, journalist Scott Carney calculated that in a region where the average Somali earns six hundred dollars per year, even adjusting for the risk of prison or death, the potential payout of a minimum of ten thousand dollars per hijacking makes piracy a better option than staying in violent Mogadishu. The best way to diminish any terrorist organization's power is to show its target recruits that there are other viable options to earn a living.

We don't need to tear down the camps to stop terrorists from making headway there. A more pragmatic solution would be to redirect aid money toward creating work opportunities instead of free stuff, so that we could give refugees, especially vulnerable young men, a sense of dignity and productivity.

Every refugee I have ever spoken to has told me that his one concern was finding or keeping a decent job. Rations are necessary, but they are also demoralizing and demeaning. Especially when you've been dependent on them for twenty years. Though many refugees in Dadaab cling to the hope that one day they will be allowed to leave the camps and start their lives anew, if only in their host countries, most are terrified of the prospect of returning to Somalia until they can be sure they have something to go back to. Can you imagine living this way? The refugees know that if they could work, they could supply all the free stuff aid organizations currently provide—food, shelter, clothes—and fully participate in and contribute to society to boot.

Sticking the victims of violent conflicts in camps with no work and no way out is a recipe for disaster, as is forcing them to go back to countries where they and their families are likely to be murdered if they refuse to fall in line with an oppressive regime, or are part of a religious or ethnic minority. Refugees who have been given the proper developmental support have seen tremendous success after establishing themselves in their new countries, furthering their education, starting small businesses, getting involved in local politics, and contributing to the economy.

This is a lesson we, citizens in the wealthier nations of the world, need to take to heart, whether we're talking about the refugees in Kenya or the masses of Syrians, Afghanis, Eritreans, and others fleeing to Europe and our own shores. We only hurt ourselves when we shut our borders, block these populations from starting over, waste their creative and intellectual potential, and keep them from building productive, healthy lives. The very foundations of this country as we know it were built by immigrants; to limit our tradition of offering shelter and opportunity to the world's poor, tired, huddled masses is a mistake we would make at our peril.

Instead, we should create incentives for companies to engage in impact sourcing, like yogurt company Chobani. As founder Hamdi Ulukaya, himself a Turkish immigrant, told the World Economic Forum in Davos, "Integration is extremely important . . . as CEOs and owners, we must open our doors just like everybody else in the community, yet we must go [the] extra mile . . . to let them be part of society and part of the workforce." He has created around two thousand jobs between his upstate New York Greek yogurt manufacturing plant and his second, the world's largest, in Idaho. Some of those jobs are given to refugees.

One of those incentives could be subsidies. Since they are performing a more effective long-term role than a refugee camp, entrepreneurs willing to tackle a humanitarian crisis by hiring refugees, in addition to locals from marginalized or poor backgrounds, and paying them local living wages, should receive a subsidy. Subsidies would help solve a huge problem in many of the countries that have large refugee populations, like Lebanon and Kenya. Local governments and citizens often express frustration because Westerners love funding refugee programs, often excluding poor locals, but we don't take many refugees ourselves. This is the situation in Lebanon, where agencies have been flooded with EU money so that refugees stay in Lebanon and don't go on to the EU. But what if instead this money went to businesses that committed to hiring both refugees and low-income Lebanese locals, perhaps in some sort of agreeable ratio, and paying them living wages? It would fight poverty, support migrants with their biggest need, and increase productivity. It would help mend relations between refugees and host communities. It would also encourage the creation of more social businesses, including businesses run by refugees that employ nonrefugee locals. "I can tell from my experience," says Ulukaya, "the minute a refugee has a job, that's the minute they stop being a refugee."

The work we make available to immigrants, or migrants, or refugees, must be the kind of work that they can realistically use as a launch pad to something better and permanent. For example, some organizations have implemented programs to teach Syrian refugees to code, but getting someone to the point where they can make good money coding is tough. At Samasource we have chosen to focus on training people to do lower-level microwork because there is an insatiable need for it in the tech sector, and you can make money quickly with this skill. And the evidence bears out that many people who learn the ropes on this type of work move up to more challenging, better-paying jobs in short order—when the opportunity exists. By incorporating the Give Work principle into their companies, the new generation of entrepreneurs and business owners can make a tremendous difference.

Over the last decade I've seen digital work dramatically improve the lives and futures of refugees in crisis, victims of natural disasters, urban slum dwellers, and the residents of rural communities. Global poverty is a hairy problem without a clear culprit, but my experiences in Africa, India, Haiti, and now Lebanon have continually reaffirmed that it is only opportunity that is spread unevenly, not potential. That's the beauty of digital work: it is borderless. It transcends ethnicity, race, religion, and gender. It transcends the artificial walls we build between humans. It seems so obvious to me that breaking down these barriers should be a priority for all of us, not just because it is the right thing to do but because it makes political and economic sense. When we provide opportunities for work instead of aid, we provide a long-term solution that not only lifts people out of poverty but gives them a say in how goods and resources are allocated. We give them a role in their political system, and a chance for them to take the lead in their own lives.

Samasource is currently in the middle of another pilot, in Beirut, which has more than 280,000 registered Syrian refugees. One of them is Fatem, who escaped with his family when his village was invaded by ISIS. They lost everything. Fatem did construction work to support his wife and six children, and a few of his children dropped out of school to work. He told me, "We are so grateful that by the grace of God the people here took us in. I will do anything, borrow any amount of money, to support my children, the girls and boys both, to get an education." I had the chance to meet him when I traveled to Beirut to talk about impact sourcing at the Banque du Liban Accelerate international conference at the end of 2016. While there, I was able to catch up with Ken Kihara. Ken is now a Samasource trainer who has helped more than 500 people from the Kibera slum in Kenya get jobs through Samasource and other local ICT companies. He had taken his first plane ride to Beirut to help train Syrian refugees to do digital work. When we spoke, he told me he couldn't believe how much his life had changed. Later, Ken would write a powerful Facebook post that crystallizes the mental shift the developed world needs to make so that we can bear witness to more incredible success stories like his:

"We see opportunities for work when they talk business, we see potential workers when they talk slum dwellers, we see technology and skills when they mention #computer. We are #samasource #samaschool #impactteam with #Leilajanah."

Chapter Three

THE CAPITAL OF HUSTLE

JULIET AYOT IS A FORMIDABLE EXAMPLE OF RESOLVE, OPTIMISM, and ambition. Yet while those qualities enabled her to survive unspeakable trauma and carve out a meager existence, they couldn't magically increase the resources at her disposal. An AIDS orphan from an area in Uganda best known for civil war, child abductions, and extreme rural poverty, she managed to survive infancy because her mother died soon after her birth, before she could breast-feed. Three of her older sisters were not as lucky. Raised by her mother's family, she witnessed the atrocities of the civil war that ravaged her homeland and displaced more than 1.8 million people. Northern Uganda began to rebuild following a cease-fire in 2006 and most of the internally displaced population returned home, yet the employment opportunities in the area remained dismal.

Juliet lived with several relatives in a dilapidated colonial-era house that had once belonged to her grandfather. In her room, where she slept on a mattress on the floor, she proudly kept a stack of the school certificates she had won; her university report card, which she'd laminated; and her high school diploma. Though she did well in school and spoke English beautifully, Juliet was unable to find a job to support herself or pay her university tuition. She resorted to borrowing money from her extended family and making extra cash through various small entre-preneurial ventures, including selling vegetables she farmed behind her house as well as foreign imports. She had bigger dreams, but without access to work that paid more than a dollar or so a day, she had no way to finance them. She was about to drop out of school when she heard that Samasource was opening a delivery center in Gulu. She was one of the first applicants for a job. When I first met her, she was tagging pho-tos of celebrities for Getty Images. We often joke about the surreal na-ture of the project: that the Western obsession with the Kim Kardashians of the world is the most unlikely fuel for an antipoverty program. It was an entry-level position, yet she was earning more than three times the average local wage. With her first Sama earnings, she bought herself her first blanket, as well as a few items of work clothing to supplement the only other three garments she owned. With the rest of her early pay-checks, Juliet bought two pigs and arranged for them to live on a farm a few hours outside Gulu by motorbike. She hired someone locally to raise the pigs until they bred, then began selling off the piglets. In short order, she was promoted several times and is now a center manager. Recently, she used some money saved from her piggery earnings to pur-chase two cows for milk and breeding. She hopes to own a factory-scale dried-fruit business one day, and she has already written a detailed business plan, including a provision for a half-million-dollar commer-cial dehydrating machine. It's a big dream, one that would require enor-mous capital, but I wouldn't put it past Juliet; she is showing incredible promise as an entrepreneur and businesswoman.

Entrepreneurs talk a lot about hustle. Americans, in particular, highly prize this quality, often crediting it as the key to achieving the American Dream, if not a highlight of American character. But believe me when I tell you we do not have a monopoly on hustle. If anyone is prepared for an entrepreneur economy, it's those whose daily lives are consumed with finding something, anything, to sell so they can earn a few dollars and live another day. Very few citizens of the developing world are just lying around waiting for handouts. It's not in rich countries like ours where you see hustle the most; it's in the world's poorest. I could see it in Dadaab, where people would scavenge in the local trading town and bring items like water canisters back to the camp to sell; in Mathare, where men like Ken cooked up moonshine; and in Gulu, where Juliet Ayot continues to breed pigs and cows as a lucrative side hustle. You can practically taste it in the air when walking the streets of Nairobi, Kenya's capital. It is a thoroughly modern, bustling city, which, like so many developing world hubs, has the best and the worst. There are lush gardens, an animal orphanage where you can cuddle baby giraffes, and incredible food and nightlife. And then there are fetid slums with open sewers and the kind of human desperation that gives you nightmares for weeks afterward. But it's a city of hope. People everywhere are striving to make life better for themselves. It's a city that inspires me in every corner at every hour, filled with entrepreneurs who literally built their businesses in trash heaps and still manage to survive. This is the kind of place where real entrepreneurship—the life-or-death, if-I-don't-make-this-business-work-I-might-die, I'm-willing-to-pay-40-percent-interest kind of hustle—takes place.

This is so not Silicon Valley. Not because people aren't smart or tech savvy. But because many of them have real problems, and cook up real solutions, rather than the kinds of 1 percent innovations we see too often in my home city. While some entrepreneurs in America raise hundreds of millions of dollars to create two-thousand-dollar toaster ovens and smart hairbrushes, and apps that let you airbrush your wrinkles out of photos (I've definitely used this one, but only really guiltily), Nairobi is busy making shit happen on a shoestring. And while this model doesn't work for all kinds of world-positive innovation, like the extremely costly process of mapping the genome, for example, it works extremely well to focus entrepreneurial efforts on the things that matter most: low-cost housing, better food systems, mobile money transfers, and ethical lending via microfinance. It is a place where great social enterprises are born or scale up. One Acre Fund, for example, provides financing and agricultural training to small-scale farmers. Branch, a microlender, offers financial services via a mobile app; and Sanergy, which "turns poop into profit," sells pay-per-use toilets to franchisees, then sells the collected waste as fertilizer.

To me, Nairobi was a catharsis. I felt at home in the madness of the city's frenetic pace. In fact, Kenya as a whole has a strong entrepreneurial, deal-making culture, which was why in May 2006 I went back in pursuit of kindred entrepreneurial spirits.

Unlike other African nations, like the Congo or Angola, which have relied so much on their ample natural resources to generate revenue that they invested little in schools or the infrastructure necessary for people to be able to work and be productive, Kenya and other coastal African countries, like Ghana, Nigeria, and, most recently, Mozambique, escaped the so-called natural resource curse by investing in human capital and creating a supportive, business-friendly climate. Kenya has a large literate, English-speaking, globally aware youth population, and is one of the most mobile connected societies on the African continent. In 2006, the government established an ICT policy designed to support Kenya's social and economic development by encouraging connectivity, and as of 2014, the Kenyan rate of cell phone ownership rivals that in the United States. More than a third of the Kenyan population uses the mobile money transfer service M-Pesa, which allows poor people to use their cell phones to conduct financial transactions despite being unbanked.

Its location along the east coast also meant Kenya would be one of the first African countries to have access to the two new transoceanic fiber-optic cables that arrived in 2009. Fiber-optic cables meant high-speed Internet and a 90 percent decrease in the cost for the average Kenyan to get online (until then, businesses used satellite connections to get online, the high expense subsidized by the World Bank). That cable was the African equivalent of the American waterways to Dutch settlers in the 1600s, facilitating and speeding up transactions and communication and carrying along economic opportunity. Large spools of red cable dotted the highways as it was rolled out across Kenya and Uganda from Mombasa, the main connection point. The national energy surrounding this milestone was palpable.

For all of these reasons, I believed Kenya would be the best place to look for my impact-sourcing business's first vendors.

I didn't go straight to Nairobi. First I went on safari in the Maasai Mara National Reserve with some good college friends: Meagan Jones, who was working for Facebook at the time (she's since become a backer of Samasource), and Timothy Thairu, a Kenyan techie. Meagan and I are big outdoorsy types, while Thairu is a man of the city and dislikes things like hiking. So he made sure we booked a lodge that was full-on "glamping"—luxury tents, daily safari game drives, and tons more food than we could handle. We must have made an impression on many of the Kenyan hotel managers, who assumed that Meagan and I were Thairu's two wives, and in one case we were even put in the honeymoon suite. The three of us, who had never dated, found this absolutely hilarious and tried as hard as we could to keep up the charade.

Like many entrepreneurs, I have a restless energy and relaxing is hard for me, but I loved the days we spent in the Mara. I had traveled all over when I wrote for *Let's Go* during my summers in college, to some of the most remote, beautiful places in the world. And still the Mara stopped me in my tracks. There is a sensation that the sky is larger there than anywhere else. It is so big and bright and blue it almost feels like an optical illusion. You can't help but wonder about our own insignificance in the face of nature, or imagine what life might have been like before our ancestors started walking bipedally. We saw so many of the "big five" animals—lions, buffalo, elephants, leopards, and rhinoceroses—that we became completely desensitized. So that by day three we were blasé when our guide showed us a group of lions feasting on a fresh kill, and by day four even baby lion cubs tussling or cuddling their mom induced a yawn. That's how incredibly beautiful and wildlife packed the Mara is. It makes the rarest wilderness seem mundane.

Besides offering unbelievable game viewing, the refuge hosted evenings when guests could gather to learn more about local culture. One evening, my friends and I sat in front of the fire while men wearing traditional red Maasai dress performed a beautiful jumping dance. I was a little uncomfortable—while I loved the performance, this was exactly the sort of clichéd cultural tourism I'd always tried to avoid. Afterward, I approached one of the dancers, who had taken off his Maasai garb and changed into pants. "Are you a professional dancer?" I asked. He laughed. "No, I'm studying IT at the local university. My dream is to move to Nairobi to get a computer job." I asked him why he was dancing. He replied, "It's a job. I have to pay for school." Of course. This twenty-year-old recognized the importance of preserving his country's cultural traditions and art forms, but he still wanted the same things everyone else does: a good job, maybe a family, and a secure future. The dance was just a show, a means to an end.

And so, as beautiful as I found the Maasai Mara, once I decided I'd had enough downtime I returned early to the capital city of Nairobi, where I hoped to scope out small businesses that I could convert to work centers, as well as find entrepreneurs who might be interested in partnering with me.

I stayed with Timothy's father, Professor Henry Thairu, a dean at the local university. Over dinner I shared my idea of connecting the poor in Kenya to the world's outsourcing firms. Internet cafés could be found everywhere in Nairobi, even in low-income areas. What if I could convince some of their owners to devote a piece of their business to outsourcing and completing data-processing projects for global companies? I'd secure jobs that would be simple enough that they wouldn't require a lot of training to complete, and small enough that I could monitor them to assure the quality myself. Like everyone else I'd met, Dr. Thairu was excited about the prospect of Internet-based development in his country. He introduced me to a Microsoft-sponsored local business incubator. Intrigued by the idea of spurring innovation with a social mission, and committed to helping Nairobi's burgeoning tech sector, they allowed me to put on a daylong workshop for potential partners, a sort of meet and greet to talk about the seed of an idea—could they use their computer centers to do data work for me, hiring only low-income women and youth? Dozens came, and I interviewed thirty different entrepreneurs. To my surprise, many women attended, some with businesses in the computer space and degrees in relevant fields. I loved that the Kenyan tech scene had a better gender ratio than in Silicon Valley (Kenyan VCs have more female partners than in San Francisco, according to friends there). One of those women was Diana Muthee Gitiba, who ran a small computer business, Adept, that did data work for Kenyan firms. Also attending was her brother Stephen Muthee.

Steve embodied Nairobi hustle. Born to a poor family with eight siblings, at the age of twenty-three he was one of countless bright, ambitious university graduates who got out of school only to discover there were no jobs to be had. So he created his own. Relying on a bank loan and some donations from family, he launched a small data-processing company he called Daproim (Data Processing and Information Management). To bring in money quickly, he started it as a tiny Internet café so he could charge customers hourly for computer time. When I met Steve, he had four employees, all with underprivileged backgrounds like his own, and had set up his business digitizing court records. A devout Christian, he was eager to grow the business not just for his own sake but to fulfill his mission to help the poor, the marginalized, and the struggling by giving them work. Steve might not have realized it, but he had already joined the impact-sourcing movement. He knew there were big companies around the world that could use his services, but he didn't have the marketing or travel money to properly compete for those lucrative contracts. He promised me that if I could connect him with a global player, he could find educated, capable employees to do the quality work I was proposing.

I saw so much of myself in Steve. We were the same age, twenty-five at the time. Like every entrepreneur I've known, he was hungry and determined, exuding a sense of optimism and possibility. A proud Kenyan brimming with vitality and excitement, he had already read about Indian outsourcing in the newspaper and was eager to prove that it could work in his country. He was excited to build up his nation and show the world what Kenya could do. I knew it would be a challenge to convince American clients to outsource work to a place they'd long ago characterized as merely a destination for their charity dollars. We would need someone on the ground willing to move mountains to prove them wrong. Launching a start-up was going to be an exhausting process that required a partner with unlimited amounts of energy. Watching Steve make friends with everyone at the event, I could see he had not only energy but also great selling instincts. He had a tiny shop, he was tremendously motivated, and he seemed open to taking risks. He could see that social impact was a differentiator that would make his firm stand apart from others that didn't have the same mission. I'd found my first partner.

I organized the first Facebook Developer Garage in Kenya, recruiting a Stanford intern to help me teach local developers how to design apps for the platform. More than a hundred people attended the event, traveling for miles by foot or *matatu*. We would later bring it to Uganda and Ghana (where a young man would tell me that he saw himself as the next Mark Zuckerberg). Over time I would continue to build partnerships with local techies and people passionate about bringing business to their country through more workshops. Everywhere I went I met people eager to work, to learn, and to produce.

I was on fire by the time I returned to the States.

STARTING UP

The only start-up capital I had was about $10,000 in savings, which I had accrued through my job at Katzenbach Partners. That wasn't going to be enough. Earlier that year I had submitted my business plan to the Business in Development Challenge, a competition for social-venture ideas funded by the Dutch Postcode Lottery, the third largest philanthropic donor in the world. It's the coolest system: people buy lottery tickets, which are identified by zip code. When the winning ticket is drawn, anyone who bought a ticket from that zip code shares in the winnings. One hundred percent of the profits from the lottery are then donated to causes selected by the public. No one ever loses—if you don't win, you have the satisfaction of donating to a great cause that you helped select, and if you do win, so does your whole community. It's genius.

I made it to the semifinals, ultimately winning second place and 15,000 euros, about $20,000. Then, in early 2008, I won another $15,000 when my plan won second place in Stanford's Social Enterprise Challenge Business Plan competition. This would prove doubly fortuitous, for not only did I get a necessary influx of cash, one of the judges liked my idea so much she would eventually join the company's board of advisers.

Thirty-five thousand dollars wasn't much, but combined with my savings it was enough for me to quit my job, which I did two months before receiving my second-year annual bonus. I was that eager. (In fact, a year later I got an e-mail from one of the company partners informing me that I actually owed the company money for some expenses I had forgotten about; I didn't have the money and he had to lend it to me!) I sold most of my possessions except for my old Miata that I'd bought on Craigslist for two thousand dollars, and moved to Palo Alto. I holed up in the cheapest place I could find, a tiny room in a house in Mountain View, also procured through Craigslist. It was much cheaper to live there then than it is now. No one had an iPhone. Uber didn't exist yet. It's kind of hard to imagine.

A former professor managed to help me secure a position as a visiting scholar in Stanford's global justice program. It didn't pay, but it provided an office space from which I could work, and gave me a little cachet. Armed with a brochure I created on my Mac and printed at Kinko's, I tapped my small circle of contacts—a lot of my Harvard friends had already moved to California to work for a young company called Facebook—and started approaching every entrepreneur and business I could find that might need my company's services. It's common for many companies to reserve funds for charity and philanthropy and have budgets set aside for end-of-year donations. Most companies also have some form of digital work languishing in a data repository waiting to get done. My argument to potential clients was, why wait? And why not reallocate that charity money to a company that would not only get the work done with a high level of quality and service but also put it directly in the hands of the people we all wanted to help—not via those people's governments, and not via aid organizations. The wealth would be distributed using the mechanism of the market. It would be a win-win: companies could get their work done on the cheap, and poor people would benefit from decent jobs that gave them the skills and confidence they needed to build careers in the digital economy. I knew I would face criticism for concentrating on helping the communities I'd worked with overseas instead of turning my efforts closer to home, but I hadn't yet figured out how to apply my idea domestically. It seemed unconscionable to abandon an idea that could offer help to so many people just because they weren't "my" people.

I quickly learned two things. First, Market for Change was a terrible name. I'd known it all along. Clunky and nonspecific, it had never felt right. The core idea behind my company was exciting and aspirational: Give work! Change people's lives! The company name needed to reflect that energy and sense of possibility. I researched all kinds of words from different cultures and languages. One that greatly appealed to me was in Swahili: *dalali*. My research told me it was the word for "broker," likely referring to those who once sold materials from the Arab world to the locals on the East African coast. It was lyrical, it was a little techy, and it had a great meaning. Then I started canvassing my friends. One, an Indian woman, made a face. *Dalali* did mean broker, she informed me, but it was often used to refer to the kind of broker who sold women, not just trade goods. Maybe I'd want to reconsider? Out went *dalali*. A little more research and I found the word *sama*, a Sanskrit word that means "equal" or "fair." Anyone who practices yoga knows that it is also the root word for many of the poses. In Arabic it means "sky." In Hindi it's the root word for "same." I loved it. The word crystallized exactly what I wanted this company to do—give all humans an equal opportunity to make the most of their lives. We were sourcing in a way that furthered the value of *sama*, and so we became Samasource.

The second thing I learned as I vied for additional funding was that my company would have to be a nonprofit. Thank goodness for business-plan competitions, because getting money from any other source was proving problematic. No one quite knew what to make of me. I was twenty-five. I wasn't enough of a traditional start-up to give private VCs confidence that they'd ever see a return on investment. I had friends in tech—I attended a lot of parties at Facebook and was friends with the Airbnb and Dropbox founders—but the tech boom hadn't happened and there was no megawealth yet to draw from. I wasn't a traditional aid group or charity, either, which meant the philanthropic organizations that might have funded me were also leery of me. When I met my friend and mentor Premal Shah, cofounder and president of Kiva, the world's first peer-to-peer microlending site, I asked him what I should do to improve my fund-raising success rate, and his advice was to do whatever I needed to do to get my organization off the ground efficiently and achieve my mission. It was clear that as a for-profit, I'd probably receive a great deal of praise and admiration, but not much else. As a nonprofit, however, we would be eligible for grant money, and the organizations holding those purse strings not only admired us but seemed willing to support our efforts, too.

There was no debate over what I should do. I applied for 501(c)(3) status and received it in late 2008.

I doubled down on grant writing, but that came with its own challenges. That is, the money itself comes with lots of restrictions. You have to be able to predict how your plan will work and what you're going to accomplish several years out, which is an especially big challenge when you're working in a rapidly changing environment like tech. What works or what is even possible at the beginning of a fiscal year could be completely different by the end, depending on what technological advancements or new platforms have been perfected. Plus, grant makers just didn't seem to get it. They were locked into the idea that poor people weren't capable of the kind of work I wanted to hire them to do, and that jobs were secondary to insecticide-treated bed nets and water. Not being plugged into the tech world, they also had a limited understanding of how far and how fast the Internet was going to take us, and they couldn't fathom what kind or how much work it was going to generate as a result. The only way I was going to prove to anyone that the people I wanted to hire were capable of performing high-quality work would be to show them the work. But for that I needed a client. I needed someone to take a chance on me.

That chance appeared in the form of a technology company called Benetech, run by a friend of mine, Jim Fruchterman, a decorated former rocket scientist and social entrepreneur. He created Benetech to apply technology to solving global problems. One of its branches, Bookshare, based in San Francisco, is the world's largest nonprofit online library for people with print disabilities, such as blindness or low vision, and reading disabilities caused by conditions such as dyslexia. Bookshare had just won its own large contract to provide textbooks to American students with disabilities, and Jim needed people to proofread the digital book transcripts to make sure they were perfect before loading them into his audio software. I loved the idea of working with another nonprofit and helping disabled people around the world gain access to more books. I gave Jim my personal guarantee of quality, and he gave me a thirty-thousand-dollar contract.

I had a client, a contract, and a vendor. And so Samasource finally launched in September 2008—the same month as the biggest market crash since the Great Depression.

Launching any start-up is brutally hard. Launching a nonprofit just as the country starts staggering through a financial meltdown can make you question your sanity. Banks were failing, people were losing their homes, and the national mood was grim. I didn't feel the financial effects—I was paying myself only four hundred dollars a month anyway, so I was essentially already living in crash mode. But it was a bad time to try to raise funds for an organization designed to help poor people on the other side of the world. The money we procured for our first contract with Benetech went straight into the overhead associated with Steve Muthee's computer center, including paying the workers he had recruited and hired. Within a few short months my savings had run out and I had left the little room in Mountain View to take up residence on my ex-boyfriend's futon. (I've always been blessed to date really good people and develop deep, lasting friendships. I've decided that's an important skill for an entrepreneur. Build your tribe, because you will definitely need one for support.)

It was one of the most depressing periods in my life. I'd gone from living in my own apartment and having a steady job at a well-respected firm to couch surfing and working all alone in a drab cubicle in a far-flung corner on the Stanford campus, trying to hash out deals one by one, some as small as one hundred dollars a month. I sat alone in obscurity eating vegetarian Top Ramen three times a day and carefully counting out the daily allotment of Red Vines licorice I depended on to sustain my energy. (Later, Kevin Jones, the founder of Good Capital, whom I'd met at a networking event and who had become a friend, set up a PayPal account labeled "protein" to make sure I ate something healthy every now and then.) Meanwhile, my friends were traveling, socializing with Silicon Valley's up-and-comers, and immersing themselves in their work at cutting-edge companies that were clearly on the verge of becoming household names. There were days when I was consumed with self-doubt. What the hell was I thinking? Did I have some kind of messiah complex? Who was I to think I could actually make any kind of a dent in poverty?

I would sometimes calm myself down and regain perspective by visualizing the people I was trying to help, and reminding myself how lucky I was compared to them. Yes, I was living on my ex's futon. Yes, I was eating only ramen and Red Vines every day and foraging the Stanford campus for events with free food. But I was doing this by choice, because I had the luxury of an enormous tool set: a good education, low-interest student loans, and a network of powerful friends who had room to spare. The vast majority of humans on this planet have had no such luxuries. And the majority of those people didn't kill themselves. So I was going to be okay, even if things often felt like they sucked.

The worst vortex I'd get into was the "If only my life were like Person X's" spiral. I'd imagine how perfect Person X's days were, waking up in a luxury condo just off Palo Alto's tree-lined main street, walking hand in hand with her boyfriend to their tech start-up jobs, which gave them stock options worth millions, leaving work at five to work out at a designer gym. This was the life that a lot of my friends enjoyed, and there were many, many moments when I craved the security of a job and the built-in social network that came with it. Especially because my friends were all literally working for the hottest social network, and even then it was clear that they were going to end up with a lot of money (we had no idea how big their bank accounts would actually grow, but many of them are now worth tens or hundreds of millions of dollars).

But maybe that's the price of following your dream—you have to be willing to say no to everything that's not your dream. In my darkest moments, I'd remember the poem "Harlem," one of my favorites by Langston Hughes, about the potentially terrible consequences of leaving "a dream deferred," and that would get me through.

What really kept me going was the immediate feedback I'd receive via Facebook from the employees working in Steve's computer centers. They were doing excellent work. I'd stay up late at night reviewing the transcripts of the books they were proofreading, fulfilling my promise to Jim Fruchterman to personally oversee that he got a quality product. And he did. Steve's hires were competent, careful, and prompt. He hadn't had any trouble recruiting good talent.

Steve was tireless. He found it easy to recruit poor youth because he'd ask the local universities for names of students in their scholarship programs. He'd also place radio and newspaper ads targeted to reach the slum communities. At one point he identified a recruiter who had a radio show for youth from the slums. To motivate them in their job search, she'd give these great talks about how to build confidence, self-esteem, and other soft skills. He also reached out to local NGOs, orphanages, and other institutions that housed or worked with youth who lacked opportunities. He told me excitedly about Jobita, a young deaf guy who wasn't able to work, as no one would hire a stigmatized kid from the slums. Steve taught him to do data entry. Jobita was excellent, with a very good eye for detail when comparing transcripts to images of text. His abilities were so stellar that he was quickly promoted. Steve loved the idea that Jobita was working on transcription for a company whose mission was to create accessible reading materials for the blind.

Though the local government never offered to assist us in our efforts, one of the ministers did attend one of our workshops, which earned us some local press. Most Kenyans, even those living in the slums, read the papers and listened to the BBC, so, like Steve Muthee, they had already heard about outsourcing successes in India. The minister's appearance helped legitimize Samasource and eliminated any reason to be skeptical of our intentions and purpose.

We had a system where I'd send files to Steve in the evening, and by morning he would send them back completed. He'd get a PDF of a book and then start a spreadsheet whereby he'd divide it up by pages. In the first row he'd list pages 1–40, in the next pages 41–60, and so on. He would then assign the chunks of pages to a worker to examine for errors. As the work was completed, he'd sample pages from each chunk to check for mistakes the worker might have overlooked. If there were none, he'd review perhaps two more pages, and if there were still none he could then assume the rest of the chunk was error-free. Then I'd perform the same routine on my end.

Thirty thousand dollars might not be enough to keep a small startup afloat for long, but it represented a fortune to my coworkers on the other side of the world. As soon as they began getting paid for the Benetech project, Steve's workers started sending me messages telling me what a difference it was making in their lives. Christmas is enthusiastically celebrated in Kenya, and I received wonderful cards from Steve with effusive notes from his employees tucked inside. I'd get on the phone for meetings and people would take the opportunity to tell me about how they were moving out of the slums, or the plans they were making for their future. Knowing that I was measurably making a difference, not just giving people charity but really helping to transform their lives in a short time frame, was the most exciting thing in the world. It validated everything I had wanted to do since I was seventeen years old. Benetech was satisfied with our execution and continued to contract with us, allowing us to spread the work to more centers in Kenya, including one run by Steve Muthee's sister Diana (who is still a Samasource partner) and another run by two incredible women who made it a point to recruit university students and recent graduates.

Once we could point to some success and offer evidence that our model was working, more contracts followed in short order. They were small, but they were something. I began to write a blog that started getting traffic, and then we got a little press, which led to phone calls from other computer centers like Steve's around the world asking if we could work together. That was exciting. It really highlighted for me how different we were from an ordinary charity. So many have a missionary aspect and approach communities with a certainty that they're going to teach the people something they don't already know, or show them the error of their ways. But no one likes to be told they're doing things wrong, or that their cultural norms are backward. The Samasource model is driven not by ideology but by economic forces, which are ultimately survival forces. We provide opportunity and leave it up to people to decide if they want to take advantage of it. You can do a lot more good in a community when they call you because they think you can bring in revenue and jobs than if you just show up and find a place to plant your flag. Businesses are much less likely to pack up and leave when they feel connected to their community, and when their employees feel invested in the work they are doing and are building reputations based on the work they do. I was always interested in building a pull model, not a push model, so when companies started reaching out to me, I was thrilled.

I was quickly able to move a piece of the business to India to work with a group trying to do something called rural sourcing, which was similar to my mission, except instead of bringing work to people in the slums they focused on bringing opportunities to people living in extremely rural communities. There wasn't any high-speed Internet in Kenya yet (the cost of the expensive satellite connections Steve Muthee and my other partners used was subsidized by the World Bank), but it already existed in India. One positive side effect of the needless fear-mongering around the computer bug Y2K—when people worried that the world's electronic systems would collapse when the date switched from December 31, 1999, to January 1, 2000, because computers would interpret "00" as "1900"—had been a heavy investment in fiber-optic cables.

I didn't know it at the time, but expanding rapidly into other countries after launching in Kenya proved to be one of the best decisions I ever made. You can't take anything for granted when you're working in still-developing countries—not electricity, not water supply, and certainly not Internet connectivity. The infrastructure in Nairobi is superior to those of most of the areas where Samasource would eventually operate, but there was no way I could predict that a year or so after our launch a ship would drop its anchor on the one cable connecting East Africa to the world, cutting off all Internet access to the country. Had we not diversified our operations as soon as we did, we would have been toast. As it was, we were able to quickly move some of the work in Nairobi to our centers in India for a spell, and though we informed our clients of the change, they didn't notice the difference.

I was still learning, though, and I made mistakes. I can be too impatient, and I have difficulty keeping track of details over long periods of time, especially if my head is in the "big picture" of recruiting board members, fund-raising, or developing strategy. I didn't know how to financially structure the organization in a way that fed all aspects of the business, so sometimes less than 10 percent of a contract might go toward our expenses and I would find that I had barely enough cash to cover my costs in San Francisco.

I'd learned a lot of business skills at Katzenbach Partners, but the main driver of success is figuring out what you're good at, and finding a team that complements that. There is no honor in forcing yourself to do work you don't enjoy and are bad at. Especially when there are many other people, like our current CFO, Tony (a CPA and former auditor), who loves to spend time on the kinds of things I hate doing, and is thus one hundred times better than I am at doing them. Those early days showed me that I need to partner with strong leaders in finance, operations, and engineering to build a solid business and match my passion with a measure of discipline and process.

They also showed me how to manage. It was hard to build teams in areas I didn't know well. We had three heads of sales in our first three years, and a lot of my early hires didn't work out. I was a brutal manager—slaving away at all hours and expecting the same of my team, and getting angry when things didn't work out. It took me a while to realize that I had inherited a lot of unhealthy ideas about leadership from my childhood. When we don't have a ton of relevant work experience, we often default at work to the relationships we saw modeled at home in our families. I wish more leaders would go into therapy or at least executive coaching to better understand their patterns and ensure that they don't carry bad habits into the workplace. I was the last person to think I needed to change, because so many outsiders told me what a great idea Samasource was, and I had heaps of external validation.

For me, hiring a team was initially overwhelming. I didn't know who I needed. I couldn't figure out people's true motivations for joining. I was naïve, undisciplined, and impulsive in the recruiting process, hiring several people too fast and then taking too long to figure out when it wasn't working. As a result, we had high attrition in the early days. It wasn't the fault of the people we hired—it was mine. I was the one who'd found them, convinced them to join, and then realized it was a mismatch. My advice to all founders is to hire slowly. Much more slowly than you think you should. Unless you've worked with someone at a prior company for several years, approach new hires the way you (should) approach romantic partnerships: compassionately, and with the benefit of the doubt, but with your head on straight. I learned to use checklists to make sure I covered all the key bases. I learned the power of reference checks. People are a company's most vital asset. I never understood that fully until things started coming apart after my first rounds of hiring. There were constant fires, causing good people to leave, and there was continual friction when the internal culture didn't gel because I'd hired people in such a rush to fill their roles.

The most important part of being a team is working well together. People need to share values and working styles. People need to have similar expectations about what they're getting into. I realized over time what defined Samasource's culture: highly analytical, thoughtful people who had some sort of catalytic moment that made them want to quit working for The Man and spend their days serving a greater, higher purpose. Nearly everyone on our staff has had some experience volunteering or serving others, or a transformative life event, like the death of a loved one or an illness, that made him or her reevaluate life's purpose.

Finances and hiring were not my strong suits; my biggest strengths were sales and marketing. I can get virtually anyone interested in Samasource. And a percentage of these people go on to become funders or customers, supplying investment or work to our organization. Cracking open a door at Microsoft or Google that leads to a $3 million contract and thousands of people moved out of poverty is really valuable, and something (one of the only things) I'm able to do consistently. It requires a kind of zeal for our mission, a sense of optimism about human nature, a reluctant acceptance of the need to speak in public (despite my introvert tendencies), and a love of people. These are attributes I have had since childhood and honed over the years. Had I instead tried to be better at building pivot tables in Excel, which I was never good at to begin with, it would have been a disaster for Samasource.

Still, at the time we were running out of money, and I was getting desperate.

LUCKY BREAK

Then in 2009, we got lucky. Facebook's incubator program, fbFund, run by Dave McClure, a famous "super" angel investor, chose Sama to join its inaugural class of start-ups. The point of fbFund was to incubate companies and technologies that would leverage Facebook Platform, which became Facebook's biggest driver of growth—this was the beginning of the "social graph" that we live so much of our lives on today. People generally loved our idea of using Platform to connect people in need with work. I also planned to use Facebook to track poverty and health outcomes and related data on our workers longitudinally—no one was doing this yet. The prevailing thinking was that people living on less than $2.50 a day were not on Facebook. But I saw the contrary in my visits to poor countries. Young people were figuring out a way to get on Facebook and social networks—even then, they saw that it was a way to connect with the outside world.

Out of twenty organizations, we were one of only two nonprofits selected. As a nonprofit we wouldn't be privy to any of the investment capital the other winners received. That was frustrating, because we needed the money as much as any for-profit did. (Recognizing this, the start-up accelerator Y Combinator now allocates grants to the nonprofits it selects.) Still, we were grateful to be chosen, because we knew the exposure and networking opportunity the honor offered would be priceless. And it was. For twelve weeks we were mentored by luminaries of the tech industry, advised by Facebook engineers, and received tons of free start-up help. Some of my early advisers, like Sebastien de Halleux (a cofounder of Playfish, which developed free social network games) and Dave Morin (an early Facebook manager and founder of the social network Path), became friends, donors, and even board members.

At the end of the summer was Demo Day, when we presented our organizations to a group of investors and the press. The room was packed with Silicon Valley royalty, like Shervin Pishevar, who became a billionaire by investing early in Uber, and Bill Trenchard, a serial entrepreneur and angel investor at the founder-driven VC First Round Capital. I demonstrated how we were using Facebook to authenticate our workers and how the digital work we provided to slum dwellers, refugees, and others living in deep poverty could make a difference in their future as well as give them a sense of dignity and hope. It didn't go as smoothly as I had hoped. I was incredibly nervous, and near the end, I froze. Everything I wanted to say just evaporated from my brain, leaving me standing there horrified, trying not to gape like a fish running out of oxygen. As I frantically tried to recover, Dave McClure suddenly stood up and said, "You're all rich. Who is going to make a donation to this woman's company? I'll start with one thousand bucks." He started literally pointing people out, putting them on the spot, practically daring them to refuse! We got five thousand dollars here, two thousand dollars there, and

I was grateful for every dime. I wanted to hire Alex, a young Stanford engineer, and Jess, my salesperson, full time. I needed them, but I had no way to pay them and myself. It was an incredible gesture for Dave to rescue me and spontaneously take the opportunity to throw some cash our way, even though we'd accepted the invitation to participate in the program knowing there would be no investor capital at the end of it. There were also a lot of important people in the audience that day, which would pay off shortly in both exposure and additional funds. The moment taught me a good lesson, too, one that would serve me well as I continued to make presentations on behalf of Samasource: as long as you're authentic and standing up for something worthwhile, people will care and respond positively, even if you mess up.

CONTROL ISSUES

Many graduates of the fbFund became quite notable, and a few, like TaskRabbit, became household names. Unfortunately, the other non-profit, Vittana, folded in 2014. I always thought highly of Kushal Chakrabarti, the founder, and his vision to bring educational loans to poor youth all over the world, because I'd seen the consequences of so many bright young people leaving high school with nowhere to go. In so many countries, loans are not available to the poor at all, let alone for educational purposes. So families sometimes go into massive debt, taking money from loan sharks at insanely high interest rates to be able to afford certificate programs, in many cases with unaccredited fly-by-night schools that promise jobs to graduates. East Africa and South Asia were full of them. Vittana's idea was to bring the Kiva peer-to-peer Internet-based lending model to educational loans. By 2014, Vittana was reaching just under ten thousand students, and their impact data was promising. But the goal they had set was to reach 1 million students by 2015. They could see that wasn't going to happen. Their board would have given them more time and money if they could have developed a new model that would achieve that goal and eventually be self-sustaining, but Vittana couldn't.

In an article for NextBillion, COO Kate Cochran wrote that boards often protect nonprofits, to their detriment, from the market-based feedback loop that normally shuts down for-profits when a product or service doesn't work. It's understandable that donors might want to keep supporting a struggling organization with money to give it a little more time to prove itself. But if the market doesn't want your product, more money isn't going to help. She wrote that at a for-profit, "The capital and talent that might have been reinvested in your company finds another company that will hopefully find a more successful path." But at a nonprofit, "[t]he donors who make the decision to give the organization more time are generally not the right people to make the call on whether this organization is the best at delivering its service. There's a break in the feedback loop that allows capital and talent to stay invested in sub-optimal approaches."

As I've watched nonprofits rise and fall over the years, one of my core learnings has been the degree to which nonprofits are driven by the agendas of board members. In the Silicon Valley landscape of for-profit start-ups, most boards are lean and mean, and the founders are able to keep a lot of control because they own substantial equity stakes in the company. The online payment processor Stripe, for example, has three board members: the two founders and their biggest investor. For a long time, Mark Zuckerberg owned a huge chunk of Facebook and kept his board as small as possible. Founders have a lot of control in for-profit companies, as well they should: they put in the blood, sweat, and tears to turn an idea into an organization capable of replicating it. Nonprofit founders are often screwed. Close friends of mine have countless stories of board members—often older and wealthy—who wrote a check in the early days, and then sought to control the board and the founder. With no ownership stake in the company (since nonprofits have no owners), founders have no real leverage other than the degree to which other funders associate them with the cause. It leads to a bizarre dynamic, wherein founders are often paranoid about maintaining control and power because they could lose it at any moment. Many are encouraged to have large boards to give their small organizations "legitimacy," and because nonprofit donors often expect to serve on the boards to which they donate.

I think we need to shift this dramatically. Nonprofit founders should have more control over their organizations. The ability to execute on a vision without a lot of distractions is the hallmark of being an entrepreneur, and social entrepreneurs are no different. Depriving them of this chance makes nonprofits bureaucratic, slow, and political. In the absence of a new legal structure for social business, Muhammad Yunus has proposed a solution to this, which is to allow for "ownership" of a nonprofit as long as the owners agree that they will not personally profit from the organization. That is, if it becomes profitable, they have to re-invest all the money or get back only what they put in in terms of loan capital, with no interest. This structure interests me. If we did that, it might encourage more great entrepreneurs to move into social enterprise, knowing they wouldn't be blocked by their own boards and have their freedom curtailed. Of course, financial accountability and transparency are crucial, but they are enforced through the annual auditing process that every nonprofit above $2 million in revenue must go through.

NECESSARY ADJUSTMENTS

As we gained funds and credibility, the Samasource model continued to evolve. Entrepreneurs, and especially social entrepreneurs, constantly walk a fine line between their ideals and their reality. While on the one hand you have to have an unwavering commitment to your purpose, on the other hand you can't be so blinded by your passion and sense of determination that you're incapable of making adjustments when your original plans don't work out the way you thought they would. Or if they don't generate the kind of revenues that will allow you to become self-sustaining. As the months went on and we got a better sense of our needs and the needs of the people we were trying to serve, we started making changes. By now we had around seven or eight partners: Daproim and two more in Kenya, a few in India, one in Cameroon, and one in Pakistan. At first I had thought I'd create a marketplace model that would draw millions of people seeking work to one site, and my job would simply be to manage the contracts. But as I had quickly discovered, the marketplace model works only when people have the infrastructure to support the work they're trying to do. For example, ride-hailing companies can function only when drivers have access to smartphones; take those out of the equation and the model collapses. Someone living in a slum with no electricity can't work on a crowd-sourcing site via computer, assuming she could even afford a computer. To solve for the twin problems of computer access and unreliable electricity, we thought about providing workers with computers and portable batteries so they could work from home. But then we found out how dangerous that could be. When you live in a community beset by abject poverty, and that community finds out that you've brought something of real monetary value into your home, you become a target for robbery or worse. Workers much preferred working in computer centers away from home, which allowed them to be discreet about the type of work they were doing and their income.

The only reliable access to the Internet was at the Internet cafés and computer centers in the cities (and even then reliability was an issue). That geographic and structural barrier automatically excluded any of the poor living too far from an Internet café to make the commute worth their time. It also excluded anyone who couldn't even fathom what "digital work" meant. I hadn't yet fully considered the psychology of the people I was trying to help. To even think about applying for an advertised position as a digital data worker, a potential employee would most likely have to have some inkling of what kind of work can be done via computer. This wasn't a case of "If we build it, they will come." If we didn't get more hands-on and start actively recruiting the lowest-income people with promises of structure and training, only the middle class would come—and the middle class didn't need these jobs. We had to be able to reach out to people who might initially be intimidated by the idea of Internet work. So we did.

We also started partnering with organizations—other NGOs, government organizations, schools—that were already in place offering job-training and life-skills programs designed specifically to help our target population. They were already working in the slums, teaching residents the basic skills everyone needs to hold down steady employment, such as punctuality, dressing professionally, résumé writing, English language skills, and presenting oneself with poise and confidence. They could be our eyes and ears on the ground, targeting promising recruits and encouraging them to apply to the Sama training courses where they could put these valuable skills to good use.

In 2010, I hired a woman named Jen Cantwell, who had previously worked at Gerson Lehrman Group setting up their India office. She was my highest-paid staff person that year because I needed an organized person on the ground who could navigate both Kenyan business culture and U.S. client needs. Once we found Jen, she put all kinds of processes in place to manage our pipeline of workers from various NGOs. We now recruit from more than fifteen local NGOs directly, in partnership with some of our funders (like MasterCard, which funds other NGOs in Nairobi), and even indirectly via referral. One great source of workers for us is our existing workforce. When a slum kid buys a laptop or moves out of the slum, that's huge news for other people around the neighborhood. Word travels fast. We are consistently ranked one of the best places to work for entry-level workers, so young people recruit their friends from their neighborhoods. Through trial and error, we started learning more about our workforce and what it was capable of accomplishing. The will was there; only the structure was lacking. Ken is based out of a local NGO in Kibera called the Human Needs Project, founded by the actress and humanitarian Connie Nielsen.

A second change I had to make was the way I managed partnerships. Initially, I'd thought that I would best help the poor by focusing my efforts on helping entrepreneurs set up and scale with the additional business and revenue I could bring them. But it soon became clear that there would always be a natural tension between the goals of most for-profit entrepreneurs and my goal of maximizing benefits for workers, especially in places where the idea of "benefit corporations" didn't yet exist. In addition, your typical entrepreneur, even in a developing country, is generally from the middle class and not living in poverty. If your ultimate metric of success is the number of people you're moving out of poverty, and your first beneficiary isn't even poor, you're already behind. We also knew there was no way we'd be able to scale if we continued to partner with tiny outfits. So we started shifting toward larger clients and thinking about opening our own delivery center, increasing the number of employees whose lives we could improve directly.

Finally, I realized that if I wanted to hire the truly destitute, we were going to have to go lower down the income stratum. This meant we had to be able to provide even less complex work, and we'd have to initiate even more training. That's how microwork was born, a concept I introduced to the world in a TEDx Talk at Stanford in late 2009. We started breaking down big digital projects, such as managing a large image database or digitizing documents—the kind of work that companies need done in bulk but that can't be automated—into small assignments. We were applying Henry Ford's assembly line methodology to Internet-based tasks. Like the assembly line, microwork doesn't require much training—a few fundamental computer skills, some basic English—to quickly get someone working and earning a paycheck, which means we could hire people with fewer skills to do the work our clients were hiring us to complete. And, like Henry Ford, we could pay our employees significantly above the standard local wages, thus attracting a stable and motivated workforce, who could then spend their earnings within their community, helping to raise everyone's productivity and standard of living. And since I knew no one wanted to spend his or her whole life doing the same task over and over again, no matter how well it paid, once we trained our employees to do the simplest digital tasks, we could gradually teach them to do more complex ones. In this way, we were truly setting people up to position themselves for bigger and better opportunities.

I hired an engineering team to build a tool that could help us scale. I had already recognized that Steve's spreadsheet method wasn't going to be sustainable as the volume of work ramped up. New clients were suggesting that it would be vastly more efficient if they could just load their data themselves rather than e-mailing us their files and then letting us take over. So we started designing a new platform that would allow our clients, our workers, and us at Samasource to work together, essentially reporting to the same virtual office. We called it the Sama-Hub, and it would prove to be the linchpin for everything we would accomplish from then on, a central platform that would allow us to manage our workforce while giving us the direct access we'd need to ensure equal amounts of efficiency and quality control, as well as acceptable work conditions, transparency, and fairness.

The efficiencies SamaHub made possible set Samasource apart from other charitable organizations and nonprofits that were working in the same geographic areas, and even toward similar goals. It was certainly what set us apart from traditional outsourcing companies. A lot of development organizations and companies that work with developing countries source through local vendors acting as middlemen, just like Samasource. But no matter how conscientious you try to be, it's very hard to know for sure that the workers manufacturing your product, whether it's furniture, shoes, or clothing, are being treated well and benefiting from employment with your company the way you have been assured they would be. That's true for any large for-profit company, too.

TECH ENABLES TRANSPARENCY

A person manufacturing a piece of clothing for a company simply works on a piece of factory machinery. His handiwork is checked by an immediate supervisor, and his name appears on the payroll, and he may even be noticed by a third-party inspector. Yet he is still invisible and anonymous to the end client. A conscientious, concerned buyer could try a work-around, perhaps by making an unannounced visit, but how many visits can a client reasonably make every quarter or even every year? You could try asking for workers' cell phone numbers, but that solution won't work if your workforce doesn't have cell phones or, as is usually the case, doesn't speak your language. Getting to the truth of what's happening locally can be incredibly difficult, so serving your ground troops the way you want to can be hard. But the beauty of a tech platform and a tech-enabled business like Samasource is that workers have to connect to the Internet in order to perform their work. They log in every day to the SamaHub so we can communicate directly and efficiently. We set up our new platform so that workers logged in via Facebook. This allowed us to reach out to them via the social network to check in or send them employment and household impact surveys. In this way we made sure that workers were being compensated appropriately and determined that they were benefiting from the employment opportunities we procured the way we hoped they would be. The transparency was extraordinarily powerful and reassuring, and allowed us to address that tension between our goals and those of our for-profit business partners.

It's not easy, but we have an ethical obligation to ensure that any company we buy things from is treating workers fairly, especially when that company operates overseas and isn't subject to the same labor laws that we have in the United States. It's also true for subcontractors that produce things for the companies we buy from, since labor abuses and human rights violations so often happen deep down in the supply chain. Even Apple, a company known for regularly inspecting its overseas manufacturers, has been criticized for contracting with sweatshops. Part of the problem is that even with an antisweatshop regulatory system in place (initiated following the revelation that television talk show host Kathie Lee Gifford's Walmart clothing line was sewn in Honduran factories that employed children as young as thirteen years old), our standards are not high enough. Businesses can honestly claim they comply with regulations, and workers can still suffer because the bar is set so low. All companies need to hold themselves to a higher accountability. If given a choice, most people will pay a little more on a purchase if they can be assured that someone didn't suffer to make it.

We required our partners to submit worker pay stubs, since they paid people via payroll. We also randomly surveyed the workers independently, comparing their responses to the pay stubs and stated compensation. We did have to fire a few entrepreneurs over the years. We conducted a pay audit and found out that one partner wasn't always paying what he said he was paying to the workers. We also found out that some employers weren't recruiting the way we required, hiring people from neighborhoods that didn't qualify as needy enough. Whenever we find that a center isn't complying with our standards or we hear complaints from workers that their employer isn't treating them well or fairly, we put the partner on review or, if necessary, let them go. Unfortunately, that's unavoidable in a model like ours. Sometimes companies will go into business with us with the wrong incentive and try to maximize what they can earn by skimming from their employees and lying to us. They don't get away with it for long, though, because we've set up a system that makes it easy for us to find out, and when we do we end those relationships right away. In general, though, as, naturally, they want to grow and expand their own businesses, the entrepreneurs we partner with are honest and genuinely eager to help their fellow citizens get a leg up.

The details are where social enterprise gets tough. The details determine whether you are reaching the people who really need help or the people who are easiest to reach. You have to learn to say no. In social enterprise, as in any other business, product is king. Without a great product, you have no business and you can't help anyone. In the early days especially, you have to make heartbreaking choices to preserve the quality of your product, so that you can build the sort of lasting business that can help as many people as possible in the long run. It's never black and white. Some partners just couldn't produce the quality work we needed. We partnered with one tiny organization in Dharmsala that hired Tibetan refugees, but they just didn't have the capacity. Their founder was traveling between the United States and India, didn't have experience running a tech business, and had little funding. And so the work we'd get back from this center wasn't always on par with what we had elsewhere.

The hardest thing in the world is to build a business with the aim of helping people and to have to turn away partners that work with needy groups. It feels hypocritical and depressing, like no matter what you do, you're failing—either the people you can't help because you don't have capacity or the people you're already helping but can't focus on because you're getting deluged with applications from others. As I learned, focus is your friend. You have to say no a lot in order to prove your model, which can take years. Once it's proven, you have to show consistent results, which can be even harder as you scale. For us, we had to develop robust partnership criteria, such as: Does this region have electricity and Internet access, or could we install reliable sources with a funder who wants to foot the bill for at least three years? Is there enough funding for us to make sure the center is up and running? Does this region have enough people who can read and write English, get to our center, and be able to work for thirty to forty hours a week? Is the government going to try to shut us down or stop us if we come here? Will the country suffer from violence or political instability? Will our people be safe if we send them there to start a new center?

Eventually, our model shifted from partner-owned and -managed delivery centers, as with Anudip Foundation in India, Daproim in Kenya, and CETEMOH in Haiti, to a mix of these and our own "SamaDCs"—delivery centers that we own and operate, starting first in Kenya, where we had the longest operating history. A lot of companies do this. Most franchises, for example, maintain company-owned stores in order to compare their own performance to that of their franchisees. The same goes for companies that maintain a network of indirect dealers that also carry their supplies. In all these cases, it's useful to have a mix of third-party providers and company-owned facilities. In the company-owned operations you can pilot tons of things, everything from seating arrangements to optimal break schedules to the number of plants per square foot of office space. It's hard to do this when working with partners, who have their own ideas about how things should be done. We'd long wanted to open a SamaDC, especially since many of our partners were for-profit and needed to extract a profit margin on top of the margin we took at Samasource to cover our costs. We wanted to understand whether we could pay workers more, offer better benefits and facilities, and also generate more margin to reinvest in more facilities and more salespeople and business growth by operating our own DC. It turned out we could. In fact, the SamaDC has achieved incredible outcomes, seeing a sixteen times increase in wages on average for the workers there, over their pre-Samasource income.

Sometimes we were compared to crowdsourcing sites like Amazon's Mechanical Turk, but there, too, we stood apart. These sites work by listing small tasks, which workers can then find and sign up to complete. The problem with that model, however, is that it leaves the worker vulnerable. A worker could sign up, do the work, and then not get paid. In addition, the work that's made available on that kind of site is usually so basic it doesn't require a lot of human intelligence, training, or care. At Samasource we realized there was a huge demand for more managed services. We screen the work that comes in and then create training manuals for the workers so they can learn the appropriate skills to complete it, even if they've never done work like that before. The worker opens the Web form, clicks on a task, completes it, and then goes on to another one. Meanwhile, the system offers feedback to individual workers to make them better. They stick with projects long term, which helps give them a sense of continuity and ownership over their work. Someone who takes pride in the work she does is naturally going to do a better job than someone who's just doing a one-off gig.

Our funding increased as we were able to show that our model was working and showing outcomes. Another reason might have been because within a year of Sama's first run of success in Kenya and India, we experienced one of our greatest challenges to date, one that introduced me to someone who gave me a heck of a powerful story to tell.

In early 2009, I had spotted an Oxfam report about some computer labs that the Danish Refugee Council had set up in a twenty-year-old refugee camp called Dadaab, located near the Kenya-Somalia border, to provide Internet access to the people living there. The refugees were using the computers to complete online university coursework. If these refugees were capable of that, I thought, certainly they were capable of doing the kind of lower-complexity digital work we brokered through Sama. I was sure we could do a lot of good for this group, and I was eager to test our model in a new environment. I decided I had to go visit the camps.

Easier said than done. It took me months just to find someone at CARE International, the poverty-fighting and disaster-relief organization that manages the camp, to take my call. (I would, many years later, join the board.) When I finally did get through, I explained that I had an idea that I thought could give the refugees a chance to gain a foothold toward a better future, and asked if I could come test it out. The response was swift and emphatic: no. It wasn't that they didn't appreciate my idea or my good intentions. It was that just getting the bare minimum done, just getting basic rations of oil, rice, and water to everyone in the camps so they didn't starve to death, was already a logistical nightmare. The last thing they needed was to be responsible for the safety of some random do-gooder without security clearance or ransom insurance. That's a thing. There are full-blown businesses built on ambushing and robbing the aid vehicles that go back and forth carrying goods and materials for refugees, which they then sell, so most organizations and companies that work in high-conflict areas have ransom insurance to protect themselves against this inevitable risk. Sama didn't have it, of course, and CARE didn't need the stress of worrying about me.

But I couldn't let it go. I assured them I had traveled a lot in Africa and knew what I was doing. It's too complicated, they said. We don't know how to get you there. You'd have to get approval from our safety officer. They threw every good reason they had at me to dissuade me. They didn't realize who they were dealing with. For six months I called and begged and pleaded and negotiated with anyone who would give me five minutes of his or her time. I insisted that this was an idea that would work and that I was worth the risk. In the meantime, I applied for grants to help fund the project. Everyone rejected me except the Rockefeller Foundation, which offered us sixty thousand dollars as a grant to get started, with the possibility of more once I reported back with initial results. Finally, CARE gave in and gave me the name of someone who could start coordinating my visit. I wasn't getting into Dadaab without first meeting the CARE team in Nairobi in person. It would be exceedingly complicated to negotiate a visit because there were so many NGOs working in camps like these. For example, the computer labs were funded by an outside NGO, but administered by CARE, which was also in charge of distributing food rations and providing other basic services. Yet another agency, the UNHCR, was in charge of managing all the funding for the camp. All of these NGOs had their own bureaucracies, and I needed to get all of them on board.

In June, I traveled with Samasource intern and Stanford MBA student Kate Brennan to the main CARE office in Nairobi, where we spent a week figuring out how we were going to get into the camps, which were about eight hours away. We used our time well, visiting Steve Muthee and checking in on the computer centers we had already set up. But even though we made good connections and got business done, it was frustrating to be so close to and yet so far from the camps, with only a car ride standing between us. Usually business happens rapidly in Nairobi. It's a city of hustlers and, unfettered by the formality that we often expect in the West, deals can get done with a handshake or via text message almost instantly. But it was also a former British colony, and the British loved their paperwork. So dealing with government and formal institutions can be maddeningly slow. And frankly, I wasn't so foolhardy not to get that if you're traveling to a place where terrorists are kidnapping people, it makes sense to be extra-cautious.

As frustrated as I was, I understood why it wasn't the NGOs' first priority to cater to what, from their perspective, might have seemed like a harebrained idea. Besides, the fact that it took us a week to arrange a relatively short ride wasn't due to any shortcomings on their part. So often these organizations are the target of criticism from people who have no clue about the circumstances they have to navigate, nor of the Herculean effort it takes for them to bring relief to the people they're trying to serve. They are doing the best they can within a broken system that has left hundreds of thousands of refugees baking in the Kenyan desert for twenty years. Everyone I spoke to and met once I got to Dadaab were stand-up people who had willingly left comfortable homes in countries like Austria, Germany, Switzerland, and the United States to work in a god-awful camp where they lived in barracks not much more comfortable than the tents issued to the refugees. That takes a tremendous amount of courage and sacrifice. And a big heart. They've taken on a brutally hard job that not many people would want.

Finally, at the end of the week, Kate and I negotiated a ride with a convoy that was already scheduled to travel to Dadaab that Sunday with supplies and CARE personnel. At 6:30 a.m. on June 21, the convoy picked us up in front of a central business district building called the Telecom House, directly opposite the soaring, cylindrical Hilton Nairobi. We climbed into a Land Rover flanked by black SUVs in front and back, manned by imposing guards armed with what to my inexpert eye looked like AK-47s. As we traveled, our Somali driver taught me a few words in his mother tongue and pointed out photo ops, like the herds of camels that greeted us once we entered the North Eastern Province. He admitted that he worried each time he drove north, because al-Shabaab operatives and terrorists would steal anything—refrigerators, food, fuel, and even cooking oil—since it was all so scarce in neighboring Somalia and Sudan.

The journey was intense. The idea of traveling with security hadn't fazed me, but once I saw the guns, the reality of how vulnerable we were really began to sink in. I tried to imagine what it would be like to live here permanently, unable to escape the sense of insecurity and danger. When we got to the camp we were given a security briefing: we had a curfew—all operations were to be over by 6:00 p.m., with no movement or vehicles until 6:00 a.m. the next day. We would always travel by police escort. We were told that in the case of an emergency, we were to assemble in front of the mess hall, near the dusty square of land that served as the soccer field. My nerves, already on edge from the trip, really kicked in when we started being shown around. By this time in my life I'd walked through some of the worst slums on the planet, yet I felt like I had stepped into a whole different world. As I looked around at the camp's appalling conditions, I wasn't as confident as I'd once been that my idea was going to work here.

Dadaab is a complex of five refugee camps, three of which I would visit: Ifo, Hagadera, and Dagahaley. It was at the time the largest refugee camp in the world, sometimes referred to as Kenya's third largest "city." Built in 1992 to house 90,000 people, at the time of my visit it was home to about 250,000, mostly Somalis fleeing civil war and ghastly violence, bringing it 270 percent over capacity. Many Dadaab residents were born there and have never known any other home. They live in curved United Nations–issued tents made of plastic sheeting, their mounds providing the only visual break to the endlessly flat, red earth. As the scorching sun beat down on a landscape reminiscent of Tatooine, the tents, along with the refugees themselves—the men in short-sleeved Western-style shirts, the women wraithlike in their long coverings and head scarves—cast the only shadows. The few straggly, thorny trees were too skeletal and bare to provide any relief from the unyielding heat and glaring light. The whole place felt oppressive. If Nairobi was the twenty-first century, Dadaab was the Dark Ages. I did notice, however, that despite the wind and the dirt everywhere, the camp residents were doing their best to keep their little plots neat and tidy. Even in the midst of chaos and desperation, they valued order and strove for a sense of dignity.

Technically, the people living in Dadaab were safe. They were fed, though their rations did not include sugar, meat, or vegetables. The warring factions of Mogadishu could not come hunt them down. But in exchange for food and safety, they had given up all their freedom. Even today, the residents of Dadaab are essentially imprisoned, living in perpetual limbo, restricted to small plots of unfarmable dirt. Fearful that the displaced will establish roots and never leave, the Kenyan government (like most refugee host countries) has barred the refugees from leaving the camps without permission, and also barred them from getting permanent jobs. Some receive stipends from NGOs and even from family outside the camp via mobile phone. People eke out a living selling what they can pick up from the closest town, Garissa, about seventy-five miles away—a few water containers here, some tea there. But for most people, there is nothing to do. Extreme boredom is a real problem.

To keep them from getting too comfortable, refugees are forbidden to pour concrete or in any other way construct more secure homes. Anything deemed too close to resembling a permanent structure gets torn down. The refugees are stuck in an impossible situation, and there is no way out.

The knee-jerk reaction upon learning about such seemingly heartless policies might be to blame the Kenyan government for these terrible conditions, but it must be noted that Kenya has actually done more for refugees than many far wealthier countries. It takes a huge humanitarian commitment to take more than two hundred thousand refugees into a country smaller than the state of Texas. And it is no small thing that Kenya gives these people sanctuary when Somali terrorist groups have threatened the government for allowing the camps to exist. Any country that does something to help people displaced by war, famine, or drought is to be lauded, because there are too many that do close to nothing.

My guide escorted me to the Ifo camp, where I spotted an anomaly, a little house trimmed in white—the computer lab. Next to it, stuck in among a tangle of vines and tall grasses, a gray satellite dish lurked like a small round UFO, surrounded by a rickety wooden fence made of sticks to keep curious hands off. Inside the computer lab, we found the tiny room crowded with two or three rows of flimsy desks topped with computers covered with special screens to help protect them from the thick sand and dust. Tangles of cords and cables lay about everywhere. We soon met our initial class of trainees, sixteen young men and women aged eighteen to twenty-seven, recruited and screened by CARE. It took Kate and me only a day or so to train them with the basic Internet and digital skills they'd need to complete the work we had lined up for them—address verification for a Silicon Valley company. (We'd gotten around the work restrictions by arguing that these refugees were doing temporary nontraditional work, so they weren't actually employees and their payments shouldn't qualify as real paychecks.) I was impressed with everyone in the class, but there was one student who really stood out—literally. At around six feet five inches, Paul Parach, with his inky matte skin, giant white smile, and purposeful expression, was striking. He had already overcome unbelievable odds. A member of the Dinka ethnic group, at the age of seven he'd become one of the Lost Boys, one of the approximately twenty thousand young orphans from South Sudan forced to flee their homes to escape being killed or pressed into combat by Sudanese rebel forces. Leaving his mother and four sisters behind, he banded together with a group of young boys and walked for weeks, braving heat, thirst, starvation, disease, and wild animals, until reaching the Kakuma refugee camp on the Kenyan side of the Sudan-Kenya border. He had hoped to find safety, but within days someone from a rival tribe shot him in the leg. He recovered in an ICU in Nairobi, but one of his legs was left paralyzed. In 1994 he was transferred to the Ifo camp in Dadaab, and he had been there ever since, one of a tiny handful of South Sudanese in the majority Somali camp, which came with its own set of problems.

Yet it wasn't just his physique or his story that made Paul memorable; it was his intellect and drive. Every day, Paul showed up to class early, prim and proper in a starched shirt. To this day I have no idea how he managed it. I certainly never saw a bottle of starch anywhere in a place like Dadaab, much less an ironing board. He had attended school in the camp and learned English.

Now, at the age of twenty-two, he just wanted to find a way out, a way to support himself so that he could leave Ifo for good. He had been using a computer for only about a month by the time I met him during our first class. Within minutes he had mastered using e-mail and Google. By the next day, he was helping to teach his classmates. All of the students picked up the information quickly, but Paul's facility with the technology made me cringe. He was too smart for this. For the first time I started to see how the work we were giving these people could be demeaning. We were essentially telling people like Paul, who under any other circumstances would be the founder of some multimillion-dollar start-up, that what we were offering was the best they were going to get, the most they could do to contribute to their community. If this program succeeded, would we be entrenching artificial divides and perpetuating a stereotypical narrative that some people saw between "us"—well-meaning mostly white Americans and Europeans who could have done anything but chose to help the less fortunate—and "them"—black refugees and Africans who were dependent on the choices and opportunities we provided them?

One of the tasks we assigned our fledgling workers was to find and document the e-mail addresses of financial aid Web sites for U.S. colleges. While completing the work, Paul happened upon a picture of a young man from Sudan whom he knew from the Kakuma refugee camp. The man had received a scholarship to a university in Maine and was profiled on their Web site. When Paul described this to me, his eyes grew big and he had the same look in his eyes I get when I'm really, really hungry. Except his hunger was for opportunity. He had to be thinking, "Why not me?" His hunger was for a chance to stop waiting and start doing. He had so much potential, and all he wanted was a shot to prove himself and build something of his own, something that could provide him with independence and safety.

I left Dadaab inspired by Paul and his classmates' tenacity, and confident that Samasource could help them achieve the independence that other aid agencies had not. My optimism was buoyed when within a week of getting home I opened my computer to find a Facebook friend request from Paul. His very first status update read as follows: "Hi. Thanks to Samasource, I'm connecting to the world." He would continue to ping me regularly on Facebook. A few months later I was in a meeting with the State Department and Paul sent me a message—as I was talking about the crisis in Dadaab. Globalization flattened the world; Facebook shrank it to the size of a smartphone.

I believed digital work was a game changer. The core problem in the camp is that refugees can't move to find work, and are also prohibited by law from working in most countries to prevent them from competing with locals for much-needed jobs. Digital work, however, would allow the refugees to earn money locally without competing with native Kenyans for a job, since the work was coming from all over the world. The work was portable, so they could take it with them if they left the camp eventually or got repatriated. And it was skill building—they'd be advancing in a career, rather than wasting their education by doing basic tasks like subsistence farming or tailoring.

The CARE staff loved the idea, believing it also solved another fundamental problem: lack of inputs to produce goods and sell them. Many CARE staff had tried to start small informal businesses to create something to do and some income for the refugees—things like making bags or clothing to sell outside the country or to tourists. But they struggled to import key supplies, like thread, cloth, and needles. These items had to be airlifted into the camp, or loaded onto armed convoys. It was hard enough getting all the rations into the camp; no one had time to worry over sewing needles. The beauty of the Internet-based work model was that the computer labs were already there, running on generators and partly on solar. The Internet was already there, thanks to 3G connections from several cell towers within the camp (incidentally, my Black-Berry, which was still in vogue in 2009, worked better in Dadaab than it did in San Francisco, probably because there was less competition for data bandwidth). The only input digital work required was brainpower, which was in abundance in Dadaab—many refugees could read and write; they just had no outlet. The work would also give recent high school graduates something to do, other than waste away.

In the winter of 2009 we launched a new project, Samasource E-Cards, also popular at the time. People in the United States could send digital cards with images, sounds, and personalized holiday greetings created by our Dadaab workers—a digital version of the popular UNICEF cards people send, each one customized by a refugee, almost like a telegram. The cards cost ten dollars, but the sale of each one directly benefited the refugees who made them. Unfortunately, they didn't take off. We sold only a few hundred and weren't able to create much revenue. We kept trying, though, partnering with the crowdsourcing company CrowdFlower to create a Give Work app. Workers could perform tasks like creating tweets or verifying photographs for copyright information, but their pay was contingent on a third-party quality check. Mobile phone users filled that role, using the Give Work app in their spare time to check on the accuracy of the work. Each verification released the payment to the worker who had completed the task. Mashable called it "one of the best and most useful iPhone apps we've ever come across." And the French senate awarded us the Prix Netexplorateur (Net Exploration Prize), which Twitter had won the year before. All along, I kept wondering how long the Kenyan government was going to allow us to keep operating, because while we'd come up with a temporary rationale for allowing these workers to earn money (we paid them via mobile phone) for one-off tasks, it was still illegal to employ refugees, and the longer we stayed, the more our organization was going to be suspected of skirting the law. Refugees couldn't get M-Pesa accounts legally, so we paid a contact in Dadaab who then gave the refugees cash payments. We'd then text or e-mail the refugees to be sure they received them.

Then tragedy struck. Or rather, it struck again, for the people in this region were certainly no stranger to it. The terrorist organization al-Shabaab had made serious threats against aid organizations in Somalia, accusing them of spying and engaging in a Christian agenda. Then, on July 18, the militia group raided the offices of Action Against Hunger, located in the Kenyan border town of Mandera, and dragged three Kenyan aid workers back across the Somali border. The Kenyan government feared that terrorists were infiltrating and recruiting from the refugee camps. As the months went on and the situation became increasingly unstable, CARE finally told us that we could not stay unless we paid for our own security, which would cost three hundred dollars per day. The grant we had received from the Rockefeller Foundation allowed us to keep training people and hire a full-time employee to help with our efforts on the ground in Kenya, but that money was to be paid out over the course of three years. There was no way we could cover the cost of security personnel without another grant. Applying for grants takes time, and time is something else that we didn't have. We didn't want to stop the program entirely, so we put things on pause while allowing the local CARE staff and other NGOs based in Nairobi to continue training the refugees and teaching them how to find work. Our hope was that we could find a local partner who could help share some of the cost while implementing the program. But as time went on the violence only increased. We just couldn't take responsibility for people's safety. The absolute saddest thing is that none of the refugees were upset when we told them we were halting the program—they were too accustomed to disappointment. They thanked us for trying, promised to stay in touch if they could, and moved on, doing what they could to keep their families going. It was heartbreaking. They had all worked so hard and had been so excited by the possibilities.

We generally like to read stories about entrepreneurs who go out on a limb, take big risks, move mountains, and succeed despite the odds. This probably doesn't sound like that kind of story, but it is. Don't get me wrong; for a long time I felt extremely guilty for letting those refugees down. I felt like a failure, until one day I realized that my guilt was misplaced. We hadn't really failed! We had proved that not only can refugees—a population from whom the world expects nothing—learn Web-based skills and produce high-quality work but also that they want to—just like everyone else. We tried something that very few people or organizations would have ever dared. That's what entrepreneurs of all stripes are supposed to do. It may be what we're born to do. I had fought like hell to get into that camp, and it was only forces completely out of our control that had forced us to back out. So now I no longer feel guilty. I've learned that when you're doing social justice work, especially in a war-torn area with no infrastructure, serving already traumatized people whose trauma is perpetuated by a lack of food, water, and health resources, you can cut yourself just a little slack if things don't work out exactly the way you planned. These experiments are worth doing, as long as you are extremely honest with the people you're working with and make sure that they understand the inherent risks, and that you even might fail and have to suspend things. Honesty counts a lot, just like in a normal start-up, where you have to be frank with your customers about your product's flaws and issues.

Some of the most valuable advice I've ever heard about running a company came from a blog post about what skills make a great CEO, written by venture capitalist and author Ben Horowitz. It boils down to a line that became famous among entrepreneurs: "Don't punk out and quit." No matter how bad things get, no matter what challenges get in your way, do not engage in self-destructive behavior to cope with the stress, and do not quit, because as long as you hang in there and fight, there is hope. Horowitz points out that often, when asked to explain their success, mediocre CEOs will reference their business strategies or acumen, but the best CEOs generally all have the same answer: "I didn't quit." And we didn't. We had seen how quickly and powerfully work could surpass aid in getting income, skills, and a sense of self-worth to the refugees in the camps. We weren't about to abandon them now if we could help it. As soon as we had more funding in place that would allow us to operate with proper security—the Rockefeller Foundation followed up with multiple generous grants—and found partners on the ground that could implement our model, we relaunched the program in 2014. We're still waiting to find out whether the camps will be shut down. As long as the camps are there, we will also try to be there.

Doubling down on my fund-raising efforts after returning to the States in August 2009, I told the story of what I had seen in Dadaab, and what we could do to help its residents, to anyone who would stand still for more than two minutes. It was while I was visiting the camps that I got the news that we were one of two nonprofits selected by the fbFund. Among the influential people in the audience during our demo was angel investor Ariel Poler. He came up to me afterward and suggested hosting a cocktail party at his home in Silicon Valley, where I could make a presentation about what Samasource was doing. I spoke to a room filled with Silicon Valley's elites. Fresh from Africa, my emotions still raw, I gave the presentation of my life, coming to the brink of tears when I recalled the bright smile of Paul Parach. Within two weeks, two people in the audience became board members and presented me with twenty-five-thousand-dollar checks.

What about Paul? We stayed in touch. He traveled to Nairobi, and I collaborated with another Sama staff member to help him fund a college certificate so he could become a customs official in South Sudan, where he is from. Unfortunately that job didn't materialize, and with nowhere else to go, he went back to Dadaab. The bright lights in his life are his wife, also from South Sudan, and his children. The family bonds of sub-Saharan refugees are remarkably strong. In fact, in this kind of environment, creating families and building attachments may be one of the only things you can do to stay sane. Family gives you someone to turn to, someone to reassure you that you are not alone in this world. Family gives you a reason to live.

Paul doesn't know what he will do if the camp is disbanded. He is weary and sad. All Paul wants to do is make his life better and support his family. He is the kind of person who should be making it. If the world is failing someone like him, who tries so damn hard, who has done everything he could and has made the best choices possible, there is something very wrong.

Making a difference in Dadaab ended up being much harder than I thought, but it didn't dissuade us at Samasource from seeking out new communities in which to try our model. Several years later, we would end up collaborating with the World Food Program and UNICEF in Beirut on a pilot to put Syrian refugees to work, and we also launched our program in Northern Uganda in partnership with Oxfam, funded by the Dutch Postcode Lottery.

MEETING DOUBLED STANDARDS

In the meantime, we were still ferociously competing for bids in the States. No matter how well we performed, we had to prove ourselves all over again with every project. On the one hand we had to prove that we were upholding our mission, but on the other hand we also had to be able to prove that we were competitive vendors. The social mission was our heart and gave me the story I needed to get people to pay attention, but the assurance of quality was the only way I could get any business. I wasn't selling pretty jewelry, furniture, or retail items that people might buy because they feel connected to the mission (or because they like what the logo says about them as consumers). I was selling data services. Only three things matter to any company: will the work get done on time, done on budget, and done right?

We're always in the peculiar position of having to rise to the highest standards of both nonprofits and for-profits, and we don't get cut any slack. Not that we need it. Perhaps one of the happiest moments of my career was in the fall of 2015, when I sat on a panel with Robert Hohman, CEO and cofounder of Glassdoor, one of our clients. During the panel, he confessed that he had found out only five minutes earlier in the greenroom that Samasource was a nonprofit. He had chosen to work with us because our salespeople were the most knowledgeable. I cheered inside. Just as our workers want to be chosen for their talent and not out of pity, we want to be chosen for our excellent quality and service, not out of charity. For our clients, our social mission should be icing on the cake. We do a great job and we help move people out of poverty. Why wouldn't you work with us?

Our business continued to grow. When I met Steve Muthee he had four people working for him, and his business was hanging by a thread, supported by the donations of friends and family, especially his mother, a farmer. The Bookshare contract was the turning point. As of his untimely death in 2014 at age thirty-two from a rare autoimmune disease, he employed 150 people and had expanded into other kinds of data-entry work. Our partnership had ended because he didn't need us anymore; he had grown—to the point where he had taken over the top floor of a building in downtown Nairobi—and wanted to work directly with customers. He was a pivotal reason impact sourcing came to Africa, and I believe that he succeeded in his mission to raise Kenya's profile in the eyes of the world.

Over the years, we built a network of more than twenty entrepreneurs like Steve in six countries. We heard success stories from many of them. In Rukka, technology services firm Usha Martin Rural Services (UMRS) started out training thirty-one students from nearby villages in Jharkhand. By August 2010, UMRS employed one hundred workers and had a four-member management team. The center operated six days a week, two seven-hour shifts per day. CETEMOH in Haiti, for another example, was a training program that got their first contract from us with a firm in Montreal. Initially we had to do a lot of quality assurance, but eventually that requirement tapered off. They recently went direct with that customer, and they've hired dozens of Haitians to work from Port-au-Prince. CETEMOH has become a local leader and a pioneer of the impact-sourcing concept in Haiti.

At this point Samasource has helped more than 7,900 people transform their lives, more if you consider the fact that most of these people become the primary breadwinners, which means all of their dependents—children, parents, relatives, and other direct beneficiaries of their monthly income—also enjoy that transformation. That brings the number of lives changed closer to 35,000, not counting all the people profoundly affected by the capital reverberating in local economies for the first time, such as the local woman who bakes bread, the local tailor who stitches clothes, and so many other small businesses in the community that are normally starved of it. These wages trickle up, rather than trickle down, lifting everyone who touches them into a higher income bracket.

Some people might see the number 35,000 and wonder whether that's really something to brag about. It's a tiny number by Silicon Valley standards. But moving someone from two dollars a day to more than eight dollars a day is literally the difference between life and death. It's the difference between multidrug-resistant tuberculosis and a clean bill of health. It's the difference between eating sugarcane and eating real food. We're not using technology just to touch people's lives but to transform them. I think 35,000 transformed lives—and counting—are indeed worth celebrating, even as we recognize that there are many more, like the Dadaab refugees, who are still hoping for their chance.

EVERY LIFE IS WORTH IT

There were times during the early days of Samasource when I felt like my efforts were just a tiny drop in the ocean of extreme poverty. It's a feeling all of us in the business of solving huge, complex social problems have faced at one time or another, and maybe repeatedly. What helped me was to remember something I'd read in *Mountains Beyond Mountains,* the book Tracy Kidder wrote about Paul Farmer, cofounder of Partners In Health. There was a kid in Farmer's clinic in Haiti with pediatric cancer. He was in very bad shape. Farmer, still a young doctor, was working at the time in a top Boston hospital. He begged the head of the pediatric oncology department to see his sick Haitian patient. When the oncologist gave his permission, Farmer called his staff in Port-au-Prince and asked them to medevac the boy to Boston. Medical evacuation by helicopter or private plane costs a lot of money—maybe twenty to thirty thousand dollars.

Some of Farmer's staff thought he was showing bad judgment. With so many other sick people to care for, that money could go a long way in purchasing medicines and other supplies for hundreds of patients. Wasn't it indulgent and emotional to blow it all on one?

Farmer was furious. He felt that life was not relative—a human life was worth the same in Boston or in rural Haiti. Junior doctors in his hospital regularly earned four times the cost of the medevac flight in their first year on the job. How could he not do everything in his power to save this child, knowing what he knew?

Farmer's logic informs a core belief, which I think we all know deep down: All human lives have equal worth and dignity. And each life we save has infinite worth. Who knows if the person he saved might go on to lead Haiti? Or cure cancer? It's impossible to predict the domino effect of doing the most good you can in a given situation.

This is where I part ways with a more strictly utilitarian theory of effective altruism—essentially, that giving ethically means doing the most good you can, measured in clear ROI—embraced by so many of today's philanthropists. That would mean not medevacing that kid from Haiti to Boston. And that would have been intolerable to Farmer. As it would have been intolerable to me.

Moral philosophy sometimes clashes with the messiness of real-world scenarios, when despite your best efforts to rigorously track outcomes and be as efficient as you can be with every dollar, you are called to do what I would call irrational good. You risk your life to save a stranger's, you donate bone marrow, you pay thirty thousand dollars to heal a child from cancer. Those moments of irrational good are how I define God. To me, divinity exists in the connections between living beings—in the moments when we lower the barriers of our consciousness to feel true empathy for someone or something. This is not to say that we shouldn't measure outcomes or track impact to know whether our efforts are working. We should do all these things. But we should also allow for irrational good.

To anyone who says that a single person or a group of ten people being helped is meaningless or futile, or not scalable enough to be interesting, I have to ask, what would you do to save your mother, father, sister, or brother? Suddenly the strict utilitarian calculus becomes meaningless. There is a limitless quality to each person you are able to personally, deeply, help.

It was that thinking that gave me the courage to try yet another experiment. On the surface it might have made little sense to the outside world to combine this with Samasource. But I spotted an opportunity, and as an entrepreneur I couldn't resist trying something new, especially when its success could mean revealing a way to efficiently and effectively direct charitable donations that actually made a permanent difference.

In early 2011, I traveled to Sierra Leone with the Women's Technology Delegation, a group of tech execs, NGO leaders, and foundation heads invited by the U.S. State Department to meet with local government officials and the heads of various organizations on the ground to discuss how technology could be used to improve the lot of women and girls in their country. The whole point was to identify where there was need, and to take action however we could to address it. I arrived hoping to find a new site for a Sama center, but I quickly concluded that our model wouldn't work in Sierra Leone because of its sky-high 70 percent illiteracy rate and unreliable electricity and Internet access. While traveling through the town of Bo, however, I was introduced to Dr. Darius Maggi. If there is a saint among us, it is he. Charming and sweet in his midsixties, Dr. Maggi is a renowned ob-gyn formerly based in Dallas, Texas. Since his retirement almost a decade before we met, he had been volunteering his services in Sierra Leone, performing obstetric fistula repair surgeries. An obstetric fistula is a hole between the vagina and the bladder or rectum, usually caused by prolonged, difficult childbirth or rape. It is a horrific injury that used to be common in the United States, but was mostly eradicated as obstetric care improved and doctors began to routinely use Cesarean sections to deliver babies during obstructed labor. It still affects approximately 2 million women in Africa, however, and is particularly common in Sierra Leone, where most women receive no prenatal care and labor alone or without experienced help days from the nearest medical clinic; where sexual violence is routine; and where many new mothers are young girls and teenagers (in 2011, the International Rescue Committee rape crisis center in Freetown, the country's capital, stated that 26 percent of its rape victims were aged eleven or younger). One of these girls had a profound impact on me. Tiangay Kiawo, who spoke excellent English despite attending a rural school, was about twelve years old when her teacher raped her. When she got pregnant, she was forced to drop out. Then, after laboring for four days to give birth to a stillborn baby, she developed a rectovaginal fistula and incontinence. She lived with the condition for four years, hiding at home and suffering from depression, until her uncle heard about Dr. Maggi's clinic and brought her in. Beautiful, friendly Tiangay made a deep impression on me, but she was just one of dozens of young women I met with similarly heartbreaking stories.

The impact of a fistula on a woman's life is devastating. Once she finally makes it to a medical center, often after having labored for days, she usually suffers the trauma of delivering a dead newborn. Afterward, she leaks a steady stream of urine and feces. The smell and the stigma make her a pariah in her community. She is often too embarrassed to go to school and can no longer easily work in the fields or at the market (adult diapers and sanitary pads aren't available), and she is even sometimes shunned by her family and sent away. If she's not, she wraps herself as best she can and farms her plot of land. But her life will be lonely.

I found out that the surgery necessary to repair the injury is relatively simple and inexpensive—costing about four hundred dollars. That shook me. For four hundred dollars a woman could have her life back. It's an astronomical sum to a woman in Sierra Leone, but I could easily raise that amount by simply reaching out to a few of my girlfriends in the States. Dr. Maggi performed approximately two hundred surgeries per year, and when not fund-raising he was using his retirement account to support his work. I thought to myself: if the Dr. Maggis of the world could spend less time fund-raising and more time scaling their clinics, they could do a lot more good, and a lot faster. I had a tech background, I had fund-raising experience, and I knew people. As a woman born in a country where I knew I'd get state-of-the-art obstetric care should I ever need it, and whose Facebook feed was starting to fill with pictures of blissful friends holding their beautiful, perfect babies, I felt I had a duty to help. Though I was completely committed to Samasource, I knew I could not rest until I got this new idea off the ground. I left Sierra Leone with a mission to find a way to fund more of these lifesaving surgeries.

I reached out to Dr. Maggi's volunteer Web site designer, Shawn Graft, and asked him if he would help me develop a prototype for my idea. Working nights and weekends, we put together a plan for a Kiva-inspired peer-to-peer donation site that would allow anyone, anywhere, to pay for the surgery of a child or woman in need of a fistula repair. Then I called together my board of directors and explained why I thought it was important that we try to create the world's first international crowdfunding site for lifesaving medical treatments. I explained how even if a fistula does not literally kill a woman through infection, the isolation she suffers because of it can be a virtual death sentence. Meanwhile, we could restore these women's ability to support themselves and return to their families. We'd still be giving work, albeit indirectly.

One of my board members gave me $25,000 to get started. We raised an additional $50,000 on Indiegogo, money that I was able to use to pay Shivani Garg Patel, a former program manager who had just quit her job at McKinsey, and Shawn to run the site, which would share the Sama brand but run as a separate entity from Samasource. The same month we closed a $7.5 million funding round for Samasource, we launched Samahope, the world's first crowdfunding site for inexpensive yet lifesaving medical treatments. We initially started funding only obstetric fistulas performed by Dr. Maggi's West Africa Fistula Foundation; thanks to fifteen generous donors, he was able to heal Tiangay Kiawo's broken body, and she was able to return home and go back to school. Then we quickly added the option of providing women with Maama Kits—safe birth kits containing gloves, a sterilized razor blade, and a clean plastic sheet on which they could deliver (doctors in rural hospitals in Uganda cannot provide these bare necessities, so women who arrive without them borrow used gloves and razor blades from other mothers in the ward, leading to the spread of HIV and other diseases). Eventually, donors could help doctors repair cleft palates and burn injuries, which often go untreated in poor countries. We even helped fund a doctor in Berkeley who needed dental kits to further his work with the homeless.

Originally, Samahope was a peer-to-peer funding site that featured profiles, including photographs, of women and children who were in need of surgeries, giving donors a chance to get to know a little bit about the people they were trying to help and their circumstances. Concerned that these profiles could be embarrassing or demeaning to the women we were trying to help (would you want the details of your private parts online?), we soon shifted our focus to creating an immediate connection between visitors to the site and the doctors—heroes, really—we featured who were performing surgeries for people who wouldn't otherwise be able to afford them. The whole site was designed to help people understand that they were facilitating something deeply meaningful every time they made a donation, by investing in a doctor fighting against all odds.

A NONPROFIT M&A

Over the next three years, we raised more than a million dollars that funded critical care for almost seventeen thousand women and children in eleven countries, from surgeries to safe births. We built a birth center in Nepal. We provided an ambulance to transport pregnant women to and from the rural clinic of Dr. Priscilla Busingye, the only ob-gyn in her part of Western Uganda, so they could deliver their babies safely. We trained birth attendants in India and awarded nursing scholarships in Uganda. But our mission had always been to treat 1 million patients, and we knew we couldn't do it on our own. So after careful vetting, we decided to combine Samahope with Johnson & Johnson's CaringCrowd platform. It made so much sense. The Sama brand was well known for giving work and impact sourcing, and few people really understood why we were dabbling in health care, assuming they even remembered. I had tapped out all my friends, begging them for donations to Samasource over the years. Meanwhile, there's hardly a better, more recognizable health-care brand than J&J; with their extensive experience, networks, and budget, they'd be able to penetrate the health-care market in a way that we just couldn't.

I had envisioned that Sama could one day be the kind of brand known for a single concept applied across multiple categories, like Richard Branson's Virgin Group. I still have that vision, but I realize now that it won't happen unless my first company is wildly successful, and any future enterprises will have to be closely tied to the mission to Give Work. Otherwise, it will be just too difficult for consumers and the press to grasp and remember what we stand for. We won't stop building other organizations under the Sama umbrella, but we will be more disciplined about sticking to causes that align with our core mission of giving work.

Had this been a traditional merger, my cofounders and I might have walked away with a sweet payout to ease the pain of letting go of this special project that was so close to our hearts, and that we had worked so hard to nurture and grow. But since we were a nonprofit, we got nothing out of the deal other than the solace of knowing that it was the right thing to do. Because of this, I'm often asked if I have any regrets. I don't, just as I have no regrets about trying to bring work to the refugees of Dadaab. Maybe you could call these efforts my own examples of irrational good. But Shivani and I know that none of the seventeen thousand people who benefited from the treatments we were able to provide through Samahope, whether birth kits, dental kits, or surgeries, would say what we did was in vain. In business, you have to be strategic, but when you're dealing in matters of life and death, it's worth trying everything in your arsenal if you think it will make a difference. And we not only made a difference, we took steps to make sure that Samahope would continue to increase its impact on the people we wanted to serve. Samahope was our acknowledgment that in some cases, such as when someone is so incapacitated by a condition (like a fistula or cataracts) that she can't contribute economically to her community, charity is the only option.

What's important to note, however, is that the root source of the misery so many women suffer in Uganda and other countries where obstetric fistulas and other easily preventable conditions are left untreated is the same as what causes so much misery everywhere: poverty. So many of the kinds of projects currently on CaringCrowd could fund themselves if the recipients just had work. For example, one organization asked for help providing female Kenyan students with reusable sanitary pads to help deter school absences during menstruation. But if the girls had jobs, or if their families had work, the students would create a market for their own sanitary pads. Another organization sought funds to help complete a safe house for the children of brothel workers in India, who face extreme discrimination due to their mothers' line of work and are at high risk of turning to prostitution themselves. Yet the children of brothel workers wouldn't be at risk if their mothers could find employment anywhere but the sex trade. My experience with Samahope confirmed that the answer to almost every poverty-driven problem we see in the world is the same: give work.

Chapter Four

HOME, AND THE FUTURE OF WORK

WHEN PEOPLE WHO MANAGE TO TRANSCEND THE DIFFICULT CIRcumstances of their birth and achieve upward mobility, such as my great-grandfather, tell their story, they usually credit at least one person—a teacher, a parent, maybe a religious figure—who noticed them, expected something of them, and pushed them to succeed. For many people in Dumas, Arkansas, Terrence Davenport is that one person. Born and raised in the Mississippi River Delta, Terrence is a rare Dumas native who, like my great-grandfather, rose, mostly thanks to a demanding and tough father with high standards. He is tall, with a goofy smile and a deep look of empathy in his eyes. A star athlete and student, he graduated from college and went on to launch his own successful Web-design service based in Fayetteville, in the northwest corner of the state. His brother's murder in 2012 brought him home. The case raised a number of questions—not the least of which was how his brother's body came to bear Taser burns—that Davenport could not get answered. "[The law enforcement officials in charge of the case] blew me off and treated me like an idiot, or a second-class citizen. How could my voice be so blatantly ignored? It gave me a new perspective."

Davenport moved back to Dumas ostensibly to care for his ninety-four-year-old grandmother, who was afraid to be alone in her house, but a fire had been lit. He started researching the history of the region to understand the forces that had shaped the town and its people. His grandmother still remembers how frequently black landowners' bank loan applications—to pay for seeds and tools to work the land—would be delayed even as neighboring white farmers got immediate approval, allowing them to plant and harvest first and thus get full market value for their crops. By the time the black farmers were able to get their crops planted and ready to sell, the value of the crops would have gone down. Eventually, most black farmers were forced to sell their land to pay off their debts. The town comprised three square miles of living space surrounded by seventy square miles of fields and crops. And yet in the middle of this breadbasket, Dumas had a hunger problem. Terrence couldn't understand how so much money could come into the county yet leave so many people with nothing, not even an opportunity to work. He was determined to figure out a way to reverse the crushing poverty and lack of opportunity that he was convinced was the main source of all the area's troubles and tensions. "I wanted to be an asset and give people a voice. If you are in a position to give people opportunity and you don't, you're oppressing them."

In America, we put tremendous value on the idea of personal responsibility and the role it plays in directing individual destiny, yet it's easy for many of us to fail to fully recognize how much we benefit from having someone in our lives who expects something of us and for us. Terrence fulfills that role for many in Dumas. We also profoundly underestimate the leveling forces in society, such as good public schools, libraries, electricity, roads, and public transportation—I could never have taken that entry-level secretarial job at the law firm in Los Angeles when I was a teenager had there not been a reliable city bus that came out to my neighborhood. Connectivity needs to be added to the list. Like roads and electrical power, broadband Internet access is vital to a twenty-first-century education and to fully participating in our economy and civil society. There is no doubt that the lack of basic infrastructure and technology undermines people's best efforts in poor countries, exacerbating their lack of opportunity. It is unconscionable, however, that such conditions exist here within the borders of the richest country in the world. Think about this the next time you curse a dropped call or a slow upload: there are people living within our midst with less access to broadband Internet than the residents of Gulu, Uganda.

I know this because in 2012 Samasource set up centers in Gulu, the largest commercial hub in the northern part of the country. Its streets were once the nightly refuge for hundreds of children who would leave the surrounding rural villages before sunset to hide from roving bands of the Lord's Resistance Army (LRA), notorious for conscripting child soldiers and forcing them to perform brutal, gruesome acts in the name of their leader, Joseph Kony. It's not the kind of place most people would associate with digital work. And yet when I met with the head of Gulu University in 2012, he was so excited by the possibilities the Internet represented, he literally jumped up and down. That excitement was shared by many of his students; the young man I met at the first Ugandan Facebook Developer Garage I organized four years before wasn't the only one who saw himself as the next Mark Zuckerberg.

A few years later Samasource would reach out to Terrence's community in Dumas, Arkansas. In many ways it shared a surprising number of commonalities with Gulu. Both are situated in isolated, rural areas; both struggle with a legacy of brutality (one perpetuated by murderous warlords, the other by the institutions of slavery and Jim Crow); both suffer from the limitations perpetuated by generational poverty and trauma. Yet no one I met in Dumas talked about becoming the next tech titan. In some ways, I discovered, people living in the poorest parts of America can feel as hemmed in—physically and psychologically—as the refugees of Dadaab. It was a challenge and a complication we did not anticipate when we decided that even as we fulfilled Samasource's mission to give work to people living in developing countries, we needed to give work to and transform the lives of people living closer to home as well.

COMING HOME

At the end of 2009, Hulu offered us and other nonprofits free advertising time on their video service. We created a thirty-second spot featuring Paul Parach and a few other refugees from Dadaab with clips we had shot at recent visits to our centers and their local areas. To the lively background beat of African drums, it announced that Samasource was working to ease the corrosive effects of 70 percent unemployment in Africa by bringing computer work to the world's poor, and that Americans could help through donations to the program or by hiring our workers. What a great way to raise awareness about what Samasource could accomplish and the good we could do, I thought. I was sure we'd see a spike in donations and interest.

I knew everyone did not agree with the focus of our mission. Only the prior year, I'd had a prickly argument with a potential funder about the fact that Samasource was promoting job creation abroad in the midst of a recession. "Why are you focused on Africa and rural Asia when there's plenty of poverty right here in America?" she asked. There it was again: "us" versus "them." As though a human being born elsewhere somehow has less value than a human being born within our own borders. That geographic proximity carries with it a stronger obligation to help. It's an idea I find repugnant. If anything, it's this cleaving to national boundaries that makes our biggest problems worse. It's why multinational companies can operate with few checks and balances in poor places. It's why the Earth is becoming a cesspool of polluting agribusinesses and highly suspect mining operations that leave their dirty laundry in those "other" places. It has contributed to the steady swell in human trafficking, making it the world's fastest-growing crime.

Enough. A life is worth the same whether it unfolds in a busy African capital, the dust of a refugee camp, a sleepy town in Arkansas, or Silicon Valley. So the idea that I have more of a moral duty to someone who lives near me than someone who lives far away is nonsensical. It defies logic. We are all part of one human race, one giant family, and we have a duty to all living beings to uphold life wherever we can. This isn't about solving other people's problems, because there are no "other people."

I did not bother sharing these feelings, but instead replied with my standard answer. I reminded her that I was, in fact, benefiting American companies by procuring high-quality work at a competitive price, which was good for the American employees of those companies. And that with a limited pool of resources, our efforts should be focused on the lowest-hanging fruit, where we could get the most bang for our development buck. That is, on the "bottom billion"—those who lived in the world's poorest countries and made less than $1.90 a day (in 2011 U.S. dollars, adjusted for purchasing power), who could barely afford food, water, or basic sanitation. The latest census data showed that the bottom sixth of the U.S. population earned a household income of about $25,740. That's about $5,000 per person per year—still about fourteen times what the world's poorest people made annually. At the time, it didn't occur to me that the same model that worked for our Kenyan workers might also work for poor people in richer countries, like the United States, who might have higher incomes but are still materially deprived and suffering from scarcity of basic resources.

The conversation stuck with me, however. Global wealth is increasing. That's a good thing. But there's no doubt that our mechanisms for ensuring that these dividends result in better quality of life for as many people as possible are outdated. Two trends, globalization and automation, have resulted in a radically different economic order. It used to be that to amass wealth, you needed to have a lot of workers. So the richest people, like the Fords and the Waltons, had to build the biggest companies in terms of head count. The market-capitalization-to-worker ratio at these companies was low. Now you have tech companies with giant revenues and market caps, like Facebook, that have very few employees. Because software has zero marginal cost (once it's built, you can make

copies of it at no cost, unlike, say, a physical good, although this is changing with the advent of robots in factories), the old rule of "more revenue
requires more people" is totally flipped on its head. These companies
have unprecedented revenue per employee. So in the world of tech, the
winners win much, much more. On top of this, globalization allows capital to move freely across borders, so a lot of wealth is now held overseas,
where it's not taxed or reinvested in the economy. Added to this is the
trend of sky-high CEO salaries. Over the last three decades, CEO pay,
adjusted for inflation, went up 997 percent; the CEO-to-worker pay ratio,
which was 20 to 1 in 1965, was 303 to 1 in 2014.

What was the role of an international NGO based in the States
when the Great Recession was eroding American livelihoods? Did we
have a duty to work with victims of domestic poverty alongside victims
of the kind of extreme poverty we were seeing in developing countries?
I was curious as to how bad the problem actually was. I realized that I
had no idea what rural poverty looked like in the United States, since I'd
lived only in Tucson, L.A., Boston, New York, and San Francisco. I
started reading the 2009 census data. It told me that Mississippi was the
poorest state in the country. So I decided to head there. The map gave
me a sense that the poorest counties were mostly in the Mississippi
River Delta region, and so I began researching where there might be
Internet facilities in that area.

Unlike Nairobi, thick with Internet cafés and cell towers, rural Mississippi proved to be a tech wasteland. The owners of the few computer-
based businesses I met, some funding their enterprises by borrowing
from family because it was so hard to get start-up capital from the state,
were barely scraping by. They persevered because it gave them something to do in the midst of an area harboring few other economic opportunities.

I drove to Cleveland, Mississippi, an area known for cotton, the
blues, and grinding poverty. Representatives from the local small business center expressed a keen interest in Samasource, but mentioned

several constraints. "In some areas, the Internet connection is so bad that companies need to purchase expensive satellite dishes to get online," said one counselor. A local professor told me, "You'd be shocked at the lack of basic language skills in the population here. Because our educational system is failing, many of the kids from Cleveland are less equipped than foreign students who come out of English-medium schools in developing countries." Another told me that many firms just didn't have a grasp of technology: "There's a huge digital divide between the rural and urban areas of this country." I flashed back to high school, and to Jonathan Kozol's *Savage Inequalities,* which investigates the long-term consequences in the United States of the massive gap that exists between the quality of the public education received by the children of the rich and the children of the poor. Just as it took a trip to Ghana to open my eyes to the depth of global poverty, it took a visit to Mississippi to viscerally understand the depth of rural poverty in America. It's one thing to read about it; it's another to see it in person.

Poor rural America was an alternate universe, characterized, especially in the South, by extreme racial injustice, lack of infrastructure including basics like broadband, decent roads, and schools, and a profound sense of hopelessness after the recession. Like most people on the coasts, I'd had little idea of what life was like for people far away from the big cities. Urban poverty is a problem, certainly, but people living in big cities have access to so much more: more nonprofit resources like homeless shelters, food banks, and job training programs; more public services funded by a bigger tax base; and more access to jobs and economic opportunity. Rural Americans miss out on much of this, and suffer from the same sort of "brain drain" that poor countries face— many of the most qualified talent leave the area in search of better opportunities elsewhere, leaving a gaping hole that doesn't exist in cities.

I took a few preliminary steps toward exploring partnerships with some of the state's business incubators. Many were interested, like the small business program at Cleveland's Delta State University, but the funding was tough to access. You had to apply for elusive government grants from the Delta Regional Authority (DRA), a federal fund set up and run by Congress. I ended up visiting the DRA leaders in D.C., but got the feeling that I'd need a full-time lobbyist in order to push a grant through. The level of red tape was staggering—arduous procurement processes for grant applications with little guarantee that they'd ever get read. So we decided to pursue private philanthropy, the only thing we'd so far been successful in obtaining. But I was worried that Samasource was just too new for us to tack on a domestic program unless we suddenly had a giant grant fall in our lap. It seemed unlikely. At the time, we hadn't even found funding for the international work we were trying to do; there wasn't enough of me to go around to start trying to raise money to open centers in the States, too, and I worried that we would confuse our brand promise. In time, once we had successfully established ourselves for a few years and nailed our core promise and commitment to donors, we could then investigate how we might adapt the Samasource model for the United States.

That reasoning came into question when we ran the ad featuring our work in Africa on Hulu. In response I got an angry e-mail:

FROM: Joe ██████ <joe████@verizon.net>
TO: info@samasource.org
DATE: Sunday, November 22, 2009, at 7:00 p.m.
SUBJECT: Your company

I am sick and tired of hearing about all these companies like yours that take work that could help our country away from us to give to other countries. The USA is falling apart because of egotistical, money hungry assholes that care more about finding ways to make more money no matter what it does to the rest of us! So as far as I'm concerned bring the work to us or keep your ads off of our AMERICAN television systems!

Stop. Breathe. Listen.

When you put your heart and soul into a job that pays nothing, takes up every ounce of your energy, and doesn't even allow you to afford basic benefits, e-mails like this one really hurt. I was still deeply in debt from student loans and barely surviving on my minuscule pay, which I had to fund-raise. In addition, once again I had to defend my organization against the assumption that giving work to the global poor was a zero-sum game. It was anything but. We were creating a win-win-win situation. Destitute people got trained for the jobs of the future and a steady income that allowed them free agency, companies stayed competitive while performing a social good by selecting a vendor with a social mission, and the poor's additional earned income meant the promise of some relief on government-aid spending funded by U.S. taxpayers. This was a bad thing only if you were under the delusion that American companies relying on inexpensive outsourcing to keep costs low and improve their profits and growth were going to turn around and give those jobs to Americans. Outsourcing is what keeps prices affordable for most American consumers. Clothes, home furnishings, electronics, cars—all of these would cost us double, maybe more, than what they do now if the manufacturers had to pay American minimum wages to produce them. Even as some of our workers moved into more advanced jobs, Samasource wasn't competing against the American worker; we were competing against for-profit outsourcing operations, ones that did not make it a point to hire women, youth, or the world's most destitute.

Outraged and self-righteous, I started to dash off an angry e-mail. But then I followed the best advice I've received as an entrepreneur: never send an angry e-mail before sleeping on it. The next morning, I thought about what I'd seen in Mississippi. At the time I was reading Trappist monk Thomas Merton's *The Seven Storey Mountain*, and I was moved by the compassion and kindness that seemed to flow out from Merton to the rest of the world. Perhaps the better angels of my nature, inspired by Merton, woke me up the next morning in a different state.

(Side note: I highly recommend that you keep a book of uplifting poetry, moral philosophy, or spiritual inspiration by your bed at night. It will do wonders for how you feel when you wake up, and how you go about your day. It's impossible to feel small and tense after reading an expansive Rumi love poem, or a lesson on compassion from the Dalai Lama.) I deleted my original e-mail, and wrote back the following:

FROM: leila▮▮▮@gmail.com
TO: Joe ▮▮▮ <Joe▮▮@verizon.net>
DATE: Monday, November 23, 2009
SUBJECT: Re: Your company

Dear Joe,

We are a nonprofit helping the poorest people in the world, including low-income entrepreneurs in the US. If you'd like to engage in a constructive dialogue about how we could help more Americans, please let us know—we'd be happy to.

Best wishes,
Leila

Three days later, we received this:

FROM: Joe▮▮▮
TO: me
DATE: Thursday, November 26, 2009
SUBJECT: Re: Your company
I live in Ohio which has one of if not the highest unemployment rate in the country. I have been looking for work unsuccessfully for over a year. There is an old Kmart building in my town that would be perfect to renovate into a building that would suit the needs of your company perfectly, which would in turn provide many jobs for my area. If there is

anything you could do to get this going, it would be greatly
appreciated! I apologize for my previous e-mail, but I hope you can
understand the reasoning behind it.

Thanks

Joe

Compassion beats contempt every time. I'm no saint, and there were days when the intense pressure I felt to make something out of our organization overwhelmed my ability to be patient or generous with my close friends and family. But on that day, at least, kindness allowed two people—one who felt mistreated, the other misunderstood—to hear each other out. The consequences would prove to be far reaching.

I saw an opportunity. I had previously brought up my travels to Mississippi with my newly formed board and asked about the possibility of expanding our focus, but they weren't sure domestic social issues were relevant to our mission, and my chairman felt it would distract from our brand building around the idea of working to end international poverty. The next time we reconvened, I shared my e-mail exchange with them and explained that Joe's reaction proved that domestic needs were, in fact, relevant, and that we should explore setting up Samasource in the United States.

I tried to find out which Kmart Joe had in mind, but he stopped following up and we lost touch. I had given him a chance to share his thoughts, but I knew he had no expertise on where the real need was in Ohio, or what kind of budget setting up a Samasource center in the States might require. One challenge nonprofits frequently have to contend with is that many people seem to think that social problems are easier to solve than they really are. Entrenched poverty in America is an extremely complicated problem. It's layers deep. You can't just point to a lack of job opportunities—it's a lack of education, a breakdown in family structure and community relationships due to the lingering effects of slavery and Jim Crow, housing and environmental problems, generational trauma, and more. When all these issues meld together, as you see in remote rural corners of America and in urban centers, the problems are so rooted and tangled it can take years to fully understand them, let alone figure out solutions.

I kept an eye out, looking for the right place to try a pilot program. Then something fortuitous happened. Later that year, in the fall, I got a call from someone at the Clinton Foundation asking if I'd like to attend the 2010 annual Clinton Global Initiative conference. I'd long wanted to go, but could never afford the more than ten-thousand-dollar entrance fee. At the last minute, someone had backed out of a main stage panel moderated by the bestselling author Tom Friedman. Yes, that Tom Friedman—the one who wrote the book that inspired Samasource. Would I like to fill in?

Naturally I accepted. I practiced my talking points for days (while walking on the treadmill in the mornings—it helps me remember things), and a week later I was talking about Samasource and explaining my thoughts on how best to address poverty and global development in front of the Clintons and a huge number of influential people who had never heard of Samasource or the concept of digital work. I managed to drive home the point that giving work could change lives far better than almost any other aid program, and that social enterprises are better equipped than large bureaucracies to make real change happen quickly.

It was a game changer. Afterward, a man in the audience who had worked at the Rose Law Firm in Arkansas with Hillary Clinton approached me, along with the head of the state's economic development agency, and asked if I thought the kind of program I was describing in Africa would work in Arkansas. There it was, the opening I'd been looking for. Coincidentally, the same day, a man in the audience connected me with the California Endowment in Los Angeles, one of the state's largest funders. These conversations continued in tandem for two long years, via hundreds of e-mails and phone calls. I must have had lunch with Kathlyn Mead, then COO of the California Endowment, at least five times, and each time she'd tell me she wasn't sure she could get her board to buy in. Then one day she mentioned she'd like to have lunch again. I flew down just for the meeting, staying in a motel next door to the café in West Los Angeles where we were to meet. We made small talk as we settled into our meal, and then, beaming, she dropped the big, unexpected news: "Guess what? I'm going to give you eight hundred thousand dollars to pilot your program in California." I was so excited I couldn't eat. Two years of legwork, and totally worth it.

WELCOME TO THE GIG ECONOMY

It made no sense to try to connect American workers to the same kind of digital work we were sending to Africa and Asia. Because a lot of data work was already being outsourced, U.S. companies weren't willing to pay a surcharge to bring the work back to America. If that seems greedy, imagine, for a second, if we tried to bring electronics manufacturing, such as for the iPhone, back to the United States. It would mean consumers would have to pay triple or quadruple what they pay now for iPhones. If Apple did that, its customer base would leave it. Personally, I wish the difference could come from executive salary decreases, but that's where pragmatism comes in—this kind of shift is highly unlikely anytime soon. As a social entrepreneur, my best bet is to focus not on what I wish would happen but on what is actually happening. What kinds of projects would customers be willing to pay for to have them done here in the United States? There were many tasks that our foreign workers couldn't do, like answering a phone in an American accent and providing a domestic location ("Hi, this is Susan from Arkansas. How may I help you?"). Jobs like sales calls require local cultural context.

Our plan, then, was to adapt the Samasource model to train low-income Americans, in particular those trying to complete their degrees at community colleges, to take advantage of the surging on-demand or "gig" economy by showing them how to earn supplemental money providing off-line services via apps like the errand-running TaskRabbit, the ride-sharing Uber, and grocery-shopping Instacart, and to access freelance work on sites like oDesk and Elance—which I describe as eBay for services (they merged and became Upwork in 2015). The pilot, which we first named SamaUSA before changing it to Samaschool, launched in early 2013 in an old police boxing gym in Bayview–Hunter's Point, also known as the Bayview, a predominantly black industrial neighborhood just outside San Francisco where 40 percent of the population lived below the federal poverty level and the unemployment rate was above 30 percent. I hired a remarkable young woman, Tess Posner, to head Samaschool. We painted the walls Samasource yellow and black and found a local from the community to start training recruits—who didn't come flocking right away. We were surprised until we realized that when you've been scammed as frequently as the people in this neighborhood had, announcements for Internet jobs that will let you earn money while you work from home were going to be met with jaded eye rolls. It wasn't until we put the logos of our local partners—the YMCA and the local community college—on our flyers that we started seeing an uptick in interest and applications.

As classes began even I, who thought I had a pretty good grasp of the disparity that existed between the poor neighborhoods in California and the ones where I had been raised, was surprised to learn just how different most of our applicants' experiences had been from mine. Many of my students hadn't explored the city beyond their own neighborhoods, and had never been to the iconic landmarks in San Francisco, like the Golden Gate Bridge or Alcatraz. They lived in isolation, partly because there was so little public transportation that reached the neighborhood (BART, our city's system, doesn't stop in the Bayview, so you have to take a separate train, and it doesn't connect with the rest of the city). Some didn't know anyone who had held an office job. For many, selling drugs had proven to be the only way to make enough money to stay afloat and even provide for others. One young man had been in and out of foster care his whole life; another had been homeless for a time. I started learning about the concept of generational trauma—trauma that can be passed on from mother to child. Research shows that stress in a pregnant woman elevates the cortisol levels in her unborn baby and has long-term implications for the child's predisposition to high cortisol, mental health problems, and even aggression, which in turn creates a number of other follow-on problems. Knowing that we can't control the hand we're dealt, how can we hold people fully accountable for their personal outcomes and not try to help when they are struggling? The eminent Stanford biologist Robert Sapolsky famously said, "'Free will' is the term we give to the biology we haven't discovered yet."

The people living in some of the communities where we were working had so many more issues than just growing up poor. Otherwise they'd have gotten out. Those left behind are usually dealing with more challenges than just a lack of work. Drug culture, broken families, substandard schooling, and, for African Americans, the legacy of Jim Crow and, before that, slavery have hurt families and kept communities down in ways that we are only now just beginning to understand. So many of the young people we trained in Bayview told me that their siblings and friends ended up dealing drugs because it was the only job they knew, and because it paid more than doing hourly work at a grocery store (San Francisco's cost of living is among the highest in the nation). In essence, drug dealers were making the same rational choice as the Somali pirates in Scott Carney's *Wired* article who chose piracy over staying in war-torn Mogadishu.

Kenya is recovering from colonialism and Uganda from the dictator Idi Amin and warlord Joseph Kony, but in those countries black people are the majority, and though they might have been brutalized and terrorized, after the colonial period it was not for their color; upon sight they are never considered separate, different, or suspect. And it instills a different mind-set when you grow up poor in a country where the vast majority is also poor than it does when you grow up poor in a rich country. If you're in the minority and you feel like the system is set up to keep you from the opportunities that do exist, it will have a different effect on your motivation and grit than if you believe that you live in a country where all you have to do is find that opportunity. The greatest despair is found in places where there is no longer hope, where opportunity died a slow death long ago. Incredibly, I have found that those places are not in refugee camps or slums, but right here in the United States.

The need of our students was eye-opening. I thought our work would be pretty straightforward—show people some Web sites they didn't know about, teach them how to set up a profile, and they'd be on their way. But that wasn't going to be enough. Our students' literacy skills were lower than we expected, and a quarter of the participants didn't have Internet access at home, even through a smartphone. According to the Pew Research Center, most people who have not adopted the Internet at home cite cost as the primary barrier. Of those without fast Internet service at home, two-thirds say that it represents a "major disadvantage" to accessing at least one of the following: "Government services, searching for employment, following the news, learning new things, or getting health information." This wasn't just a question of familiarizing people with a new kind of work, but of getting them onto the twenty-first-century grid. Of those who had some experience with computers, most had never used them for professional purposes, and even some with extensive computer experience had been unable to find steady work. We found the same circumstances in Merced, where we opened a center later that year. In 2012, *Forbes* named Merced one of America's "Most Miserable Cities," and a year later *Time* listed it as the most polluted city in the country.

The situation was even worse in Dumas, where we launched about a year later. Rural Americans are more than twice as likely not to use the Internet as those living in urban areas. More than thirty thousand people die annually from addiction to opiates, often in rural and disconnected communities. Where hopelessness prevails, people seek to numb the pain of living. Ordinary people no longer feel that the powers that be respond to their needs, and so they check out. This is the setting in which despots come to power.

Located in the Delta region of the state, Dumas, a town with just over forty-five hundred residents, is caught in a stranglehold. The meagerly funded public schools struggle to educate a student body of which the majority qualify for free or reduced-price lunch. High school seniors regularly test at a fifth-grade reading level; 50 percent of the people who take the workforce development basic skills test fail the literacy component.

We came in with a curriculum that assumed a basic understanding of computers. After all, all the schools had computer labs. Still, some of our students didn't know what a URL was. It blew my mind that a student in the Mathare slums would be more comfortable with technology than someone born in the United States. The Internet connection was so sluggish, we might as well have been back in post-earthquake Mirebalais.

There were pernicious psychological barriers, too. We started out with extremely low expectations when we trained in Africa and Asia, and especially in the refugee camps. But it was only our expectations that were low; our trainees' own expectations were still quite robust. They were so eager and hungry for opportunity that literally only the threat of death (theirs or ours) stopped them from completing their training. There were enough stories circulating about people who'd gotten out and gotten asylum, jobs, scholarships, and new lives to allow them to believe that they, too, could do it. It wasn't a matter of if, but of when; all they had to do was hang on long enough to be able to take advantage of the opportunity that would surely come. Even those born in the camps didn't view their circumstances as permanent; they were going to get out somehow, someday. But in Dumas, where few people knew anyone who had left or gotten more than a high school education, where the best job you could get was at the gas station or McDonald's, where people regularly chose between eating and gassing up the car to get to work, all while living in the richest country in the world, the mood was one of resignation. A life of taking hits wears on a person. When you've got enough to eat and a small nest egg or support network, it's not the end of the world when something goes wrong. A simple mistake or misunderstanding, say, some lost paperwork, can be resolved, even if it takes a few weeks of angry phone calls. Life goes on. But when you're scrabbling for existence, one mistake, one hospital bill, one flat tire, can set you back years. Life stands still.

And there is no question that racism and discrimination are still daily slaps in the face for many in this community. Due to the historically preferential bank loan practice favoring whites that was witnessed by Terrence's grandmother, today African Americans own a fraction of the land surrounding Dumas and only .5 percent of local businesses, even though they make up 70 percent of the population. One Samaschool student took a job at a local furniture store only to find out that she was being paid 30 percent less than her white coworker. During the writing of this book, the KKK held a rally and burned a cross in a town center not a half hour away from Dumas, and a sign hung outside another warning blacks to stay away after dark. That same year, while checking out some newly published history books from the chamber of commerce, accompanied by a film crew he'd been showing around town, Terrence Davenport was warned by a grandmotherly white woman behind the front desk, "You'd better bring the books back or we'll tie a rope around your neck."

This is not the full story of Arkansas, of course. The state has a remarkably progressive side, and many people and organizations, like the Walmart Foundation, the Women's Foundation, and the Walton Family

Foundation, are working toward racial and economic justice, especially for the descendants of slaves and sharecroppers, and are investing efforts to move people out of poverty in rural parts of the state. But there is still a lot of work to do.

In the meantime, even in the motivated groups that applied to Samaschool, the smallest failure or setback caused people's attendance rates to falter and even made them drop out. Sometimes logistics got in the way, such as when a spouse took seasonal fieldwork and needed the family car to get to and from the job. It was very common for people to pick cotton in the summertime, even while they were in school before graduating—the rhythm of the cotton fields still pulsed through the community. Cotton had once been the region's biggest export and hope for a brighter future.

Sometimes we got feedback that the courses were too hard. Occasionally we never saw or heard from the students again and never knew why they gave up. With little demand for services via apps like Uber, the students mostly concentrated on the freelance opportunities available on sites like Upwork. But the average worker on Upwork had a master's degree; students just couldn't compete, and employers expected workers to be higher skilled if they were going to pay more.

Ironically, our students faced stiff competition for the more low-skilled work they were qualified to do from international workers who demanded less pay. In many ways they were less equipped than the Kenyans in terms of schooling, connectivity, and sense of possibility. It felt awful that we were operating in an island of poverty in the midst of the United States. And it felt even worse that there was so little funding interest for this rural community. Dumas felt foreign to me—more foreign, even, than Nairobi, because here were people who'd uttered the same Pledge of Allegiance as I did in elementary school but had been served up a dramatically different fate.

Accustomed to job training programs that also helped with placement, students were demoralized by how many proposals they had to write and applications they had to put in just to get one hit. For people who needed work urgently, it took too long to see any reward for their efforts. Poor people often cannot afford to be patient.

The lack of infrastructure was a real block, too. A few of our promising students had offers rescinded when the hiring company tested the Internet in the area and found that the upload speed in Dumas wasn't fast enough to meet the jobs' requirements. The service providers simply weren't serving rural communities with the same products they provided to more profitable and more populated areas, cutting poor people off from desperately needed income. Fortunately, today there are public, private, and legislative fixes to this problem in play that could prove beneficial to future Samaschool students. For example, in late 2015, the Federal Communications Commission announced that it would pay millions of dollars to telecommunications carriers throughout the country, via the Connect America Fund (a revamped version of the Universal Service Fund, which brought telephone service to rural areas in the twentieth century), to provide high-speed Internet access to rural areas. Progress will be slow, however; the carriers aren't expected to cover 100 percent of their targeted locations until 2020.

Once our first cohorts graduated, we took note of our mistakes and shortcomings and made changes to the curriculum. We implemented additional basic writing modules and sample projects. We partnered with the career development departments at local community colleges and other organizations so we could connect students to their support services and therefore improve the rates of class attendance and completion. And in the end, we developed two models to serve the distinct needs of our urban and rural communities.

In urban communities, like the ones we serve in California and now New York, there is plenty of opportunity to make money through on-demand services like Uber, Instacart, TaskRabbit, and other platforms that connect people to temporary gig work. So we offer short workshops geared toward getting people with some computer knowledge up and running to provide services on these platforms as fast as possible. We teach our students how to gauge the pros and cons of various platforms, how to create a strong online profile, and how to build an online reputation that generates word-of-mouth recommendations and steady work.

Our rural model, however, focuses on getting people remote work opportunities, services that people can supply even when they don't live where the demand is, like customer service, telesales, and social media marketing. Once again, this is the beauty of digital work—no boundaries. Over the course of a ten-week boot camp, our students cover everything from the soft skills of work readiness, such as showing up on time, to crucial English and digital literacy skills to creating attention-getting résumés filled with the right keywords to setting up a LinkedIn profile.

We were so bombarded with inquiries and applications, however, that we started an online educational program at Samaschool.org, one designed to serve anyone, anywhere, with a modicum of digital skills— a self-paced four-hour crash course in monetizing already existing skills for online freelance work on sites such as Upwork. As of this writing, more than 25,000 people had enrolled.

Though our programs focus on giving work first, we do our best to fill in the training gaps as well. On evenings and weekends in Dumas, for example, Terrence offers additional intensive writing instruction, plus classes in WordPress Web design and graphic design—anything, he says, that can provide more hope and prepare his students for the new economy with the tools they need to build careers and propel their lives forward. (I always encourage our local instructors to be entrepreneurial and do what they want to get better outcomes for students, as long as they aren't overworking themselves.) Meanwhile, he believes his students will ultimately succeed if we find their first opportunities for them, the same way we do for our Samasource workers in Uganda, India, Kenya, and Haiti. He therefore actively seeks to make connections with companies that specialize in the kinds of work students can start as soon as they get their certificates, such as customer service (one of the few traditionally offshore services U.S. companies are bringing back to the States) for virtual call centers like Arise, which employs home-based domestic workers. Once you eliminate the costs of gas and child care, you open up a wealth of opportunities to people in rural America.

My best hires at Sama have been people who could easily have started their own companies (some have)—they're people who take ownership, lead from a place of deep conviction, and sweat the small stuff. They aren't managers; they're doers. Like so many entrepreneurs, Terrence has The Fire. He has a million ideas for making things better around him, and no fear. He doesn't care if his idea gets shot down, if other people think it's stupid, or if there are too many looming obstacles. Terrence knows that in a place like Dumas, things don't change without a glass-half-full philosophy and a willingness to deliver drop-kicks to the system. Every company can use more of what Terrence has.

We have failed the people of Merced and Dumas and places like them. There's no excuse for any community in the United States to have bigger infrastructure challenges than in developing countries. It should not be possible for our educational system to turn out a populace with such weak literacy and English skills that it was harder to find our initial pool of qualified candidates for the pilot program in rural Arkansas than the one in Nairobi.

Yet we've seen our students achieve in ways that give us great hope for the future. The benefit to this model is that it's much cheaper to train people to be successful because a lot of them have traditional skills that can be repurposed really quickly for moneymaking. Our urban students find so much work on big platforms like TaskRabbit that instead of introducing the site and training for it during the final week of instruction, like we used to, we introduce and train for it during our third week; many students start landing jobs there even before they graduate. We see people rapidly repurposing skills they already have into new jobs. For example, one of our younger students loved working on cars but he'd never held a formal job. He got a job on TaskRabbit installing car stereos and earned several hundred dollars in about a month. In Merced, California, single mom Kristen Logan found work as a virtual assistant for a company in New York. In Arkansas, where the cost of center-based child care for two kids can eat up more than half of a single parent's income, Robinette Franklin, a mother of four young children, was grateful for her job as a work-from-home virtual customer service representative for Comcast. Another student in Dumas, Gary, a former marine who came back to Arkansas to care for his aging parents, once worked for a dog food factory that closed. The replacement job he found was two hours away, making it economically unfeasible when he calculated the cost of gas. He completed our training and wound up with a full-time customer service job earning two dollars more than the minimum wage, and left only when he found a truck-driving job that paid significantly more. Another Dumas student, Ernestine, buoyed by the support and confidence she got through Samasource, parlayed her new writing skills and social media dexterity into a burgeoning online business designing and selling high school sports–themed hair bows to fans around Arkansas. And yet another, Carrie, who came to class with somewhat stronger writing skills than the average student and some unusually strong hustle, was regularly getting hired as a social media marketer one month after she graduated.

We have to measure our success differently than we're used to. Unlike in the other countries where Samasource operates, the money our students earn through the online jobs we train for domestically is rarely life changing. The money just can't go as far. On average after the boot camp, which lasts eighty hours or so and can be completed on nights and weekends, our students' income increases by about fifteen hundred dollars within three months. That doesn't sound like much, yet it represents a 10 percent income increase for the one in six Americans who live under the federal poverty line. The real payoff is that as the students gain skills that serve as building blocks to help them move on to the next job, they start to earn more and gain more stability. Our mission is still to give work, but we have recognized that Samaschool must also serve as a career incubator, a place that offers not only training but support and encouragement, too. Where there is generational trauma and poverty, patience is the only option (giving up is not).

We know that most of the jobs our students find are not the kinds anyone would want to do for the rest of their lives. But that's the case with most entry-level, unskilled work. I certainly didn't want to clean toilets for the rest of my life, but I did it in college because I knew that it would pay my way toward something better. Gig economy platforms like Lyft and TaskRabbit are neither exploitative nor saviors. Technology is amoral. It's how we use it and shape it that defines its legacy. We can build around these platforms and create tools like portable benefits (government programs that support benefits that move along with workers, as opposed to being tied to an employer), better savings and retirement programs that aren't employer dependent, and better access to collective pooled resources, like what Sara Horowitz has built with the Freelancers Union or what Ai-jen Poo is working on with the National Domestic Workers Alliance. Workers need more freedom; employers need more flexibility. The average person doesn't need a full-time personal assistant, but as office employment hours have increased and work has spilled into nights and weekends, many could use help managing their lives. They need someone to deliver groceries once a week, or walk the dog, or babysit, and they want to know they can get home safely after a night out, no matter where they went or how much they had to drink. The gig economy is simply a market response to human needs that have not been met through the traditional economic system.

That said, it would be remiss not to acknowledge that many of the jobs people are training for today are vulnerable to offshoring and mechanization. That's why I believe the industry with the most long-term promise for our domestic workforce is the care economy. Care-taking jobs, especially the ones that require empathy and a human touch, won't be totally protected from automation, but they will be among the last to go. Elder and child care, housekeeping, art instruction, cooking, pet care, and a number of other jobs are often done by unpaid caretakers but have immense social value and diminishing returns if they're outsourced. (How long will it be until you're comfortable having your child raised by a robot? Probably awhile.) In these fields, empathy and physical affection, human ingenuity, and creativity are prized—and hard to deliver remotely. And so in the future I think these types of jobs will have newfound meaning, especially as robots do more of the economically valuable and productive work that is less artistically and emotionally enriching. The drudgery and routine will be done by the robots, leaving the humans to do work that matters in a very different way. In 2016 we began discussion with partners like Ai-jen's organization, NDWA, to create a "care institute," where low-income people can be trained for caregiving jobs, the first program of its kind to focus on this rapidly growing sector of the gig economy. We're formalizing informal work, offering training, support, and the opportunity for day laborers to build the same kind of online professional reputation that white-collar workers have benefited from for years.

Despite the gloom and doom, I think gig platforms are really good for workers. Most low-income people tell me they love that these jobs give them the freedom to set their own schedules and allow them to decide when and where to make money according to their needs. Many creatives, entrepreneurs, and others looking for flexible income supplement money from other sources—taking the portfolio approach to income, common among the poor. The only thing they need now is security. At the dawn of industrialization unions offered laborers protection and bargaining power. We need to reinvent the labor union for this new era. The National Domestic Workers Alliance is the first organization to give low-income informal caregivers the same kinds of benefits they would receive in a union. We need more forward-thinking players in this exploding space.

So far, Samaschool has trained more than 650 people in person. To my knowledge, we are the only training program in the country to educate workers on how to find and excel at jobs within the tech-driven gig economy or for online caregiving platforms. But succeeding on any online platform is not just about the professional skills candidates bring to the table; it's about the amount of resilience they bring, too. And that skill, along with a certain stick-to-itiveness, is proving to be harder to teach than anything else. The new economy depends on people to act as independent contractors—to have hustle and find their own "gigs" on the new labor platforms. The old corporate model is going away and being replaced by freelancing. And that essentially means that more and more people have to learn to be entrepreneurs. The best way to equip future generations is to develop a keen ability to identify and articulate problems that haven't yet been solved, to teach kids how to work in teams to achieve big goals, and to instill in them a comfort with failure. Sara Blakely, the famous founder of Spanx, tells the story of her father and his nightly dinner table question: what did you fail at today? She and her siblings would have to report on what they tried and failed at. If they didn't fail, their father wasn't happy—he wanted to see them pushing out of their comfort zones.

I can't think of better advice, other than encouraging your child to find a job: something that she can practice failing at and commit to even when she doesn't fully enjoy it, and that will teach her how to manage even tiny amounts of money. Failures are woven into the fabric of entrepreneurship—any good leader will tell you her war stories, and many come from unglamorous jobs (selling knives door-to-door, flipping burgers, or babysitting) that test your mettle. Those who can't hack it and quit when things get difficult are the only ones who really fail. Everyone else has minor setbacks.

Terrence sees the payoff. He says, "It's hard to paint a clear enough picture of how rampant discouragement is among the poor. And yet my students show up, and from the first day of class I make it my goal to keep them there. The retention is not easy, but if I can keep them here and motivated, they'll get that inspiration to get to work, even in something other than digital. Some people drop my class, not because they can't cut it, but because they develop new habits and get something else. The Samaschool classes inspire and motivate them to believe they can succeed. That's what I try to do for people." With these words, Terrence gets at the crux of why so many charity and aid programs can't move the needle: the key to raising people out of poverty isn't just creating, training for, and securing jobs, it's also restoring people's sense of dignity and self-worth.

A NEW SYSTEM

The loss of dignity caused by unemployment also explains the frustration and anger felt by so many people in the West, and the rising appeal of nationalist, xenophobic, and isolationist movements. Stanford biologist Robert Sapolsky has written that these instincts are triggered primarily by fear, and there is no greater fear among primates than status anxiety. Most of the countries where Samasource works have always known a huge, almost unbridgeable divide between the haves and the have-nots. But here in the States, where the middle class came to hold a great deal of political and economic power after World War II, most Americans have grown up expecting that if you work hard and stay out of trouble, you should be able to afford the basic necessities of life. It's a fundamental promise of the American Dream. But for more and more people on the lower economic spectrum all across the country, it's an empty one, which is why we now find ourselves in a dangerous place. The effects of large-scale unemployment cascade into all aspects of our society, revealing themselves in everything from a disenfranchised, angry, and fearful populace to overcrowded emergency medical facilities to the diminishment of our collective morale. Companies move freely across borders, but workers cannot, so workers are always going to be at a disadvantage. The system is failing our citizens and is woefully unprepared to ready them for a new reality.

So we need a new system. Global trade is here to stay. Retreating from global governance and moving toward isolationist and protectionist policies is only going to make things worse for workers and cut us off from the rich spectrum of products and services that modern consumers love. (Try to imagine your life without coffee or pepper.) In the short term, jobs in certain industries would be protected, but in the long term there would be fewer jobs and lower standards of living. The answer, therefore, is more global collaboration, not less, and more rules on how companies operate transnationally. Our current trade agreements have benefited wealthy corporations and their owners by encouraging them to send their companies' manufacturing to the cheapest places possible and hire the cheapest labor, which tends to mean low standards for working conditions. There are no incentives other than consumer pressure to pay living wages, source materials sustainably, or invest in the workers' communities. We have to establish reasonable regulations and tax policies that reflect the nature of the global world we're living in.

The government would play a dual role in the new system I'd like to see. The first would be to create job-training opportunities for poor and disenfranchised people to do the kinds of work that should be safe from offshoring and mechanization, primarily found in the care economy—caretaking jobs that require a human touch and tremendous empathy, like child care and elder care. The second would be to incentivize companies to give these previously overlooked groups a chance to participate in the economy. For example, rewarding platforms that already exist, such as SeniorCare.com, for recruiting people who would otherwise be unemployed and turning them into care workers, perhaps by subsidizing those new workers' wages or providing vouchers to care recipients, redeemable on social enterprise care platforms. In this way, you encourage the platform to keep innovating.

The government and philanthropic organizations could work together to support social impact companies and entrepreneurs committed to helping our most vulnerable, such as Hot Bread Kitchen, a Harlem-based nonprofit that hires and trains recent immigrant women to bake internationally inspired breads and prepares them for culinary careers. They could give entrepreneurs a reason to tackle markets that seem too risky to profit-oriented start-ups, the way Samasource did eight years ago. They could redirect the billions of dollars we spend on aid programs to tax breaks for businesses that not only promise to recruit low-income people here and abroad but also are able to prove they are achieving the goal of raising them over the poverty line and keeping them there. Companies focusing on the environment or conservation would be rewarded only to the extent that they could prove that their initiatives were effective in protecting wildlands, for instance, or in deterring poachers. There are lots of businesses that could be built to accomplish these goals, but they've never been imagined because we haven't set up incentives in such a way as to reward entrepreneurs for doing it. Of course such a system would come with challenges—building infrastructure in poor areas is expensive, for example, and people with no work history often require soft skills training to help them integrate smoothly into an office environment—but they are not insurmountable.

The best entrepreneurs live to solve these kinds of problems. Rose Broome would walk by homeless people on her way to work at a San Francisco health start-up and feel frustrated that the tools she was building at her company weren't solving this local problem. She wound up starting HandUp, a local Kickstarter-like for-profit where you can donate directly to a homeless person in need in your community. Rose saw a problem, and instead of looking around for someone else to fix it, she tried to fix it herself. She used technology, as I did, but you don't have to. If you're an entrepreneur, ask yourself what you can do to give work in your community, and start an enterprise that does that. If you're a business owner, rethink your philanthropic donations and figure out how you could allocate that money toward creating employment for the poorest in your community.

And remember that it's not necessary to go big. Muhammad Yunus laments that so often we think that we have to create something huge, and that it's not worth doing if it's not scalable. That kind of thinking is flawed. If you can create good living-wage employment for five people in your community, or even only three people, especially from low-income populations, you're making a difference in greater, untold ways than you realize. It's not about achieving massive scale or being on the cover of a magazine; it's about sleeping well at night knowing you're part of the solution.

That said, there is one big uncomfortable fact looming ahead for Samasource, Samaschool, and any other organization trying to tackle poverty. You've probably already figured it out: at the pace of innovation, the work for which we are currently training people will likely be obsolete in five to ten years. Whereas at one time we at Samasource were training people to convert PDF images of text into text files, machines can handle that now. Our workers are currently tagging pictures taken with cameras attached to car bumpers to help create programs that will tell a self-driving car when a human being is walking in front of it. But once the algorithm is created, humans won't be needed for that job anymore. In just a few short years, those same self-driving cars are going to throw the Uber and Lyft drivers now bedeviling the taxi and hired-car industries out of work, too. Many of our U.S. Samaschool students currently training for the gig economy are going to join the tens of millions of people who lose jobs to those cars, as well as to Internet bots that automate low-end customer service positions like help-desk work, and to actual robots that perform menial tasks like home cleaning. A lot of the jobs available through gig economy platforms have been part of the work landscape for only the last decade and are just stopgaps supplying much-needed supplemental income, but their absence will be deeply felt. And while the cost of labor is still so low it might take awhile for mechanization to reach countries like Uganda, where people still do the majority of farmwork by hand, the technology that has taken over agriculture in the West will eventually reach developing countries, too.

So in this new world where machines can do the same work humans can do and produce the same amount of economic output, how do we make sure the people who used to do these jobs have a future? The answer is not to fight progress by regulating tech. The answer is to accept reality. If work were to become irrelevant, what would you give people so they could build comfortable, productive lives?

Money.

There are some fancy terms for this, like direct cash transfers and universal basic income. It's all the same—cash handouts. The only real solution to the looming specter of massive unemployment and poverty would be to pay everyone a universal income every month to afford them the basic necessities to live a dignified, fulfilling life: three meals a day, education and culture, and the freedom Martin Luther King Jr. spoke so eloquently about in his 1969 Nobel Prize acceptance speech. We could replace the expensive, bloated layers of bureaucracy we currently have in place to keep track of who qualifies for welfare programs and what they do with their benefits, and simply regularly distribute the same amount of cash to everyone to do with as they choose. By giving cash, we simulate an income and allow all the other market mechanisms to take effect. Versions of this idea have been piloted in Canada, the Netherlands, Finland, and Belgium with encouraging results, and other countries, like Spain, have expressed interest in trying it. In addition, many development programs in Asia, Africa, and Latin America have experimented with giving the extreme poor direct cash transfers—one-time payments, as opposed to regular income—for years. The evidence shows that when unburdened from the stress of starvation or housing insecurity, people gain the mental bandwidth to make basic investments in health care, education, and other essentials that enable them to be more productive in school and in their work performance and to search for employment. School attendance goes up and child labor goes down. Men's annual income increased by 64 to 96 percent of the amount of direct cash granted to them. Notably, repeated studies show absolutely no evidence that poor families are inclined to spend cash transfers on so-called temptation goods such as alcohol or cigarettes.

The obvious question here is, when provided with a guaranteed income, what motivation would people have to develop themselves, innovate, and create? The question assumes that humans are intrinsically motivated by money, yet all the studies on happiness have shown that people are happiest when they're working toward a goal bigger than themselves. We can look to our own retirees, too, for evidence that money doesn't drive productivity. Very few people who can afford to stop working because they can count on a steady level of income just hole up at home on the couch. They volunteer, they find ways to share their knowledge, or they dive into their passions, like perfecting their golf swings; they spend more time with grandchildren, take care of elder family members. They create art. As long as people have their health and a sense of security (their three meals a day and their freedom), they generally continue to work on themselves in ways that are perhaps not commercial, but that do benefit society (their education and culture).

We would need to think harder about the psychology of work, what spurs intrinsic motivation beyond a steady paycheck, and learn to separate the value of work from its economic output. In this new world where we need to motivate people to contribute to society and culture, it would behoove us to find value in contributions that weren't properly valued before. Babysitting the prekindergarten kids in your neighborhood or caring for an aging grandmother would be a properly recognized respected form of contribution. Perhaps it could even be paid accordingly through tax dollars and cash payments for these new types of work. That's the kind of innovation that solves market needs: in this case, the needs of the people who need care, and the needs of the unemployed worker. We could increase the cachet and value of thousands of jobs that are simply not given the respect they deserve today, and create new work for jobs we didn't even know we needed. We've done it before. After all, to this day Americans continue to reap the benefits of the nontraditional jobs that created the infrastructure, art, music, literature, and historical preservation made possible by the Works Progress Administration, the work relief program that served as Franklin D. Roosevelt's answer to the country's crushing and demoralizing Depression-era unemployment. It would be a failure of our collective imagination to refuse to design that new world. It's not inevitable that everyone will descend into laziness. In fact, I predict that we'd see a more motivated, healthier, longer-living society in this new world, but it would of course require different ground rules and open-minded, thoughtful policy makers.

When we donate goods and services that we think people need, like coats, instead of what they really need, which are living-wage jobs, we don't address the core problem of why people can't afford coats, which is that they are very poor. It puts a Band-Aid on the problem. The day you bring someone a coat may be the day that what they really need is breakfast. Or maybe they'd rather use the money you put toward their coat toward schoolbooks. (That doesn't mean you shouldn't donate or recycle your used coat. The point is to closely examine the traditional model of doing what we think is beneficial, and try wherever we can to give people an opportunity to decide for themselves what will actually make a difference in their lives. The beauty of the market is that it allows people to tell us what they need, rather than presupposing what they need. There's a lot of efficiency built into such a system. When poor people receive direct cash transfers, they create the market for whatever it is they're missing. The lack of certain infrastructure and goods in communities, from water pumps to books to shoes, is a symptom of poverty.

So instead of giving them water pumps or books or shoes, we should be developing long-term solutions that allow us to provide them with the income they need to build or make or buy those things on their own. If that income can't be created in the form of work, then there shouldn't be any squeamishness about creating it in the form of guaranteed monthly income. Creating government and philanthropic systems that promote self-determination would be a much healthier way for communities to interact and to make sure that everyone's needs are met.

Some entrepreneurs might squirm at the idea of a world in which work is irrelevant. I'm an optimist. If that were to happen, I believe we'd do what humans have always done: we'd adapt. Such a scenario could head the dawn of a fantastic new era. Once liberated from the daily preoccupation with earning a living and providing sustenance for oneself or one's family, I think we might find that our brains are freed up to make more frequent breakthroughs. Problems would be solved faster, which would free us up even further to take the time to develop a more nurturing, compassionate, mindful society. I'd love to live in that world.

Chapter Five

BEAUTY FOR HUMANITY: A NEW BUSINESS

S CIENTIST FRIENDS OF MINE TELL ME THAT SOME OF THE WORLD'S greatest discoveries and breakthroughs, especially those in fields like string theory and molecular biology, were made possible with a little help from consciousness-expanding psychedelics. It's not surprising. Humans learn through pattern recognition—that's how neural pathways form. Our brains are wired to retread the same patterns over and over, making it extraordinarily difficult for us to change our behavior or way of thinking as we get older and the grooves wear deeper. That's why it can take a radical outside influence to help us see things a fresh and different way. If that's true, then Priya Haji was my acid trip.

I met Priya in 2007 when I attended the first Craigslist Nonprofit Boot Camp, an event put on by founder Craig Newmark and his team in Berkeley. Priya was one of the speakers. Like me, she was an "ABCD" (an American-Born Confused Desi, what Indian Americans jokingly call first-generation sons and daughters), born and raised in Bryan, Texas, where her parents were doctors. Like me, she believed that the best way to help the poor was by giving work. She'd often traveled to India to visit family, and while there she was struck by the beauty of the handicrafts in the market, and how cheap they were. She'd go back to the States and see a similar piece for sale that was just as beautiful but much more expensive. So, she thought, why not create a U.S. market-place for these developing-world artisans? Using a combined ten thousand dollars in savings, she and a friend, Siddharth Sanghvi, founded World of Good, Inc., a social venture that sold beautiful handicrafts from artisans working with NGOs, cooperatives, and other nonprofits in the developing world, while ensuring that the artisans were paid a living wage. She wanted "to demonstrate that you could create a market-based model in which you could align the customer's interest and the opportunity to generate income with the solving of a social or environmental problem. This way, as the business grows and as the market grows, you are actually solving the problem in a self-renewing manner."

There was so much that was remarkable about Priya, but at the time what I found especially cool was the unusual way she'd structured her business. Priya wasn't just interested in helping however many artisans whose work she could sell; she also wanted to improve the fortunes of countless others in the developing world by providing labor, goods, or services to U.S. companies. So at the same time that they launched World of Good, Inc., she and her business partner started a nonprofit, the World of Good Development Organization. While the for-profit created work, the nonprofit managed and monitored the for-profit's supply chain, made sure the artists were paid fairly, and developed fair wage-tracking tools. The nonprofit funded itself, but it also received 10 percent of its sister company's profits.

World of Good took off. A Stanford grad before getting her MBA from UC Berkeley, Priya started with the Stanford bookstore and got them to let her open a kiosk where she sold artisan-made bracelets, key chains, and other small items. From there she got into Whole Foods and then other mainstream retailers, like Hallmark, Carnival cruise ship retail stores, and Disney. She then started working with eBay to develop an ethical online marketplace for artisan goods—the first of its kind. Meanwhile, working with academics at Berkeley, World of Good Development Organization created a guide to help retailers and workers calculate fair wages and pricing. It became the free Fair Wage Guide, and Samasource, along with hundreds of other companies in at least twenty countries, still uses it today. By the time I met her, Priya had a warehouse in Oakland and thirty employees. Meeting Priya and seeing what she'd accomplished by applying the Give Work concept to her artisan producers in developing countries was what finally compelled me to quit my job and launch Samasource—she opened my mind to a new way of being.

I thought about structuring Samasource as a hybrid business like World of Good, but it was a complicated process, and my friend Premal Shah advised me to take the route that would get me up and running as fast as possible. Besides, I had no capital. So Samasource became a nonprofit. But I loved the idea of the hybrid model Priya had pioneered, of a social business structure that would allow for impartial standard setting and measurement on the one hand, in a nonprofit, and for a clear business model and investment opportunity on the other, in a for-profit, and I always kept the concept in the back of my mind. Finally one day I saw the chance to put it into play.

It was 2012, and I was traveling through Uganda. I've always loved to travel, but the thousands of hours I spend in airplanes takes a toll. I'm constantly looking for ways to reduce the effects of jet lag and dehydration on my face and body. One symptom is parched skin, a condition made worse by the hot climates I spend time in. In Northern Uganda, however, I'd noticed that despite the harsh environmental conditions and economic deprivation, many local women had gorgeous, smooth skin. One day, at a cheap local market next to a gas station, I spotted, right next to the toothpaste, some local shea butter for sale. I bought a few ounces.

I had used shea butter before—it's a common ingredient in many mass-market hand and face lotions, soaps, and hair products—but this stuff was something special. The usual shea butter (which comes from West Africa) is thick and waxy and needs an emulsifier and added ingredients to make it usable on one's face. The stuff I found in Uganda was naturally creamy and buttery, and it sank immediately into the skin, as if it had been created in a high-tech lab. I marveled over my find for several months, and then started asking around about it and doing some research. The butter had been pressed from nuts harvested from the beautiful leafy shea trees I'd seen dotting the landscape all around this fertile, verdant region, home to Lake Victoria, the source of the Nile River. Often referred to as "women's gold," shea nut oil and butter have long provided an important source of income for women, who are traditionally the ones to collect, process, and sell it, and who use it for everything from baby massage to cooking oil to burn remedies. Different species of shea trees grow across a wide band of Africa stretching almost from coast to coast, but because of the civil war on the eastern side of the continent, the majority of exported shea comes from a species of tree called *Vitellaria paradoxa*, found in West African countries like Ghana, Mali, and Burkina Faso. In Northern Uganda, however, where Samasource was establishing digital work centers, the nuts were sourced from a rare subspecies of tree called *Vitellaria nilotica*.

Whereas West African nut extracts come out as an oil, or thick and waxy like a chunk of clay, thus requiring added chemicals to get a spreadable texture, pressed Nilotica is naturally soft and buttery and requires no additives. The lab studies I found revealed that its nutritional and chemical properties are incredible, with exceptionally high levels of vitamins A and K and 25 percent more oleic acid—an amino acid that increases the skin's permeability, thus allowing deeper absorption—than the more common type of shea found in almost all commercial products, including popular formulas by brands like L'Occitane and L'Oréal. I had stumbled on a product that was pure, that was wild, that was effective, and—here's the part that had my mind spinning—that had never gone mainstream in the United States. Just a few weeks earlier the U.S. ambassador to Benin had told me he thought the key to stopping child trafficking in that country would be to increase the export market for shea, and I'd thought, well, someone else will have to do it—I'm not interested in starting another West African shea butter brand. This, though, was different.

My instincts had proven me right once before. Back in the spring of 2002, while visiting Brazil, I'd fallen in love at first taste with the Amazonian superfood açaí in a Rio de Janeiro juice shop. I was disappointed that I wouldn't be able to get it once I returned home, and told a bunch of my friends that someone could make a fortune if they started exporting it to the States. As it turned out, a company called Sambazon, started by two brothers who'd also gone crazy for the fruit, was already exporting frozen açaí puree, and it went mainstream shortly after I returned from my trip after being touted as a superfood in a bestselling diet book, on *Oprah,* and in *People* magazine. As it so happens, the company also takes great pride in its commitment to the triple bottom line, putting social responsibility and environmental sustainability on par with profit, buying from more than "10,000 independent family growers," and taking steps to minimize their ecological impact on the Amazon.

I felt I was onto something similar: this Nilotica butter could be the next açaí berry, and the company that exported it could be a Samasource for skin care. Women were selling a rare superfood so pure it was safe to eat and to slather every day on babies' skin, yet their sales still earned them so little, families were increasingly turning to ecologically harmful slash-and-burn methods to make charcoal, which can be sold quickly and easily on the side of the road, and to clearing plots of land for subsistence farming. The Nilotica shea trees, which take up to twenty years to mature, were in danger of disappearing, and with them an important natural resource, not to mention the surrounding wild lands. Why not develop a Give Work business model around this precious raw ingredient? Why not create a conservation and economic incentive to save the trees by showing farmers that they could significantly improve their income by selling the nuts? And then, why not take it a step further and create a luxury social impact brand, with great design and beautiful storytelling? Most fair trade products have a somewhat crunchy aesthetic, with a "natural" smell and a waxy or oily feel. You can easily find them in recycled earth-toned packaging at places like Whole Foods. Yet if anyone is interested in natural products free of dimethicone or yellow #5 or parabens, it's the luxury consumer who shops at high-end retailers. I wanted to make a product for women who follow popular beauty icons like Kim Kardashian, personalities known more for their eyelashes than for their activism. It would be a truly natural, good-for-you product, packaged as a beautifully designed high-end experience—with a fabulous hidden perk.

Women would be drawn to the product's exclusivity, its rarity, and its efficacy—and we'd sneak in the social impact and environmental conservation angle. I'd learned at Samasource that that impact was, at best, icing on the cake for the consumer. You had to have a great product first. I kept thinking, why is there no social impact luxury brand? Nine out of ten millennials are willing to switch brands to one associated with a good cause. As they start earning more money, they want to move beyond mass-market products and purchase luxury beauty, apparel, fragrance, and home goods. And as far as I could tell, there was no Chanel of social impact.

My determination was buoyed by the success of other brands in the category. Luxury brand Chopard now makes a watch made of "Fairmined" gold, a certification that guarantees the gold was extracted responsibly and the miners were paid fair wages. Missy and Scott Tannen were so horrified by the ravages of the cotton and textile industry in India that they decided to start the ethically sourced "fair and transparent" luxury bedding company Boll & Branch. Sheet sets are priced around $250; in 2015, their first full year of business, Boll & Branch did $10 million to $15 million in sales. Former U.S. presidents and Christina Aguilera have been customers, but Scott says their clientele runs all over the map: "It is not only wealthy people that purchase our products . . . we also have people tell us that they don't usually buy luxury products, but decided that they believe in how we make things. They won't spend $75 on a set of sheets from a big box store that was most likely made in substandard conditions."

I was also encouraged by the success of companies within the fashion industry. I had always wanted to build the same kind of following for Samasource as that of TOMS, one of the first American companies that successfully bridged the chasm between business and social impact by creating a fun consumer brand that attracted its own tribe. It turned out to be ridiculously hard to make a data-services company sexy, but I was sure I could do it with a retail beauty brand. TOMS was the pioneer of the "buy one, give one" business model, donating a pair of shoes to a needy child for every pair purchased. Sold at high-end stores like Neiman Marcus and Nordstrom, the brand's success in promoting "compassionate consumerism" made founder Blake Mycoskie a millionaire (full disclosure: Mycoskie is one of my investors).

The company did get heat when it became known that they were sourcing from countries like China, not where the donations were distributed, and thus undermining local shoe manufacturers. To his credit, Mycoskie listened to his critics: "If you really are serious about poverty alleviation, [they] said, then you need to create jobs," said Mycoskie in a 2013 interview with the *Huffington Post*. "At first I took that personally—we're doing so much already!—but then I recognized that they were right. If we really wanted to have an impact on poverty alleviation, using our model to create jobs was the next level." By 2015 he had evolved his business so that at least one third of all the company's shoe manufacturing was done in the countries where it donated, and it has committed to sustainable, fair sourcing for all of its products, which now include coffee and eyeglasses.

Ultrahip eyewear company Warby Parker also followed the buy-one-give-one model, but in a way that somewhat shielded it from the criticism lobbed at TOMS. Before starting Warby Parker, cofounder Neil Blumenthal had worked with VisionSpring, a top-notch NGO that trains women to administer eye exams and sell glasses to their communities. In fact, Katzenbach Partners did some pro bono consulting for the organization while I was there, and I remember meeting Neil and feeling inspired. Not long after, I got to see him make the leap from NGO leader to for-profit CEO. The impact model for Warby was genius: rather than donating glasses to the poor for every pair of glasses purchased, Warby Parker makes a financial donation to VisionSpring, among other nonprofits, to produce eyeglass kits that allow local people to repair and sell eyeglasses, both giving work and addressing a critical health need. The company was valued at $1.2 billion in 2015, and Vision-Spring reports $280 million in economic impact around the world.

Yvon Chouinard's Patagonia, too, had long been an inspiration to me and thousands of other entrepreneurs who were passionate about starting sustainable businesses that didn't just avoid doing harm but proactively pursued doing good. Despite sometimes running ads that discourage buyers from purchasing Patagonia jackets because of the environmental costs of producing the garment (as minimal as possible, per the Patagonia mission, but still there), and despite paying workers an "additional premium" that can be used as a bonus or for a community development project, and despite donating all $10 million it brought in (five times more than it anticipated) after announcing it would donate its 2016 Black Friday proceeds to environmental groups, and despite providing on-site child care and flex time for its employees, the privately held company has a cult following and remains a powerhouse adventure brand. Chouinard combines an activist mind-set with a pragmatic philosophy, and describes himself as a reluctant businessman:

> I've never respected the profession. It's business that has to take
> the majority of the blame for being the enemy of nature, for de-
> stroying native cultures, for taking from the poor and giving to
> the rich, and for poisoning the earth with the effluent from its
> factories.

Yet business can produce food, cure disease, control population, employ people, and generally enrich our lives. And it can do these good things and make a profit without losing its soul.

Clearly, weaving a social and environmental mission into the core of a health food or fashion brand could pay off. But would the idea fly in the beauty category? I couldn't wait to find out. I loved Samasource. We were five years in and growing fast, but I was too passionate about this new idea to give it up (as is so often the case, this tendency is both my Achilles' heel and my greatest strength). When I approached my board with a pitch and a business plan, I wasn't asking permission to start another company. The decision was made—I was going to do this. My question was, rather, how could I do it in a way that would complement my work as Samasource's CEO, structure the new business so that it would support the nonprofit, and ensure that I had enough reinforcements to run both companies well? I knew the board might be surprised to hear that I was launching a new separate company, but once they understood my vision and how it could benefit Samasource in the long run, I knew they'd be behind it.

And so my first for-profit company, LXMI, pronounced "Luxe-me" and inspired by Lakshmi, the Hindu goddess of beauty and prosperity, was born. My team would develop luxury products based on rare, wild botanicals and artisanal traditions that give work to women and protect the planet. We started in beauty with a collection based on the ingredient I loved, which we branded Nilotica Reserve to differentiate it. "Reserve" meant that our nuts were harvested from groves of trees in a single origin that produced the highest-quality Nilotica nuts, hand selected and cold-pressed using traditional methods. LXMI's organic certification would guarantee that the soil in which the trees grew was pristine and pesticide free, and that the land was safe from harmful slash-and-burn farming methods. Only nuts grown in this unique terroir, which can enhance or diminish a raw ingredient's chemical and nutrient profile, would earn the Reserve designation. I borrowed the concept from the wine industry, thinking it was high time we began applying the same consideration we give to what's in a fancy bottle of wine to what we put on our face every day. LXMI consumers would support fair trade and further the Give Work mission by providing a lucrative income stream to our women harvesters, who were guaranteed to earn three times more than the average local wage for collecting these nuts and selling them to us.

I set up the company and applied to be a B Corp (a for-profit certified by the nonprofit B Lab for meeting high standards of "social and environmental performance, accountability, and transparency"). I also donated a third of my personal shares to Samasource via an LLC, which gave me the ability to donate them without the nonprofit board controlling the company, which might scare off potential investors. I'm pretty sure we're the only luxury skin-care brand partly owned by a 501(c)(3) nonprofit. Despite the high price tag, I hired the lawyer who wrote the B Corporation legislation in California, and he and I created founders' preferred stock, which allowed me to anchor the social mission with special voting rights. This way, future investors wouldn't be able to take the company in the wrong direction or make decisions antithetical to what we stood for. In addition, this structure tied LXMI to our mission of giving work to raise people out of poverty, and guaranteed that Samasource would benefit materially if it should ever go public or be sold. It could happen.

Around 2008, Priya Haji had started working with eBay to develop an ethical online marketplace, and launched WorldofGood.com by eBay. It would be "the world's largest multi-seller marketplace for socially and environmentally responsible shopping," available to more than 84 million active eBay users. In 2010, she sold the World of Good brand to the online selling giant. But she had made sure to protect her company's mission. All products, producers, and sellers would continue to be vetted and verified by a group of forty-one third-party "trust advisers," like the World Fair Trade Organization and the Rainforest Alliance. Customers could easily review a product's sourcing with a simple click. World of Good Development Organization—World of Good, Inc.'s nonprofit arm—would be renamed and rebranded, but it, too, benefited financially from the sale, and would continue to be partially funded by the for-profit.

I set up a complex legal structure for LXMI because I wanted to provide for Samasource and protect LXMI's mission. But it might surprise you to know that it came at a very high cost. It was the right thing to do in the long run, but for the short run, it made things much harder than they needed to be. The biggest threat to starting any business is running out of cash, and this was an expensive move. Paying tens of thousands of dollars in legal fees right away is not the best way to avoid running out of money before you produce a product or service that people like.

The challenge to doing good is that it's hard and complicated to do the ethical thing at the outset. It's a lot easier and less expensive to just pollute the stream than to build a company with a sister nonprofit or a built-in mission to clean up the pollution at the same time. Or to develop new technology or systems that prevent you from polluting in the first place. That's why most people just opt to pollute and deal with the consequences later. My advice? Keep things as simple as possible, but don't compromise on your core values. How you structure a social business will depend on several variables, but my recommendation would be to follow the philosophy of *The Lean Startup* by Eric Ries: ask yourself, what is the simplest way to get this idea going at minimal cost? From there, create one simple entity, like a B Corp. Test your product. Listen to your customer feedback. Make sure you have a product that people actually want. As Muhammad Yunus wrote in *Building Social Business*, "A social business has to be a business in the first place." And then second, accept that you won't be able to solve every problem at once. I'd make a simple, firm commitment at the outset (like a percentage of shares or profit you're donating), and then phase in additional solutions over time. With LXMI, for example, I donated my shares at the outset but realized I couldn't launch with entirely biodegradable packaging, as I'd hoped—it would be too costly and require major buy-in from retailers. But we put it on the road map anyway. In the short term, just do what works. Reid Hoffman, the cofounder of LinkedIn and an investor in LXMI, has a famous saying: if your product has no issues right out of the gate, you waited too long to launch. The idea is to get something out there and iterate rapidly, continually learning and improving.

That's what my friend Kristin Dickerson did. Her lifestyle brand Raven + Lily was created as a nonprofit to help alleviate poverty for women around the world. But then Dickerson realized that in order to grow and scale—and have the greatest impact possible—the company needed to be a for-profit social business. She launched an e-commerce site, and within two years online sales grew by 150 percent. Her partnerships with women in other countries have changed hundreds of women's lives, from ostracized AIDS victims to single mothers in conservative Muslim communities. One told her, "Now when . . . the women in my community give birth to girls, they no longer mourn but rejoice, because they see the value that girls can bring to our society."

I started making the rounds, talking to people about my idea in the hopes that they'd want to invest seed capital. Possessed with evangelical zeal, I worked my contacts and networks as relentlessly as I had seven years before when I began fund-raising for Samasource. But what a contrast between then and now.

First, I quickly learned that I had to appeal to a completely different incentive. Earned revenue and financial sustainability would be crucial to the survival and especially the effectiveness of Samasource, yet my donor pitch had focused almost entirely on the social impact of our mission. Any mention of potential earned revenue could have been misconstrued as an attempt to profit from a nonprofit. When pitching LXMI, I could tell that a great many people truly believed in our Give

Work mission, but I also knew they wouldn't invest if they didn't also think it was a good place to grow their money. ROI was everything.

There is a lot of Silicon Valley capital available to a for-profit business if you are lucky enough to be connected. That was the second difference: this time around, I knew people. In general, it takes cash and connections to successfully build an organization, and when I first launched Samasource, many people were surprised to find out that I had neither. But hustle and passion inspire people. More than once, donors and even people who declined to fund Samasource told me to get back in touch should I ever start a for-profit, because they'd invest. They could see how hard I was working to make Samasource sustainable, and they thought, if she can do that with a nonprofit, imagine what she might do with a for-profit. Sure enough, when I did come back around seeking seed money, doors opened quickly, and people seemed excited to work with me. Not all, of course. Some investors did assume my nonprofit experience meant that I couldn't possibly be "that interested in making money," as one actually said to me. Many times people would tell me they'd come into the next investment round, and then back out.

The third difference was the size of the pool of capital available to start for-profit companies. It wasn't easy, but in a few months I was able to raise $2 million for LXMI's seed round. It took me years to raise that for Samasource. With a few exceptions, most of LXMI's investors were putting in $100,000 to $250,000; at Sama, the vast majority of our early donations came in $5,000 to $10,000 increments. My team and I were grateful for every one of those small donations, but it's obviously more efficient to fund-raise via a single large commitment than multiple small ones. The difference between getting funding for a for-profit company and a nonprofit one was the equivalent of filling a swimming pool with a water truck instead of Dixie cups.

Finally, getting that cash all at once allowed me to hire people who already knew what they were doing. In Samasource's early days, I couldn't afford experienced people. This meant we were all learning on the job, and I felt, for better and for worse, that I had to micromanage every detail to make sure we stayed on track. Only once we had a run rate of $1 million a year was I able to recruit experienced staff who could manage different parts of the business. It also helped having been around the block once already. When you're seasoned, you can recruit people right away who have more expertise and contacts than you do. LXMI's CMO, Thea Kocher, for example, has worked in the beauty industry since we graduated from college, so she knew all the competitors, merchants, and market dynamics before she walked through LXMI's door. I'd never had the budget to hire someone with equivalent credentials for Samasource in the early years of our operation.

I'd often heard that no matter what kind of business you were in, it would be crucial to build and nurture good relationships with everyone in your network, from friends to coworkers to customers. That had proven true when my friend Jim Fruchterman at Bookshare agreed to give Samasource our first contract, and it again proved to be true in getting legs under my new for-profit. Unbeknownst to me, a former Samasource client from Google, Corrie Conrad, had moved to Sephora to set up a new office of social impact. She had no idea that I was starting a skin-care line when she called me to announce her move and ask if we could catch up over coffee. That relationship was pivotal to getting LXMI through the door of a major retailer. In fact, because of that connection we became one of the eight inaugural members of the Sephora Accelerate program, an incubator set up by Sephora, the French chain of cosmetic stores, to support female-led beauty start-ups with a social impact.

I was so enamored with our product that it was a bit of a shock to discover how much I didn't know. For example, we had developed three gorgeous formulas—or so I thought. The mentor team at Sephora gave the nod to only one of them, and then informed us that our formula was not up to par for the discerning skin cream buyer. The scent wasn't quite right; the texture was still too thick. What? I loved the scent! I loved the texture! I was floored, but I wasn't about to argue with the experts. I was hungry to earn a partnership with Sephora, even if it would mean they had exclusive rights to distribute our launch product for the first six months. We had thought a lot about different distribution models, and some of our investors believed we should go with a direct sales model like Avon. I loved that idea because it would allow us to provide additional work to local women in the United States. Unfortunately, we could see that the initial cost of building our own direct sales force might be too high, and that we could quickly run out of cash. So we hung on to the idea, hoping that once we'd launched in retail channels and received more exposure we could try again later. My face was all over our online marketing materials and content because my story and social impact mission were key to the product's appeal, but I wasn't Jessica Alba or Tyra Banks—we needed a big retail partner to give us reach.

Back to the drawing board we went. In fact, we had to interview a number of new labs and hire a product formulation expert. We must have gone through thirty different iterations before finally getting the product right. And then, after getting approval from Sephora, we discovered that our new lab partner could not make the formula that our chemist had developed. Apparently the formula, which was very simple—a suspension of our Nilotica and cape aloe, an ingredient from South Africa—was unpredictable. If heated, it could melt into a watery soup, and it could also solidify unevenly into a lumpy mess. The labs didn't want to be liable if we shipped this goop all over the country and had to recall it. So out it went. We went to ten or twelve labs asking for help. In the end, with Sephora's guidance we were able to develop a different formula the labs could produce that would remain stable. It became our first product, a lightweight moisturizer enhanced with hibiscus for exfoliation and gently sweet Ugandan vanilla, both fair trade and certified organic ingredients, which we took pains to procure from nearby regions of Uganda rather than finding cheaper versions elsewhere. We called it Crème du Nil.

We got another huge break thanks to a different relationship I cultivated with someone who had insight and contacts within the beauty industry. I met Margarita Arriagada, the former chief merchant at Sephora, through a mutual friend. Around the same time, I was profiled by *T: The New York Times Style Magazine* in a surreal piece called "The Greats" (which earned me a lot of flak from my friends). It was capped afterward by a celebrity-studded cocktail reception at West Hollywood's Chateau Marmont. I was totally intimidated until I realized this was my opportunity to get Margarita interested in LXMI. So I invited her as my date, borrowing a dress for the occasion. I'd never tried this tactic with a stranger before, but it worked: by the end of the evening, Marg and I had become friends, and she'd agreed to join my board and help us develop our relationships at Sephora. A few weeks later, she casually e-mailed a friend at QVC, the home shopping behemoth, about LXMI, and scored us a meeting.

I didn't know much about the TV shopping channel. Growing up, we didn't have TV at home, so I didn't know what home shopping was until I started seeing the channel at friends' places and in hotel rooms. It wasn't until I saw the movie *Joy*, about inventor Joy Mangano, who created a business empire after inventing a self-wringing mop, that I really understood what QVC could do for a product. It is one of the biggest-selling channels in the world, with yearly sales of $7.5 billion. And it doesn't just sell household goods, like mops—it's a driver for premium and luxury goods, too. As I built LXMI, I realized that a lot of other brands, even high-end ones, had started out at Sephora and on QVC. Why not mine?

I was all nerves on the day of the pitch. Luckily our CMO, Thea, drove down to the QVC headquarters in rural Pennsylvania with me and reassured me—she'd once sold a product on QVC's competition, Home Shopping Network (HSN) and knew the drill. We walked through an immense hallway, feeling tiny and hoping our strategy would work, before sitting in a small conference room. We passed out some LXMI product boxes filled with chocolate truffles Thea had made the night before from an improvised recipe. While the QVC team ate, I told them what I tell our customers now: that LXMI is beauty in action. It gives the luxury consumer who doesn't want to compromise her morals or her beauty regimen an ethical way to indulge. Single origin and single ingredient, our Pure Nilotica Melt, made with Nilotica Reserve shea butter, is one of the purest products you can put on your skin—so pure in its raw form you can literally eat it. And that's when I let them know that the chocolates they had just popped into their mouths were made from the product we wanted to sell on TV. Their reaction was even better than I'd hoped. Immediately, the lead skin-care merchant said to me, "This is so cool! Let's get you into the queue for an air date. Leila, you'll have to go to training."

Wait, what? One of the reasons I'd brought Thea with me was because to my eye she would be the perfect spokeswoman for LXMI on screen. Beautiful and blond, the Oklahoma native was a beauty junkie, a former high school cheerleader who had grown up watching QVC. I didn't think they'd see me, a minority social entrepreneur from San Francisco, as appealing to their core demographic. Even as an entrepreneur used to breaking down racial and gender barriers, I had subconsciously decided the producers wouldn't be interested in me. I was so wrong. The reps were adamant. Think about all the women watching TV, they said, who would love to be transported to Uganda, who want to do something meaningful with their lives, who want to travel and make a difference. What an amazing thing to learn they can do that through the power of their purchase. Whether you look like them is irrelevant. What's important is your beautiful message about empowering women, and you as the founder need to share it with them.

QVC was right—there is power in a founder's story and personal brand. And that doesn't change just because you're doing social good. When I post a picture of myself, especially if I'm wearing makeup and nicely dressed after a talk or media appearance, it gets tons more attention than, say, a thoughtful blog post on how Samasource work benefits refugees, or how Samahope was a pioneering example of mergers and acquisitions in the nonprofit sector, or how LXMI is able to pay the women who source our Nilotica nuts three times the local wage. And this doesn't just hold true for my posts. When our communications team pitches a story on Sama to a journalist, it often turns into a story about me and my life, complete with a glossy photo spread. It can be embarrassing, but the thing is, it works. People like personal interest stories more than they like data. My friend Brit Morin has made her likeness the core of her media company, Brit + Co. She told me once, "Millennials want to identify with a person, not a brand." She's right. It's people who make brands come alive. Think about Oprah, Martha Stewart, or Sara Blakely. They aren't known to be humble wallflowers. They tell their stories proudly, and use their personal brands to build empires.

DITCH THE STEREOTYPES

It's time we social entrepreneurs stopped being so self-effacing. Because the truth is that those of us who run social businesses and nonprofits that try to fix major problems in the world—who don't mind making less money than we could elsewhere, who tire ourselves out raising funds, giving speeches, and advocating for the less fortunate—are not that different from the entrepreneurs who make bank-building tools to solve the problems of the 1 percent. We are every bit as nose-to-the-grindstone and intense as profit-oriented entrepreneurs. We have egos and can behave selfishly. Many of us are narcissistic. We dream big. We are perfectionists and type A's. We crave adrenaline. That actually might explain why we are willing to get into this work. It's high stakes—we not only carry the weight of running a company on our shoulders, we also carry the additional risk of knowing that should we fail, we'll let down vulnerable people. No one who likes to play things safe would ever go into this field. In fact, some of my best social entrepreneur friends are daredevils, like Mike Chambers, who ice climbs and sets mountaineering records on weekend breaks from his job as executive director of Summits, a breakthrough Haitian school; or Jane Chen, the founder of Embrace Innovations, which makes low-cost infant warmers, who travels the world in search of surf spots to satisfy her need for adrenaline. Teresa Goines, the head of Old Skool Cafe, a violence prevention program in San Francisco, is a bodybuilder and former corrections officer. Before Hanli Prinsloo founded the I AM WATER Ocean Conservation Trust and its sister for-profit boutique travel company, she had broken every South African free-diving record.

It was a bit surreal, but I did my best to channel my ego into a Vanna White–worthy television performance. QVC gave me a lot of help. I attended their mandatory daylong training on their massive campus in rural Pennsylvania. There I learned how to be a proper "guest." There's no direct selling ever on QVC. You are welcomed on air as a product expert, and you and your "host" are supposed to have an authentic chat about your product without ever telling anyone they should buy it. It's designed to feel like a community shopping experience, like the kind you'd have if you were to accept a cup of coffee at your neighbor's home and ask what kind of coffeemaker she'd used to make it so perfect. It may sound easy—I mean, talking about the product you love should be easy, right? But it really takes a lot of practice to pull this off naturally. You have to be very careful what you say, because if you make an inaccurate or exaggerated claim, QVC will pull your airing and your product.

Just a few weeks later it was showtime. I showed up on set alone—Thea had just given birth to her second child—and met host Sandra Bennett. I was surprised—Sandra, an elegant brunette, was wearing a T-shirt touting her vegetarianism. She wasn't the kind of person I expected to be in home shopping. My world opened up after speaking with Sandra, who was so touched by the social mission of LXMI. Shortly afterward we were live on her weekly show, *Friday Night Beauty*. It was one of the most nerve-racking things I've ever done. You're meant to look straight into the camera while describing your product, but there were four cameras moving constantly, and I couldn't, for the life of me, find the right one. I kept forgetting what I'd already said, and what to repeat from my list of unique selling points, which the training team had me develop. I'd been coiffed like a doll, with braids and curls and a Stepford wife–type tea dress that I'd never wear in real life (the production team had urged me to ditch my normal black for color). I was sweating. I swear, my seven-minute segment was over in six seconds.

Still a bit dazed, I walked back to the greenroom to check our numbers. Eight computer terminals displaying every data point on the latest products on air dictate the fate of major brands—success on QVC is measured by how much revenue you make per minute. If you don't hit the target, you're cut. So I was relieved to see that we'd exceeded QVC's expectations, selling close to fifteen hundred units of Pure Nilotica Melt. It was an auspicious start. That same week, we launched at Sephora.

Now, I've just made it sound as though the path from design to finished product to launch was smooth and uneventful. It was anything but. After QVC told us they wanted to slot us in on air as soon as possible, we were suddenly under tremendous pressure to get our final product out. We made our deadline, but it was only after the first production runs made it to our offices that we discovered that the French language text on the packaging was mangled. We'd caught the mistake earlier—my French friends had helped me rework it—and as far as I knew the problem had been fixed. But we were in such a rush to make the delivery window that somehow the printer used an old file. I was so embarrassed. To compound everything, I couldn't turn to Thea, the only person at our company with any significant experience in this domain, the person to whom I would have turned for help under ordinary circumstances, because I was committed to respecting her maternity leave and building a company that women would want to join. My team and I were on our own for the next two months.

And the mistakes didn't end there. We had tested the product thousands of times on ourselves and our friends. We had also spent hundreds of hours examining and refining the packaging, which was black and sophisticated and, to my mind, utter perfection. We'd even included a little code on the box that allowed the customer to track the provenance of that particular batch and see how much money women were paid to make the product. But the one thing we hadn't done was stress test the packaging. As soon as LXMI hit the Sephora shelves I started visiting stores all over the country, and I found that in each one the paint on the tester lids and jars was rubbing off from repeated exposure to the cream on people's hands. I was crushed. We had spent so much money and so much effort to make everything perfect, and here we were with a gorgeous jar, a spot in every Sephora store, and a great story, all ruined by a bad paint job. I felt like I had failed my team. There was nothing I could do but own up to the mistake. As soon as I realized the problem, I e-mailed Sephora and assured them we were on top of it. We raised hell with the manufacturer, who solved the problem immediately by doing double coats of paint on the next run of jars.

Still more steps along the way did not go smoothly. Once again, as at Samasource, I had difficulty gelling with some of my early hires. I learned that as much as colleagues may like and respect one another, and even be great partners in other aspects of their lives, their work styles must complement one another's or they will frequently find themselves at odds. While I love meditation and yoga, I can be pretty intense, especially in the early stages of a business. I deeply internalized the burden that all for-profit and nonprofit start-up leaders carry—we have to recruit people, lead the team, raise the money, instill a sense of security and safety (shielding the team from the volatility of sales, fundraising, if applicable, and shocks to the business), inspire people to work hard even when we can't afford to pay them well, and all the while not go too crazy. It's enormous, grinding pressure. Some entrepreneurs I know cracked. One committed suicide. Two ended up in the psych ward for a short stay. Several got divorced or had epic breakups. This stuff isn't easy or glamorous. The stories we see on the outside—the start-up competitions won, the glowing press, the sleek profiles in business magazines—all of that happens at the surface level. What goes on below can be much, much dirtier.

In the end, I learned this universal truth: if you're doing something new and innovative, you will make mistakes. If you don't, you are not pushing the boundaries enough. If everything around the LXMI launch had gone smoothly, if no one had challenged my thinking, if my for-profit hadn't caused me as many countless sleepless nights as my non-profit, it would have been a sign that I wasn't breaking new ground, and my brand therefore was probably not destined to create the impact I desired. But it is. Initial sales for Crème du Nil were solid. Sephora placed an order for our next product, Nilotica Melt, which we'd launched on QVC months earlier. And our press continues to grow, keeping us top of mind in premiere beauty magazines like *Allure,* *Vogue,* and *Cosmopolitan.*

People frequently ask me whether it's uncomfortable to move back and forth between the impoverished communities I'm trying to help through Samasource and LXMI and the rarefied, privileged world of fashion and luxury skin care or the posh conference circuit where I fund-raise. Of course it is. I always felt the same strain when shuttling between the world of donors and corporate executives and the places where we do the work at Samasource, like Kenyan slums and rural America. So I was not new to the contrast. One of the hardest things about social entrepreneurship is this constant back-and-forth between two worlds—it reminds me again of the movie *Elysium.*

But we fill a valuable role: as messengers. Stories have power, and when I tell the stories of the women who find work with LXMI, or the young men like Ken who transform their lives working at Samasource, people are compelled to listen, and in some cases, change their purchasing behavior.

The companies occupy two very different worlds, yet, though LXMI is Samasource's glamorous sister, they share the same mission. And while it does take an emotional toll to cross the line between Davos or the Chateau Marmont parties on the one hand and the cotton fields of Dumas or the slums of Nairobi on the other, I'm happy and lucky to do it. Navigating these two worlds allows me to take the Give Work message to a different, wider audience than the one I would reach if I were to limit myself to the Samasource market. QVC reaches 100 million households! Sephora has about twenty-three hundred stores located in thirty-three countries around the world. If I want our message of empowerment to transcend the confines of the nonprofit or corporate world, building a consumer brand makes sense. In fact, there should be more people like me here. This is where the future lies.

The NGO people and the international aid community of development geeks, poverty scholars, and economists inhabit a different world from that of the beauty and fashion mavens. But the former group often discounts the impact that the latter can have by influencing consumers to change their behavior. It's the same story with corporate executives—most development scholars don't see their work as connected to, say, the CEO of Salesforce. But if that CEO decides to commit to impact sourcing, to hiring companies like Samasource to do digital work, he can directly and permanently move tens of thousands of people out of poverty. These two worlds—the world of consumers in rich countries and that of would-be workers in poor regions—are inextricably linked. But we've tended to operate in silos. The NGO people are skeptical of for-profit companies. Beauty mavens think many fair trade products are ugly and ineffective. Corporate executives don't count ending poverty among their top priorities. But by seeing the bigger picture, social enterprises can weave these disparate worlds together, harnessing the power of capitalism to meaningfully address poverty and the large number of social and environmental issues that stem from that root.

In order to solve the big problems of the world, those of us who really care about these important issues need to infiltrate the industries that have never made it their mission to solve social problems beyond hosting the occasional star-studded fund-raiser, including luxury apparel, beauty and skin care, fitness, and travel. We need to stop assuming that self-indulgence, beauty, and glamour are anathema to social justice. It's a divide we must cross if we are ever going to scale social impact. Nonprofits and NGOs do great work, but they can't solve the world's problems on their own. We can't leave it to development economists and people who geek out on poverty statistics, like me; we need everyone to put aside their judgment, roll up their sleeves, and make a difference wherever they can. Like Kristin Dickerson of Raven + Lily. And Shannon Keith, who founded Punjammies, a loungewear company whose product is made by former sex trafficking victims training to be seamstresses, thus learning a new trade that will allow them to support themselves and leave their painful pasts behind. Then there's Rebecca Smith, who turned a hobby into a Detroit-based custom handbag company, Better Life Bags, which hires local American and immigrant women experiencing barriers to employment. And many, many more.

All business leaders will have a greater chance of succeeding in the long run if they invest equally in employee and customer happiness while taking steps to treat the earth and its people gently, especially if they can tap into the burgeoning LOHAS (Lifestyles of Health and Sustainability) market, which encompasses everything from wellness to conscious eating to social justice and is populated by the millennials, whose numbers—81.1 million by 2036—make them the biggest generation in U.S. history. But even if your business isn't LOHAS-y, you could holistically break the traditional business model by applying the impact-sourcing concept to the retail space; by forgoing stock ingredients and the cheapest packaging and labor practices, instead choosing recycled or recyclable packaging; and by pushing the limits on organic ingredients, hiring low-income or marginalized people, and ensuring living wages at all levels of the supply chain by sourcing from fair trade suppliers. If you're making products for big box chains, there are a few things you can do to move the needle incrementally. But the premium and luxury market is a different story. Consumers have indicated that they are willing to pay more for ethically produced products. Let's give them more options!

The LXMI seal depicts the circular economy with the goddess Lakshmi's four hands: two giving, and two receiving. Every transaction is a form of human communication, and by virtue of these transactions we are in a relationship with everyone in our supply chain and everyone who touches our product, from the consumer to the worker to the business owner. Both Samasource and LXMI were created to provide a useful service. Both rely upon a direct and transparent connection between workers and consumers. Both were designed to create opportunities for people with few options to reap more benefits from the fruits of their labor. We want to make sure that everyone we work with—whether it's a Kenyan data worker or a Californian social media marketer, a factory worker labeling a bottle in New Jersey or a woman sourcing nuts in Uganda—is treated fairly, and ensure that their connection to our company or product allows them to live decent lives.

You can do it as well, even if yours is a big, established business that isn't in the luxury market. For too long we've been working with the idea that the best way businesses can do their part is to maximize their profits so they can make bigger and bigger philanthropic donations in the form of money, goods, or services. But if you're a business leader, you can ensure that your company does more good and make far more long-lasting changes with simple tweaks to your business practices, starting with your supply chains. You can impact source, and in doing so, change the world. You can hire vendors committed to recruiting from the bottom of the pyramid. You can partner with social enterprises to help increase those smaller organizations' reach. And in doing so, you'll likely find that doing good does good for your bottom line as well. When Walmart followed Yvon Chouinard's advice to improve its environmental sustainability, like "reducing its packaging and water consumption," it reported that it saved money. "We are very focused on lowering prices for our customers," said Mary Fox, head of Walmart's global sourcing, in an article for the *Wall Street Journal*. "There were some investments we needed to make at the beginning, but the returns were quick enough that it came back in a reasonable time frame."

I hope that Samasource and LXMI will serve as inspiration for the new generation of entrepreneurs who don't want to choose between doing well or doing good, although for some it may be a bit like having it all—possible, just not necessarily possible all at the same time. There are enough millennials and Gen Z-ers carrying their strong belief in social justice, equality, and conservation into the workforce that we are starting to see increasing numbers of new for-profit businesses building social impact into their foundations. For our generations, purpose is no longer something to be pursued on nights and weekends; it's everything. As they seek to incorporate it into their work lives, young people are increasingly turning down typical corporate jobs or turning away from corporate career paths in order to spend time doing what they love or working for a cause they believe in. There's nothing wrong with launching a successful start-up and then, once you're comfortable, starting a social enterprise. It's good to do a traditional job first. In fact, I think my management-consulting job provided me with the best training a social entrepreneur could have asked for. I learned how to quickly assess data, how to read a profit-and-loss (P&L) statement, how to write Excel programs, how to build a presentation, and, most important, how to articulate a well-reasoned argument. I strongly urge anyone interested in doing social impact work to get those seminal business skills, and make sure that they're contributing the best of their heads, and not just their hearts, to the cause.

When you have nothing to lose and you fight tooth and nail to build something good that makes a real, measurable difference in the world, people notice. And they'll remember when you come back with your next amazing idea. Indeed, that may be the main important trait shared by do-gooders and entrepreneurs: we're almost never done.

Business has traditionally focused on the short term, while the social impact business model is about the long-term win, which means it's a path that won't lead entrepreneurs to quick profit. But that doesn't preclude them from being middle income or even wealthy someday. Gone are the days when a career of doing good meant a lifetime of living extremely modestly. Though most of us who go into this work don't need to own private jets or mansions—we're happy earning enough to take care of ourselves and our families—there's good money to be made in making great products and solving the world's problems (for what it's worth, there's even better karma). If you have a good idea and you think it's going to create change, then you have an obligation to do something with it. Start a nonprofit. Start a for-profit. Join an existing social enterprise and lend your skills to a clueless entrepreneur like me. It doesn't matter. Just stay true to your values and your mission, and start.

Chapter Six

THE MOVEMENT IS NOW

Just as the commandment "Thou shalt not kill" sets a clear limit
in order to safeguard the value of human life, today we also have
to say "thou shalt not" to an economy of exclusion and inequality.
Such an economy kills. How can it be that it is not a news item
when an elderly homeless person dies of exposure, but it is news
when the stock market loses two points?

As a consequence, masses of people find themselves excluded
and marginalized: without work, without possibilities, without
any means of escape.

—His Holiness Pope Francis

I N EARLY DECEMBER 2016, ALMOST A YEAR TO THE DAY THAT VA-
nessa Kanyi made her appearance at Samasource's first un-gala, I
boarded a flight to Rome. My destination: the Vatican. My host: Pope
Francis. This holy-sh*t-I'm-meeting-the-pope moment started with an
e-mail I'd received about a month prior from Adam Lashinsky, an editor at *Fortune* magazine: "Would you like to address a group of CEOs in
Rome and present ideas for social impact to Pope Francis?"

He added that I'd be joining a very small group of CEOs from Fortune 100 companies to discuss ideas on how to address poverty, job creation, the environment, education, health care, and financial inclusion. The theme was "The 21st Century Challenge: Forging a New Social Compact." At the end of the conference, participants would be given a private audience with Pope Francis. *Fortune* would pay for my travel expenses.

There were two remarkable things about this invitation other than the fact that I was lucky enough to get one:

1. The pope was convening the world's most influential business leaders to talk about social impact.
2. It wasn't the first invitation from Rome I'd received. A month earlier, I'd been asked to attend an Impact Investing Summit, also to be held at the Vatican. I couldn't go because the sponsoring group wouldn't pay for the travel expenses, but I was surprised that a generally conservative institution like the Vatican was so interested in new tools for social justice.

Social impact was on the pope's mind. And he was using his influence, leverage, and moral authority to bring these antipoverty strategies to the attention not only of the 1.4 billion Catholics he leads but of the world, through a forum that would welcome some of the biggest names in global business.

My parents, who'd both attended Catholic school in India, had become skeptical of the church after witnessing a great deal of abuse firsthand. And so we didn't have much of a spiritual tradition at home. I had a yearning for spiritual direction, and joined the Unitarian Universalist church in high school. Despite the role that Jesuit moral teachings played in my father's upbringing, and by extension in mine, I was always turned off by the Catholic Church's official stance toward the LGBTQ community, non-Catholics, and women. It didn't feel like an open and accepting place. Yet during the years I worked with moral philosophers

Thomas Pogge and Josh Cohen after college, I immersed myself in writings by faith-based social activists and leaders, like Thomas Merton and Dorothy Day, both Catholic, and Martin Luther King Jr., whose religious conviction gave moral authority to the civil rights movement. I also learned that Dr. Paul Farmer, who'd studied religion at the Harvard Divinity School, became the Paul Farmer we know today because of liberation theology, a social justice movement championed by Latin American Catholic priests in the 1960s and 1970s to fight for the poor. Argentine cardinal Jorge Mario Bergoglio was part of this tradition, so much so that many in the Catholic Church thought he was too extreme, getting involved in areas outside the church's typical purview, like economic reform and housing rights. But when Bergoglio was elected to the papacy and became Pope Francis, millions of non-Catholics rallied around him. A lot of my feelings about the institution changed under his leadership and moral example. Here was a pope who lived humbly, spoke truth to power, and wasn't afraid to exhort world leaders to put their faith in action.

I read his first exhortation, *Evangelii Gaudium,* as one reads poetry. It's a beautiful piece of writing, composed in the elegant, high language of a Supreme Court judgment. His was a message of acceptance and tolerance. Most striking to me, he asserted that the typical handout model wasn't enough, that we needed to address the root causes of poverty and inequality by fundamentally reforming capitalism:

> Welfare projects, which meet certain urgent needs, should be considered merely temporary responses. As long as the problems of the poor are not radically resolved by rejecting the absolute autonomy of markets and financial speculation and by attacking the structural causes of inequality, no solution will be found for the world's problems or, for that matter, to any problems. Inequality is the root of social ills.

Francis is a pope for the millennial generation, and while there are certain issues I wish he'd fight harder to support (like women's position within the church), he's done more to inspire action against poverty than any contemporary religious leader. I admire him deeply for choosing to focus on the sort of "effective altruism" that impacts billions of people: fighting inequality, poverty, climate change, and various linked issues, like homelessness. I wasn't going to pass up the chance to meet him.

I arrived in Rome to an intimidating group of VIPs. Christy Turlington was there with her husband, Ed Burns (both Catholics and, it turned out, as stunning on the inside as on the outside). Ginni Rometty, the CEO of IBM, was there. So were Virgin's Richard Branson and Darren Walker, president of the Ford Foundation. The heads of Siemens, Johnson & Johnson, McKinsey, PepsiCo—this was my audience as Adam interviewed me on the subject of "Bringing the Rural Poor into the Digital Economy." My impostor syndrome flared up that week in the presence of so many of the most powerful leaders in the corporate world. We spent the day listening to panel sessions and interviews, and then broke out into working groups to discuss what solutions we could present to challenges such as "How can the private sector use its financial muscle to stem the generations of young people now being lost to unemployment?" "How can companies broaden Internet access beyond the 10 percent of schools now connected?" "What bold action can the private sector take to foster and encourage outside-the-box thinking around entrepreneurship—especially among start-ups that are tackling issues directly related to poverty and that intersect with their own business interests?" Under normal circumstances this kind of discussion gets me fired up. On this day, in this place, surrounded by these people thinking deeply about the questions to which I'd devoted my life's work, I was giddy.

When we convened at the end of the summit to discuss recommendations to the pope, I was shocked to learn that most of the corporate attendees felt the single biggest lever for change was their supply chains, where billions of spending could be marshaled for good. If you want to end modern-day slavery, for example, you can take steps to ensure that no one in your supply chain is a bonded laborer (the recent controversy surrounding the Guggenheim Museum's expansion in Abu Dhabi highlights how difficult this can be in the case of international operations, which are often subcontracted to local firms that may be tough to audit). If you want to end poverty, hire poor people and pay them a living wage—and extend this not just to your employees but to everyone your supply chain touches: food service workers, janitors, factory workers overseas. Much of the good and the bad that companies put out into the world depends on how they run their supply chain and procurement. And here were all these powerful people recognizing that it wasn't enough to avoid doing bad, polluting the proverbial stream, they also had to do proactive good—even if it meant reevaluating aspects of their businesses.

A cynic might say that it was all lip service, that these people went home afterward, tossed away their notes, and went about business as usual. But I'm more hopeful than this, because at the end of the day corporations are just people, and people are capable of remarkable change. Modern neuroscience confirms that we are hardwired for empathy; we are naturally empathetic toward those we know, but it takes a few positive interactions to raise our empathic brain responses toward strangers. In other words, empathy can be learned. And now that we are more connected than ever before, our circle of empathy is widening to include all the people we see, hear, and interact with digitally—those workers deep in the supply chain toiling away in mines and factories are as present to us now as our neighbors are. I believe this will create a sea change in business, as leaders feel responsible for these newly visible classes of people. Pope Francis wisely realized that his presence would be a commitment device, making it more likely that the declarations this group made would stick. Once you've committed to something before the pope, it's hard to go back on your word. Talk to the pope, and it feels like God is a witness.

Larry Summers, the former U.S. treasury secretary, might be surprised to hear that he provided the second-most moving moment of the event for me. When I was an undergrad at Harvard during his tenure as president, I wrote an op-ed piece criticizing his position on shutting down the Center for International Development. Earlier, he'd opposed a student-led living-wage campaign, one of the biggest battles fought on campus in the late nineties and early aughts. Even before Summers took over as president, the Progressive Student Labor Movement had been pushing Harvard for years to enfranchise all the contracted employees at the university—like the janitors, cooks, and food service workers—who received none of the rights and benefits enjoyed by official university employees. Such a big institution as Harvard spends a lot of money, so how they contract with their laborers can make a big difference to workers. Some students rallied behind the labor movement, even staging a twenty-one-day sit-in. Others didn't, like the Winklevoss twins (the same guys who, years later, sued Facebook founder Mark Zuckerberg for allegedly stealing their social network idea), who hung a banner outside their window on Harvard Yard that read MO' MONEY, MO' PROBLEMS. It was a fascinating time.

Yet now, fifteen years later, Larry Summers walks out on a stage at the *Fortune-Time* Global Forum, and he tells us that one of his biggest regrets as Harvard president was that he didn't do more to recognize the university workers who were involved in the school's operations yet couldn't have full benefits and rights. He went on to say that companies cannot marginalize the people in their supply chain. Even if they are contractors or factory workers, we have a responsibility to treat these people as human beings, not widgets. Here was a brilliant but controversial economist echoing the words of the pope in front of the world's biggest CEOs.

Hearing those words come out of the mouth of Larry Summers

made me realize that hearts and minds do change. And so can the fortunes of everyone in the world. The problems we struggle with as a society are not fixed. They're not dictated by the laws of physics, like gravity—there is no universal, immutable poverty constant. The laws of economics are human laws, laws that we have complete power to change. Human behavior is far more malleable than we think. We used to believe humans operated according to a fixed economic model based on the white male homo economicus. Behavioral economics research pioneered by Daniel Kahneman and Dan Ariely has shown us that standard economic models bend and twist depending on the circumstances, including different belief systems. It's important to realize that many of our laws and social policies are the product of historical circumstance and outdated economic theory. We have the power to change them, just as our leaders change their minds about issues as vital as contract labor rights.

The next day, Saturday, we had an audience with His Holiness. He spoke briefly about the role of business in social justice, and then listened as a *Fortune* editor shared the group's commitments—to rethink their supply chains, for one. Remarkably, we each got a chance to shake his hand and be photographed with him (another brilliant commitment device—who can forget a promise she made to the pope, immortalized in an official Vatican photograph?). When my time came, I kept my remarks simple. "Thank you so much for all the work you do in the world," I said, taking his hand. He looked me in the eye, smiled gently, and replied (in Spanish), "Pray for me."

I said this earlier and it's worth repeating: God exists in the love and connection between beings. Prayer is simply reflecting on this truth: separateness is an illusion. We are all tied together as living beings. Nearly every world religion has some version of the quote "God lives within each of us" as part of its core ideology, and we now know that all living beings are constructed from the same code, DNA—the same four letters (A, T, G, and C) are the language of life. For me, prayer is doing work that upholds the idea of our common humanity, work in the service of something bigger than us. I do my best through Samasource and LXMI, which I hope will scale to inspire more companies to adopt impact sourcing as a viable business strategy.

When I first started Samasource almost nine years ago, impact sourcing didn't exist. Today, it's being discussed at the Vatican. And the World Bank. And even the IMF. In fact, during a panel discussion in 2016, IMF managing director Christine Lagarde implied that in the interest of bringing affordable, even lifesaving innovations to the public more quickly, it might be time to reform the patent system, which currently gives patent holders twenty years of exclusive rights. I could have hugged her. The IMF, an institution often criticized for siding with business interests over the needs of people (especially the poor), was challenging a business leader on patents. It was a bold, impressive statement, and an indication of just how far we've come.

Today, any business leader can put his procurement dollars behind the sorts of vendors who can create change for good. And more and more businesses do. It's because of this forward movement that in April 2016, the same year as my trip to Rome, Samasource hit a rare nonprofit milestone: we had our first break-even month for sales revenue. We've always been in the black thanks to the contributions we procure in the form of grants and donations, but to do it via earned income, the money we make from selling our services to companies, and in only eight years, gives me tremendous hope for the future of our model. Many nonprofits working on social problems survive by eking out a tiny existence, barely scraping by on donations, staffed with a few part-time employees, an army of volunteers, and loads of goodwill. Samasource's success shows that there is another, more sustainable, more practical way to solve those problems (while still channeling all that goodwill). We operate similarly to any other business except for the fact that we were built with social impact at our core. By the end of 2016, we'd grown to more than $10 million in sales and eleven hundred full-time workers across central California, rural Arkansas, Haiti, India, Kenya, and Uganda, doubling the prior year and shattering our company goal. While we're still a tiny business by most measures, this growth gives me so much hope.

There are already many others like us trying to think creatively about how to train the poor, the forgotten, and the left behind to provide the work today's economy relies on. Some are nonprofits, like Mercy Corps and Digital Divide Data. And some aren't, like Web design, mobile app, and game design start-up Bit Source in Kentucky, founded by two native sons working to retrain unemployed coal miners to code and develop software. They've even discussed creating an app that could help restore the beauty of the mine-stripped Appalachian hills. You're going to see more companies like these in the next few years. As we've discussed, millennials and the up-and-coming Gen Z want to see social impact woven into a company's DNA, not tacked on as a feel-good afterthought. I'll be interested to see what my fellow forum participants are inspired to do after their trip to Rome. But even those business leaders not intrinsically motivated by philanthropy or social justice now feel the pressure to go beyond simply adopting CSR initiatives, once-per-year volunteer days, and matching charity donations. Their customers demand it.

The economic shifts that roiled labor markets for the last few decades were not anomalies. We're going to see more of them, so we need to do a better job of ensuring that people are trained to market needs so they're not victimized every time. This is where government must step in. Not by banning imports to protect threatened industries or taxing some companies so high they have to shut down, but by mounting a competitive response to the threat. As a model, we could use Germany's response when it started losing manufacturing to China. The government there doubled down on providing technical and vocational training, creating a system where students could split their time between the classroom and working at a company where they practiced applying their new skills and knowledge. The strategy allowed the country to develop specialists who could create higher-quality industrial goods that could effectively compete with those from China. Today you can graduate from a German vocational school without a four-year degree and earn a decent living as a respected tradesman. Why isn't this happening across the spectrum of new digital work opportunities, in fields like machine learning, computer vision, and data analytics? We're training young people to code, but there are hundreds of thousands of jobs in noncoding fields that might have lower barriers to entry for full-time work. And there's the gig economy, which is increasingly appealing to people who want to have total control over their schedules and make time for creative, family, or other pursuits during the workweek. Why aren't we training more workers to market themselves on these new gig employment platforms? Getting people up to speed for the new economy is a must, not just for workers but also for employers eager to find people with relevant skills and competing in global markets.

And beyond the tech-enabled economy, we should look to the social enterprise model to fix many of the social problems that government and nonprofits alone have failed to solve. For example, one of the biggest social justice issues of our time is mass incarceration, a trend that began in the 1970s and got progressively worse, especially once private companies began running prisons and concessions. What started under the guise of making prisons more efficient morphed into a massive problem of perverse incentives: private prison companies, including the firms that supply food, clothing, and other services, make their money based on the number of prisoners behind bars. (The same incentive holds for prison guard unions, which fight to keep prisons open because they provide the only jobs in many small towns.) No prison company wants to support programs that might shrink the number of people living behind bars. In fact, they've spent millions of dollars to support legislation that sweeps more people into the prison system. Investigative journalist Seth Freed Wessler of the *Nation* found that prisons often cut costs by shaving health-care expenditures down to the bare minimum, leaving sick inmates in the hands of medical "support staff," not registered medical practitioners. In August 2016, the Justice Department announced that due to evidence that the security, services, and fiscal efficiency of privately operating prisons "compared poorly" to those run by the Federal Bureau of Prisons, it would not renew private prison contracts, and would reduce the scope of existing contracts until they expired. On the campaign trail, President Trump promised to reinvigorate private prisons, using the argument that they're more efficient than government-run facilities.

But the federal government and the states might be able to achieve both goals if they contracted instead with social enterprises. A social enterprise's profitability goals would encourage efficiency and innovation, while the lack of personal profit motives would ensure that the organizations' objectives and efforts were aligned with public good rather than private interests. Bringing in social enterprises could be a poverty-reducing initiative as well, since the majority of prison inmates are usually living below the poverty line or unemployed at the time of their incarceration. (I suspect that many prison guards, before they're hired, come from a similar economic background.) You'd see organizations working together to support social and educational programs that help to keep at-risk populations out of jail and reduce the recidivism rate by helping ex-convicts get work, build for the future, and achieve stability. Rather than waste away, prisoners could provide useful output to society. What if every prison was a social business, producing goods and services that would boost local GDP?

The government's role should be limited to funding the most effective social enterprises to solve a given problem. Privately run entrepreneurial organizations with a bent toward innovation would inherently be more efficient, spend less money, and do a better job of fixing social problems—but to ensure that incentives are aligned with the public's, those enterprises can't allow for the accrual of private profits. The "nonloss, non-dividend" social business model championed by Muhammad Yunus is the ideal entity to solve tough issues like mass incarceration. To make it work, stringent, impartial oversight would be imperative, and it would be equally imperative to remove profit motives from the equation. There's a difference between being efficient with resources, as we are at Samasource because we want to break even, and cutting corners to make a few points on the margin to please investors. Remove the incentive of profit from the social goal and impose high standards and oversight, and we'd remove the corruptive influences and loopholes that have plagued ideas that theoretically should work, like charter schools. Government and aid programs should act as venture capital firms, allocating funds to the most effective social enterprises that demonstrate, through controlled trials and other third-party experimental data, high social return on investment. This is the type of radical new thinking we need to apply to all of our social problems, whether it's homelessness, shoring up the education gap, or any other sector where public needs aren't met.

But in the end, at the root of so many of these social problems is poverty. And to address poverty, we need to put people to work (or, failing that, accept a universal basic income model). Anyone interested in training poor people for jobs must understand how the new economy works: survival depends on workers' adaptability, flexibility, and determination to stay ahead of the knowledge curve by pursuing self-directed learning. Most people know that it's been a long time since anyone could count on an industry remaining so unchanged for decades that workers didn't need to learn new skills. The difference today, however, is that the process has sped up, probably beyond most people's comprehension, including most of the people who have until now designed new job-training programs. Many live in the same places as the people they're trying to help, places where seismic shifts in the market aren't felt right away. When you live in an economy as innovative as that of the United States, there's bound to be a lag time between innovation and getting enough people up to speed to handle it. That's why we need more social entrepreneurs to get involved in solving these problems, because they have an advantage over almost any other institution or organization. It's in their nature. Even entrepreneurs who don't actually live in innovation zones like San Francisco, like I do, where we often get the first glimpse of new technology, are always paying close attention to trends and can see what the market is about to bring before the rest of the country. We're agile and able to move much more quickly than a program run by, say, the Department of Labor. As fast as new technology or innovations develop, social impact organizations like ours can shift our training curriculum to make sure our workers can continue to compete. When Samaschool started out in 2012, we were the only job-training program preparing people specifically for the gig economy. At the time of this writing, we still are.

So if you're an entrepreneur, what are you going to do? Building a social impact company is not easy. Is it really worth it to work this hard to build a company that will ultimately deliver no big payout? Think of it this way: you're on this planet for only so many breaths (about 672,768,000 for the average eighty-year-old). That time will pass faster than you can imagine, and, for better and for worse, it will be filled with unpredictability. The only thing you get to choose at the outset is how you are going to behave as you navigate through whatever it is life has in store for you. Choosing social enterprise gives you the satisfaction of doing something real and measurable with your limited number of breaths, not just for the people in your immediate circle whom you love and who love you back but for people you may never get to meet, who may never even know your name, generations from now.

That's true for anyone working in environmental conservation, too. Your ambitions don't have to be enormous in scale. Anyone has the power to measurably effect change for a small group of people, and that's where every powerful movement begins (Yunus gave his first microloan to ten women, and inspired a movement of hundreds of millions). Teachers already know this. So do doctors, police officers, and others who spend their days helping people. And once you enter the world of social enterprise and see what a difference you can make, you'll know it, too. You'll find that at the end of even the worst day, you get to go to sleep knowing you spent your breaths committed to something that had meaning and purpose. This isn't limited to the entrepreneurs— please don't think you have to rush out and start a new company. The biggest contributors to Samasource and LXMI's mission are the talented people who left jobs at Oracle, KPMG, and Estée Lauder to apply their skills to our social mission. Early-stage employees at social enterprises are the real leverage points, the people who pivot entire industries toward social good.

What if you're already in business? One big step you can take, as we've already discussed, is to give work. You can adopt impact sourcing and change your hiring or procurement practices to ensure that you include low-income people in your supply chain. If you're a small company and can't hire many people, or you need highly specialized, educated workers, think about other ways you can broaden your outreach. Maybe the next time you plan a company party, you could use a caterer that gives work to fight poverty, such as Delancey Street, Old Skool Cafe, or Homeboy Industries. If you manage data or product, maybe you could hire a data-services vendor like Samasource. Every time you make a purchasing decision—whether in business or in your daily life— look for a way to work with a company that hires marginalized people: low-income workers, veterans, former prison inmates, or people who've been rescued from sex trafficking. There are so many ways to give work, even if you can't directly hire someone. For help getting started, go to Givework.org/guide, where you will find the Give Work Guide, a list of vendors that give work across every industry, from caterers and home movers to construction firms, data companies, and beauty brands. We're building a B2B platform and a media site where consumers can discover new social impact brands that give work.

There is no bigger, more world-changing cause than eradicating poverty. The only practical, affordable long-term solution to poverty is to give people an income. Entrepreneurs who weave a Give Work strategy into the fabric of their businesses from the start—whether by committing to hiring low-income people or even merely by seeking opportunities to work with vendors who do—align themselves with the likes of Richard Branson and other well-known capitalists who recognize that, in the words of Marc Benioff, "The business of business is improving the state of the world." Shareholder success matters, but so does the success of your stakeholders, which includes your employees, your customers, the community in which your supply chain operates, the community in which your actual business operates, and the people at the bottom of your supply chain, most of whom would be excluded in a traditional profit-oriented model.

The idea of stakeholder capitalism—that businesses have a responsibility to create value for all the groups they touch, not just owners and shareholders—isn't new. It is, unfortunately, an idea that is still nascent in the United States. Yet now more than ever, customers and employees are demanding that businesses challenge the status quo and go beyond prioritizing profit. In fact, according to a study by Cone Communications, "just 6% of consumers believe the singular purpose of business is to make money for shareholders." There's a whole new world of sustainable social models on the rise, run by people determined to make their businesses succeed with the bar set far higher than just "do no harm." As news of Samasource's and other social impact companies' success spreads, I predict a new wave of entrepreneurs will be inspired to launch similar social impact organizations, tackling problems such as mass incarceration, climate change, homelessness, and virtually every other major social and environmental issue that plagues our society and our world. More entrepreneurs will come to realize that it can be just as rewarding, in all ways, to build a great company that solves a social problem as it is to build one that sells an app.

Since giving work is our best solution to eradicating poverty, I will continue to grow and build my own companies. Samasource doubled in 2016, and I want to get us to more than $100 million in sales and more than one hundred thousand people moved out of poverty permanently in the next decade. We're building an advisory team that helps other organizations, including local governments around the world, implement Give Work strategies in their own regions, and building new delivery centers in the United States, Uganda, and India. This year, LXMI is launching a slew of effective, plant-based formulas that give work, including a few that will retail at Sephora and on QVC—a facial mask, a makeup-treatment hybrid for glowing skin, a facial oil, a dry powder for purifying and detoxifying, and a lip product, all based on our signature fair trade and certified-organic ingredient Nilotica Reserve. Our research and development team is exploring a men's line and building our next regional collection, spotlighting one of two underserved regions, Myanmar and the northern part of the Amazon rain forest. In both of these places, biodiversity is threatened and local communities face massive poverty. We're also hoping to develop a collection based on botanical ingredients from here in the United States, to preserve our own indigenous plant species at risk of going extinct. While we already manufacture our products at local labs here in the States, and use a local family-owned distribution facility, we're also figuring out how we can expand our mission and hire people with low-income backgrounds to join our sales force as we get large enough to warrant one.

Where and how to implement the Give Work philosophy seems boundless. For example, we could explore ways to provide local employment opportunities that also drive wildland protection and ease the consumption of our natural resources. We've seen the EPA partner with fishermen in California to conserve fisheries and ensure that they will still have a livelihood in fifty years. We've seen groups dedicated to protecting gorillas develop vibrant luxury tourism economies that create economic incentives for African communities to stop poaching and preserve gorilla habitats. These are models that work, but we can't leave these causes exclusively to the nonprofits anymore. What about an adventure travel brand to compete with luxury firms like Abercrombie & Kent that would give work to more local guides and tourist operators, rather than suck up all the margin at the top? In consumer industries like tourism, personal care, apparel and accessories, and home goods—fields that are still dominated by brands that don't create social good—the world needs more well-designed and well-marketed social enterprise brands. Imagine if we could transform those industries the same way we've transformed coffee, where fair trade, artisanal brands are growing by leaps and bounds. There's a sneaker brand called Veja, made with fair trade materials, and an Android phone, the Fairphone, that is entirely fair trade, from the minerals sourced for the battery to the parts, and it's made in a factory that pays living wages. Our best hope for a bright future for the citizens of the world, and for our planet, lies in dissolving the traditional boundaries we've drawn between doing good and doing good business.

JOIN ME

Not long after Priya Haji sold World of Good to eBay, she launched a new company, this time a financial Web site and app called SaveUp. It was designed to incentivize people to save money. She also decided to have two children, an adorable girl and boy, with a sperm donor. It was a choice she never tried to hide. She was a force of nature—a real badass. One early summer evening I came to visit her for dinner at her condo in San Francisco, and as I sat on the floor and played with her kids while she cooked dinner, I was struck by the strong sense of domestic tranquillity that surrounded her. I said, "Priya, you've got it all." And she said something interesting. She told me that at first she was a little sad about the way her life had turned out, because it was supposed to be plan B. When she decided to have kids on her own, she'd rationalized it as the second-best option after having a partner. But then she realized that she had only one precious life—the one she was living. She admitted, "I had to mourn the original life I had in my head for myself, the fictional one that existed only in fantasyland." And then she told me, "Once I did that, I realized something powerful. This life I'm living, with two beautiful kids and a close circle of friends and a full, passionate career isn't plan B! This is plan A! Because this is the life I actually have, and it's a gift." It was such a beautiful thought. Screw the naysayers who told her she didn't "have it all" because she hadn't met Mr. Right. So many of those people might be married and miserable, or in a happy couple but unfulfilled at work. "Having it all" at the same time (in our thirties and forties) is a giant myth that is so often lorded over women as a means of confirming what we all already suspect—that we're not enough. Priya was my proof that there are many roads to joy, especially if you spend your working hours building something meaningful.

Priya died tragically of a pulmonary embolism at the age of forty-four, about a month later. Her two children went to live with her brother's family in Texas, close to their loving grandparents. Her example is never far from my mind. She influenced my businesses, for sure, but, much more important, she profoundly changed my ideas about how to design a life, especially as a woman. Priya was one of my few role models. There are female politicians who have struggled mightily whom I admire, and a few corporate tycoons, like Sheryl Sandberg, but their experiences are so different from the entrepreneur's journey. I can look to founders like Oprah or Spanx inventor Sara Blakely for inspiration, but these women built business empires first, not social enterprises. There are almost no contemporary women social entrepreneurs who've had massive public awareness. We just don't have that many stories on which to model ourselves. That's why it's important for those of us doing this work to tell our stories. Because otherwise there's no way you can conceive of the world being any different, there's no pattern-breaking acid trip of a story that convinces you that what you grew up thinking is all wrong and needs to change. That awareness can make such a huge difference in how our lives and ambitions unfold. And I want to see more of you out here with me.

Not long after I launched Samasource, my father returned to India and visited his mentor, a well-known civil engineer in Mumbai who had done very well financially and supported a lot of social programs in the slums. My father expressed a bit of ambivalence that his daughter would give up a promising career to start a nonprofit. His mentor replied, "Why are you worried? What she is doing will outlive her." In an instant, my father realized that I was on the right path. And on those days when I'm tired, or I'm worried that I've set an unattainable goal, or the work starts to feel like a grind, I remember those words and am grateful for the chance to wake up every day believing that I'm making a contribution to the world that's greater than myself. Maybe, if all goes well, it could be greater than my lifetime. At least I will be able to say I tried. That's all I'm asking of you. Just try. Make it your business to figure out what good needs to be done in the world, and then do it.

ACKNOWLEDGMENTS

This book would not exist without Stephanie Land's empathetic ear. She guided the manuscript from a nest of incomplete thoughts to a polished, coherent argument for giving work. Thank you to Molly Atlas, my wonderful agent at ICM, whose thoughtful critiques and guidance on many iterations of the outline made me confident that I wasn't embarking on a fool's errand. I'm grateful to our trio of Stephanies—Stephanie Frerich, my #girlboss editor, who encouraged me to stick to my guns despite many fears (and who passionately supports young women leaders); Stephanie Abou, who helped navigate brutal revision schedules; and Stefanie Rosenblum, publicist extraordinaire.

Too many people to fit in a few pages helped me launch Samasource and LXMI and keep them going over the years. I am sure I won't do them justice, but I would not be able to do what I do without the daily kindness, patience, and leadership of our management teams: Tony MacDonald, Wendy Gonzalez, Lindsey Crumbaugh, Thea Kocher, and Ashley Grabill. The current and former directors of Samasource and LXMI do much more than guide the companies—they've helped me find my path as an entrepreneur and shaped me into a better leader. Thank you to Deborah Conrad, Ben Parr, Johann Schleier-Smith, Lloyd

Taylor, Olana Khan, Bill Unger, Bıll Trenchard, Sebastien de Halleux, Dan Benton, Margarita Arriagada, Katherine Berr, and Tim Koogle.

I think often of Samasource's early days and the gifted people who helped me shape the company before we had money to pay them properly. Joy Sun, Chelsea Seale, Jill Isenstadt, Dave Yoon, Shivani Garg Patel, and Martin Anderson deserve much of the credit for getting us off the ground. Our early donors and advisers Jacquelline Fuller, Zia Khan, Reeta Roy and the MasterCard Foundation team, and the TripAdvisor team believed early on in Samahope and supported Samasource for many years.

And finally, my tribe: Ashwin Jacob, Angie Janssen, Katie Zacarian, Doriena Wolff, Meagan and Conrad Jones, Jerry and Judy Jones, Lisa Kavanaugh, Silvia Console Battilana, Jenny Stefanotti, Thairu, Raja Haddad, Mark Kinsey, Paul English, Molly Graham, Tracy Fong, Nachson and Arieh Mimran, Muneer Satter, James Lindenbaum, Katharina Volz, Sierra Campbell, Teresa Goines, Adrienne Bragdon, Charlie Cheever (whose early support made all the difference in founding Samasource), Sahadev Chirayath, Ved Chirayath, and Loïc Le Meur, who has taught me more about entrepreneurship in three years than seems possible. And to Anna Chan, my in-case-of-emergency person, who does the job of five people with unmatched grace.

RECOMMENDED READING

BOOKS ARE MY SAFE PLACE, AND MY TEACHERS. AND WITH THE ME-
dia highlighting so few stories about women leaders and social entrepreneurs, I sometimes use them as my mentors, too, drawing
inspiration from the stories of people who lived a long time ago, like
Beryl Markham, or using them to better understand people I admire
today, like Wendy Kopp. Reading provides us with broader perspectives
and deeper wells of creativity—two necessary qualities for any entrepreneur. The books below are some of the ones that have served me best.

SOCIAL ENTREPRENEURSHIP

A People's History of the United States by Howard Zinn—the classic history book
that reexamines American history from the perspective of those who lost
out, rather than those who triumphed. A good start for understanding social
problems of today.

Banker to the Poor by Muhammad Yunus—the autobiography of the iconic
Grameen Bank founder. Required reading for all aspiring entrepreneurs with
a social conscience. This book inspired me to start Samasource.

Bearing the Cross by David Garrow—a meticulously researched biography of
MLK during the era of the freedom marches.

Behind the Beautiful Forevers by Katherine Boo—hands down the best book on
poverty you'll ever read. Boo, who previously won a Pulitzer Prize for her
reporting on American poverty, spent two years conducting in-depth inter-

views of more than two hundred people in a small slum near the Mumbai airport. What emerged is a story that's more gripping than most novels.

Building Social Business by Muhammad Yunus—a companion to *Banker to the Poor*, this book outlines Yunus's key lessons for social entrepreneurs. It contains a ton of useful information for entrepreneurs of all kinds looking to make the world a bit better.

Disgrace by J. M. Coetzee—this fictional account of a crime in South Africa helps outsiders understand the brutality of apartheid. Coetzee is dark. Be prepared.

Eating Animals by Jonathan Safran Foer—a modern, very readable version of *Animal Liberation*, Peter Singer's classic work from the 1970s. Foer's book familiarizes us with the suffering of 50 billion farm animals, links our eating habits to global warming, and makes it impossible to look at a piece of pork without wanting to throw up.

Gang Leader for a Day by Sudhir Venkatesh—this book is a phenomenal example of the power of real listening. Venkatesh is an academic who decided to live with gang members in Chicago in order to understand their behavior. In the end, he shows that much of what they do is guided by a rational response to extremely challenging circumstances, rather than a predisposition to criminal behavior.

Good Work by E. F. Schumacher—a classic read by the brilliant mind behind the design classic *Small Is Beautiful*, with a meditation on the importance of work and the challenges of dealing with an increasingly educated global population.

Half the Sky by Nicholas Kristof and Sheryl WuDunn—this isn't strictly about social entrepreneurship but rather describes the global epidemic of violence against women, and the efforts of many social entrepreneurs to address it.

How to Change the World by David Bornstein—hailed as "the bible for social entrepreneurship." Bornstein visited my consulting firm in 2006 and I was taken with his ideas. Two years later, I quit and started Sama. Let that be a warning to those of you who buy his book!

Just Mercy by Bryan Stevenson—a vivid memoir by America's foremost criminal justice reformer, told through the lens of death-row inmates and juvenile prisoners. Gripping and memorable, not least because Stevenson is a gay black man living in Alabama.

King Leopold's Ghost by Adam Hochschild—the shocking and true story of King Leopold's bloody reign in Central Africa, including his brutal legacy of enslaving and killing millions of Congolese people in order to extract rubber from the colony. A must-read for understanding the colonial legacy in Africa and making sense of current relations between Europe and sub-Saharan Africa.

Mountains Beyond Mountains by Tracy Kidder—documents the life and work of Paul Farmer, the world's strongest advocate for first-class health care for poor people. From New Orleans, he fought the death penalty and inhumane prison conditions in the Deep South.

Nickel and Dimed: On (Not) Getting By in America by Barbara Ehrenreich—to better understand how the U.S. economy is shifting from the perspective of low-wage workers, read this. It's a startling and incredible work of journalism by a powerful woman writer.

One Day All Children by Wendy Kopp—describes the founding of Teach For America, one of America's most successful nonprofits.

Poor Economics by Abhijit Banerjee and Esther Duflo—two MIT development economists transform the way we think about aid and argue that we should apply the same kind of scrutiny to development interventions that we do to clinical drug testing.

Portfolios of the Poor by Daryl Collins et al.—the authors show how low-income people around the world make ends meet by holding multiple jobs, mostly in the informal economy. For anyone interested in understanding why poor people remain poor and have little access to work, this book provides helpful data and real-world analysis.

Savage Inequalities by Jonathan Kozol—this book, by an education reformer, shaped my thinking about access to opportunity in the United States, and dispelled the myth that we live in a meritocratic society. Kozol's account of poor inner-city schools is a must-read, especially for young people.

The Last Hunger Season by Roger Thurow—a chronicle of Andrew Youn's work with the One Acre Fund, a highly effective organization that fights rural poverty for smallholder farmers who missed out on the Green Revolution.

The Lean Startup by Eric Ries—now a Silicon Valley legend, Ries shaped the way thousands of start-ups and big companies think about scaling an idea. He advocates for an experiment-based approach using as few resources as possible before something "sticks" and warrants further investment. His philosophy applies to nonprofits, government agencies, and any organization looking to boost innovation.

The World Is Flat by Thomas Friedman—this book, now a bit dated, shaped our common understanding of how the Internet would change the nature of work. I still refer to it in talks and speeches, because Friedman captured a fundamentally different economic system based on the free movement of labor via the Internet.

We Wish to Inform You That Tomorrow We Will Be Killed with Our Families by Philip Gourevitch—an overview of the 1994 Rwandan genocide and the factors that led neighbors and families to turn on one another.

Workers by Sebastião Salgado—this Brazilian photographer first picked up a camera at the age of thirty, after he'd been in grad school. His work covers displaced people and low-wage workers around the world.

MORAL PHILOSOPHY AND FAITH

A Theory of Justice by John Rawls—the seminal book on justice and how it impacts policy (or should). If you didn't read it in college, it's not too late.

Dorothy Day: Selected Writings—Dorothy Day was a journalist and social activist who later became a nun. Like Thomas Merton, she was passionate about social justice and used her faith to advocate for better policies for workers and the poor. Pope Francis and many other liberation theologists draw inspiration from Dorothy Day.

Evangelii Gaudium, Pope Francis's apostolic exhortation—my favorite lines appear at the top of chapter 6.

Status Anxiety by Alain de Botton—he is not a philosopher on the level of Rawls or Kant, but Alain de Botton writes relevant and timely books on the challenges of our day. Worth a read when stress gets you down.

The Life You Can Save by Peter Singer—Singer is a moral philosopher whose current work—on how even small donations can make a lifesaving difference—inspires us all to give with confidence.

World Poverty and Human Rights by Thomas Pogge—a more nuanced look at why we have a moral duty to end global poverty. Pogge was Rawls's graduate student at Harvard and a mentor of mine.

LEADERSHIP

A First-Rate Madness by Nassir Ghaemi—lest you think you are the only crazy one, read this book, which chronicles leaders who are on the bipolar spectrum and discusses ways they've harnessed their unique brains to both good and evil ends. (Crazy fact: Hitler shot himself up with amphetamines in increasing doses as World War II escalated. Some suspect this drove him to the heinous crimes of the Holocaust.)

Benjamin Franklin: An American Life by Walter Isaacson—I especially like Franklin's values, which he posted in his study, and learning about the habits that made this practical early American a hero. My only critique of this book is that it doesn't cover enough of Franklin's flaws, such as his womanizing during the years he was in Paris.

Bossypants by Tina Fey—another feminist figure in entertainment, and arguably less feared than Shonda Rhimes, Fey describes her career in TV and film.

Endurance: Shackleton's Incredible Voyage by Alfred Lansing—I almost counted Shackleton as a social entrepreneur because he pursued crossing the South Pole as a benefit to the public at large without concern for personal gain. This is a gripping book recommended by Howard Schultz.

Joy, Inc. by Richard Sheridan—software engineer and founder of Menlo Innovations, Sheridan describes how he built a workplace that fills his employees with joy. Recommended by my colleague Jason Rogers, who worked for Sheridan.

Lean In by Sheryl Sandberg—a mentor to many women in the Valley, and millions more through her book, Sheryl Sandberg talks about how women can claim their rightful positions as leaders in every aspect of life.

Lincoln's Melancholy by Joshua Wolf Shenk—one of our nation's greatest presidents suffered from severe episodes of depression. This book describes how Lincoln channeled his moods for the good of the country.

Margaret Bourke-White by Vicki Goldberg—Bourke-White was a close friend of my great-uncle Sunil Janah, and a legend. At age twenty-nine, her photograph of industrial America took the cover of *LIFE* magazine. She was known for dangling from rooftops and scaffolding to get a good shot, and never settled for a boring married life.

Not That Kind of Girl by Lena Dunham—Dunham is vulgar, somewhat annoying, and self-important. But so is every male comedian, and she's funnier and a better writer. This book made me snort on the plane and vow to be more self-confident. If you learn anything from Lena, it's to be yourself with no regrets.

Rubies in the Orchard by Lynda Resnick—the founder of POM Wonderful and FIJI water describes her creative vision and how she and her husband built several multimillion-dollar businesses in unexpected categories.

The Hard Thing About Hard Things by Ben Horowitz—I loved reading this book because Horowitz doesn't glorify or glamorize entrepreneurship. He describes his real struggle to grow a start-up and what happened next.

The Hidden Life of Trees: What They Feel, How They Communicate—Discoveries from a Secret World by Peter Wohlleben—this book offers a fascinating view into the world of trees and forests, which behave (in more ways than you'd ever expect) like people and communities. There are many leadership lessons packed inside for the discerning reader.

This Child Will Be Great by Ellen Johnson Sirleaf—Africa's first woman president discusses her life and struggles running Liberia.

West with the Night by Beryl Markham—hailed as one of the best memoirs Hemingway ever read, *WWTN* is my favorite book. Markham was the first aviatrix (love that word) in East Africa, and she set a record flying west over the Atlantic in 1936, in the early days of aviation. Her memoir is full of gorgeous images of Africa, Los Angeles (her second home), and horses, her second love.

Wildflower by Mark Seal—a book about the life of Joan Root, a celebrated wildlife filmmaker in Kenya (and a woman of the land, much like Beryl Markham). This book describes Joan's later years as a conservationist in Lake Naivasha and her struggle to live alone after a devastating divorce.

Year of Yes by Shonda Rhimes—though Rhimes, the creator of the hit TV shows *Grey's Anatomy* and *Scandal,* is sometimes over the top (her production company, for example, is called Shondaland), she's hilarious, daring, and lovable. She describes her career ascent, having three kids on her own, and the BS underneath "having it all." I love her message to women.

YOUR BRAIN: UNDERSTANDING AND PROTECTING IT

The next real frontier is within our minds. I've learned a ton about my brain and about techniques for caring for it better in the last few years, as Sama and LXMI have grown and as I've had to deal with more challenging situations at work and at home. From meditation to medication, these books will help you understand how your most important organ functions and what to do to keep it working optimally.

An Unquiet Mind by Kay Redfield Jamison—Jamison explores bipolar disorder as a brilliant doctor and writer who struggles with the disease herself. She creates a portrait of manic depression that highlights the gifts that come along with the costs.

Consciousness Explained by Daniel Dennett—Dennett, who happens to look like Santa Claus, is one of our great philosophers. He presents various analyses of consciousness, and dispels myths about the brain's functioning using rational arguments instead of neuroscience. It's a long read, but fascinating.

Flow by Mihaly Csikszentmihalyi—ever wonder how great performers get "in the zone," or why some people seem to derive so much joy from their work? *Flow* describes the optimal brain state for producing great work and how to create the right conditions for flow in your mind.

How to Meditate by Lawrence LeShan—the fastest way to figure out how to meditate and start a daily practice. I was gifted with this book in 2013, and it changed my life.

Incognito by David Eagleman—the most brilliant neuroscientist of our generation writes about the profound effects of the subconscious on our behavior.

Karma and Chaos by Paul Fleischman—essays on Vipassana, a Buddhist mediation technique descended from Buddha's original teachings. Fleischman describes the benefits of daily practice in a series of compelling essays, and links Buddhism with contemporary neuroscience.

On Intelligence by Jeff Hawkins—a book about neuroscience and computing by the developer of the PalmPilot.

Phantoms in the Brain by V. S. Ramachandran—V. S. Ramachandran is famous for figuring out how to "fix" phantom limbs (amputated limbs that the brain believes are still present, a source of anguish for afflicted people) using mirror boxes, essentially tricking the brain into thinking that limbs that had been destroyed in accidents have reappeared.

Sapiens by Yuval Noah Harari—Harari describes why so many customs and traditions are the result of random coincidences in human history and how many of our ideas about race and genetics are dead wrong, and questions key assumptions about our brains and our future. A modern update to Jared Diamond's book *Guns, Germs, and Steel.*

The Body Bears the Burden by Robert Scaer—another great read on trauma and how it's stored in the body. I believe trauma is at the root of a great deal of current conflict, interpersonal problems, and violence. By understanding how trauma unfolds in the brain and body, we're empowered to design better solutions.

The Brain That Changes Itself by Norman Doidge—this book made a huge impression on me. Doidge is a psychiatrist and science journalist who interviewed top neuroscientists to understand how the brain can change and how we can keep our brains plastic as we age (best strategy: dance!). It's full of interesting quotes and helpful tips to avoid getting stuck in a mental rut.

The Hypomanic Edge by John Gartner—ever wonder why so many entrepreneurs seem to exhibit similar behaviors, like unusually high energy, a constant stream of new ideas, and irritation with people who move more slowly? Gartner argues that hypomania is rampant among entrepreneurs, and that immigrants (who constitute most of America's population going back a few generations) are unusually likely to be hypomanic.

The Noonday Demon by Andrew Solomon—this is one of my favorite books of all time. Solomon, like Kay Jamison, suffers from depression and describes his mental suffering as only a gifted writer can. Solomon's father was a pharmaceutical executive who developed early antidepressants, and Solomon writes about the importance of drug therapy as few other writers can, speaking from experience. A must-read.

The Wise Heart by Jack Kornfield—a leading teacher of Buddhism in the United States (it's interesting that so many American Buddhists are Jewish—a testament to that faith's open-mindedness), Kornfield helps the average person understand the key tenets of one of the world's oldest and most profound religions. Buddhism isn't really a religion; it's a way of life and a framework for thinking that has incredible benefits for the brain and for interpersonal relationships.

Waking the Tiger by Peter A. Levine—many entrepreneurs and leaders I know endured trauma of some kind, and most of us working in the social sector are impacted by larger-scale trauma inflicted by abuse, poverty, and violence. Peter Levine describes the conditions in which trauma occurs and the most powerful ways to address it in ourselves, our loved ones, and communities. An essential read for understanding patterns like generational trauma, and how historical injustice impacts the world today.

LIFE SKILLS

Difficult Conversations by Douglas Stone—this book helped me figure out how to use language more effectively. Most of the time what I say isn't the problem, it's how I say it. Worth reading to be a better negotiator, friend, manager, and lover.

Eat to Live by Joel Fuhrman—want to create a better world, lose weight, and feel incredible? Stop eating animal products, and start loading up on green vegetables. This is the premise of *Eat to Live,* the best book I've read on nutrition and health. Fuhrman's work is backed by science and, though he doesn't discuss it, moral philosophy—I believe factory farming will one day be regarded as one of the great evils of human civilization, alongside slavery and apartheid.

Getting Things Done by David Allen—as a chronically messy and disorganized person, sometimes I reread this classic book on personal organization to train my brain to think differently. Mostly I don't, but I think it's a good idea to try.

How to Be an Adult in Relationships by David Richo—a great reminder for all the important relationships in your life, even if they're going well. I always regret not rereading this annually.

Rework by Jason Fried and David Heinemeier Hansson (DHH)—authored by the founders of Basecamp and parent company 37signals, *Rework* inspires readers to think differently about being productive. Learn to avoid meetings, use laziness to your advantage, and build a small, profitable business instead of a giant, bloated start-up. Check out "Reconsider," an article by DHH on the same topic.

Spinster by Kate Bolick—after her *Atlantic* piece "All the Single Ladies" went gangbusters, Bolick followed up with a book about reclaiming the term "spinster" to refer to women who follow their hearts and dreams, finding fulfillment in themselves rather than in their men. All women, regardless of their marital or relationship status, need to read this. She also chronicles the fascinating lives of women like Edna St. Vincent Millay and Edith Wharton, iconic spinsters.

The Artist's Way by Julia Cameron—I read about this book in Walter Isaacson's Steve Jobs biography and bought it immediately. Cameron describes several habits that spur creativity; some of them, like the "artist's date" and morning pages, have changed my life.

The Life-Changing Magic of Tidying Up by Marie Kondo—this has become a cult favorite among decorators and organizers, and messy slobs like me. Reading the book gave me a new appreciation for the joy of a clutter-free life and home, and for something even more important: the peace of mind that comes from owning less stuff. Decluttering isn't about decorating. It's a life philosophy.

Words That Work by Frank Luntz—want to write and speak more effectively, reaching more people? Read this, and John McPhee's article in the *New Yorker* on the importance of omission, entitled "Omission: Choosing What to Leave Out."

NOTES

INTRODUCTION

2 **youth unemployment in Kenya:** Eduardo Zepeda, Fatou Leigh, et al., "Kenya's Youth Employment Challenge" (discussion paper, United Nations Development Programme, January 2013), 15, http://www.undp.org/content /dam/undp/library/Poverty%20Reduction/Inclusive%20development /Kenya_YEC_web(jan13).pdf.

2 **"It was kind of a funny conversation":** Interview with Vanessa Kanyi, April 5, 2016.

3 **"I looked around and thought, 'Cool!' ":** Ibid.

4 **In 2015, the United States alone donated:** Charity Navigator, "Giving Statistics," http://www.charitynavigator.org/index.cfm?bay=content.view& cpid=42.

4 **around 10 percent of the global population:** World Bank, "Overview," http://www.worldbank.org/en/topic/poverty/overview (last updated October 2, 2016).

4 **That's more than 2.8 billion people:** World Bank, *Working for a World Free of Poverty,* World Bank Group, 1, http://siteresources.worldbank.org /EXTABOUTUS/Resources/wbgroupbrochure-en.pdf.

4 **Three hundred thousand women die annually:** World Health Organization, "Maternal Mortality" (World Health Organization fact sheet), http:// www.who.int/mediacentre/factsheets/fs348/en.

4 **Millions of children suffer brain stunting:** UNICEF India, "Stunting," http://www.unicef.in/whatwedo/10/stunting.

4 **783 million people:** Water Project, "Facts About Water: Statistics of the Water Crisis," https://thewaterproject.org/water-scarcity/water_stats (last updated August 18, 2016).

4 **2.5 billion don't have:** Centers for Disease Control and Prevention, "Global Water, Sanitation & Hygiene (WASH)," https://www.cdc.gov/healthywater /global/wash_statistics.html#two (last updated April 11, 2016).

7 **design thinker E. F. Schumacher:** E. F. Schumacher, *Good Work* (New York: HarperCollins, 1979).

7 **the UN reported that more people:** Ken Robinson, "Do Schools Kill Creativity?" TED Talk, TED2006, Monterey, California, February 2006, http:// www.ted.com/talks/ken_robinson_says_schools_kill_creativity/tran script?language=en.

CHAPTER ONE: FROM THE GROUND UP

26 **In the United States, poverty is defined:** U.S. Dept. of Health and Human Services, "2014 Poverty Guidelines," https://aspe.hhs.gov/2014-poverty -guidelines.

26 **Extreme poverty is currently defined:** World Bank, "World Bank Forecasts Global Poverty to Fall Below 10% for First Time; Major Hurdles Remain in Goal to End Poverty by 2030" (press release, October 4, 2015), http://www.worldbank.org/en/news/press-release/2015/10/04/world-bank -forecasts-global-poverty-to-fall-below-10-for-first-time-major-hurdles -remain-in-goal-to-end-poverty-by-2030.

28 **a case against the California State Board of Education:** ACLU of Southern California, "Suing State Education Offices and Inglewood Unified School District on Behalf of Students Denied Equal Access to Advanced Placement (AP) Courses," July 27, 1999, https://www.aclusocal.org /aclu-of-southern-california-sues-state-education-offices-and-inglewood -unified-school-district-on-behalf-of-students-denied-equal-access-to -advanced-placement-ap-courses.

29 **historians like Samuel Huntington:** Samuel P. Huntington, *Who Are We? The Challenges to America's National Identity* (New York: Simon and Schuster, 2004).

32 **explain how the brain changes:** Sendhil Mullainathan and Eldar Shafir, *Scarcity: Why Having Too Little Means So Much* (New York: Times Books, 2013), Kindle edition.

35 **Courtney Martin wrote:** Courtney Martin, "The Reductive Seduction of

Other People's Problems," *Development Set,* January 11, 2016, https://the
developmentset.com/the-reductive-seduction-of-other-people-s-problems
-3c07b307732d#.va2gfnisc.

36 **a "portfolio approach":** Daryl Collins, Jonathan Morduch, et al., *Portfolios
to the Poor: How the World's Poor Live on $2 a Day* (Princeton, NJ: Princeton
University Press, December 2010).

42 **Grameen has disbursed:** Grameen Bank, "Introduction," http://www
.grameen.com/introduction (last updated December 2015).

CHAPTER TWO: AID: WHAT WORKS, WHAT DOESN'T, AND WHY

50 **The scenes set on Earth:** Lauren Williams, "Matt Damon: We Literally Ate
S*** Filming in a Mexico Dump," *Metro,* August 16, 2013, http://metro
.co.uk/2013/08/16/matt-damon-we-literally-ate-s-filming-in-a-mexico
-dump-3924984.

52 **before achieving independence:** U.S. Department of State, "Mozambique
(11/04)" (information last released online January 20, 2017), https://2009
-2017.state.gov/outofdate/bgn/mozambique/40304.htm.

53 **trauma begets trauma:** Peter A. Levine, *Waking the Tiger: Healing Trauma*
(Berkeley, CA: North Atlantic Books, 1997).

53 **$13 billion was poured:** Barry Eichengreen, "Lessons from the Marshall
Plan" (World Bank World Development Report 2011 background case note,
April 2010), http://web.worldbank.org/archive/website01306/web/marshall_
plan.html.

54 **one of the first of the Millennium Development Goals:** World Bank,
"Overview," http://www.worldbank.org/en/topic/poverty/overview (last updated October 2, 2016).

54 **It left 2.8 billion:** World Bank, *Working for a World Free of Poverty,* World
Bank Group, 1, http://siteresources.worldbank.org/EXTABOUTUS/Resources
/wbgroupbrochure-en.pdf.

54 **with more than half of them:** World Bank, "Overview."

54 **More than $1 trillion has been invested:** Daron Acemoglu and James A.
Robinson, "Why Foreign Aid Fails—and How to Really Help Africa," *Specta-
tor,* January 25, 2014, https://www.spectator.co.uk/2014/01/why-aid-fails/#.

57 **But forty-three years of Belgian rule:** Alison Des Forges, *Leave None to
Tell the Story: Genocide in Rwanda* (Human Rights Watch, 1999).

59 **majority of the World Bank's private investments:** Oxfam, "84% of
World Bank's Private Investments in Sub-Saharan Africa Go to Companies

Using Tax Havens" (press release, April 11, 2014), http://www.oxfam.org.uk /media-centre/press-releases/2016/04/84-percent-of-world-bank-private -investments-in-sub-saharan-africa-go-to-companies-using-tax-havens.

60 **clear targets for extreme poverty eradication:** World Bank, "Speech by World Bank President Jim Yong Kim: The World Bank Group's Mission: To End Extreme Poverty," October 3, 2016, http://www.worldbank.org/en/news /speech/2016/10/03/speech-by-world-bank-president-jim-yong-kim-the -world-bank-groups-mission-to-end-extreme-poverty.

63 **her facilities actually exacerbated:** Christopher Hitchens, *The Missionary Position: Mother Teresa in Theory and Practice* (New York: Verso, 1995).

63 **Moral philosopher Peter Singer:** Peter Singer, "The Logic of Effective Altruism," *Boston Review*, July 6, 2015, https://bostonreview.net/forum/peter -singer-logic-effective-altruism.

63 **a perspective not shared:** Hitchens, *Missionary Position*, 82. Or: https:// www.washingtonpost.com/archive/lifestyle/magazine/1981/10/18/amazing -grace/80c3d328-1270-4f50-90d8-ba72dc903b90/?utm_term=.dc0de39e1fb5.

64 **More than eight hundred studies:** J-Pal, "Evaluations," Abdul Latif Jameel Poverty Action Lab, https://www.povertyactionlab.org/evaluations.

70 **taking up $4.5 billion:** Robert Kennedy, Shateen Seth, et al., "Impact Sourcing: Assessing the Opportunity for Building a Thriving Industry" (Ann Arbor, MI: William Davidson Institute, May 2013), 33.

70 **one initially grounded in seven principles:** Muhammad Yunus, *Building Social Business: The New Kind of Capitalism That Serves Humanity's Most Pressing Needs* (New York: PublicAffairs, 2010), 2–3.

72 **In 2006, the Peace Dividend Trust:** Nick Rockel, "Scott Gilmore Makes Peace Missions More Effective," *Globe and Mail*, December 14, 2010, http:// www.theglobeandmail.com/report-on-business/25/the-25/scott-gilmore -makes-peace-missions-more-effective/article1836128.

73 **Building Markets has facilitated:** Building Markets, "Afghanistan: Overview and Impact," June 2014, http://buildingmarkets.org/our-impact/afghanistan.

74 **85 percent of workers continue:** Samasource, "2015 Annual Report," http://media.wix.com/ugd/e4cc5f_0198092661bf449ea0429a24f0b838f0 .pdf.

75 **Women make up 60 percent:** United Nations Development Programme, "Fast Facts: Matters of Fact," February 2014, http://www.undp.org/content/ dam/undp/library/corporate/fast-facts/english/FF-Gender-Equality-and -UNDP.pdf.

75 **Their labor force participation:** Jeni Klugman, Lucia Hanmer, et al., "Gender at Work: A Companion to the World Development Report on Jobs," World Bank, 2013, http://documents.worldbank.org/curated/en/884131468 332686103/pdf/892730WP0Box3800report0Feb-02002014.pdf.

75 **women continue to earn:** World Food Programme, "Key Facts," 2017, https:// www.wfp.org/our-work/preventing-hunger/focus-women/overviewm, http:// www.uis.unesco.org/Education/Documents/fs26-2013-literacy-en.pdf.

75 **women make up the majority:** UNESCO Institute for Statistics, "Adult and Youth Literacy," September 2013, 1, http://www.uis.unesco.org/Education /Documents/fs26-2013-literacy-en.pdf.

75 **Women in the United States:** Jasmine Tucker and Caitlin Lowell, "National Snapshot: Poverty Among Women and Families, 2015," National Women's Law Center, September 14, 2016, http://nwlc.org/resources/national-snapshot -poverty-among-women-families-2015/.

75 **But as of 2011:** Betsy Brill, "The Power of Investing in Women," *Forbes*, March 28, 2011, http://www.forbes.com/2011/03/28/women-led-philanthropy -intelligent-investing.html.

75 **less than 10 percent:** Jacki Zehner, "State of Philanthropy: Women on the Cusp of Transformative Power," LinkedIn, March 25, 2014, https://www.linked in.com/pulse/20140325115637-25295057-state-of-philanthropy-women-on -the-cusp-of-transformative-power?articleId=8408159838777807202.

75 **Yet women are likely:** Women Deliver, "Invest in Girls and Women: The Ripple Effect," May 2016, http://womendeliver.org/wp-content/uploads /2016/05/Invest_in_Girls_and_Women_2.pdf.

75 **Those good head starts:** Samasource, "2016 Year in Review," https://www. samasource.org/impact.

76 **Research and impact reports:** Sandesh Sharanappa and Leila Chirayath Janah, "Microwork for Macro-gains: Evaluating the Social Impact of ICT-based Job Creation in Rural India" (background paper, Samasource, 2010), https://docs.google.com/file/d/0By_WYPOCGnBkZGM5ZmVlYTctZTBi Mi00ZjdhLTlkMDktNTQzMmJkODMxMzE2/edit?hl=en_US.

76 **"I thought empowerment":** Ibid.

77 **The PlayPump, for example:** Amy Costello, "Troubled Water: Story Synopsis," *Frontline World*, June 29, 2010, http://www.pbs.org/frontlineworld /stories/southernafrica904/video_index.html.

78 **Of those interviewed:** UNICEF, *An Evaluation of the PlayPump Water System as an Appropriate Technology for Water Sanitation and Hygiene*

Programmes, October 2007, 10, https://www-tc.pbs.org/frontlineworld /stories/southernafrica904/flash/pdf/unicef_pp_report.pdf.

78 **Women said they found:** Costello, "Troubled Water."

79 **"Earlier the thinking was":** Samasource, "Samasource 2013 Annual Report," 9, https://media.wix.com/ugd/e4cc5f_7116f47359a34e5fa4d64b48ade 41862.pdf.

79 **Neha Parveen, a doe-eyed:** Samasource, "Samasource Field Cam: Neha Parveen, India," YouTube, November 30, 2011, https://www.youtube.com /watch?v=WZ8lstt3Avk.

81 **In Jharkhand, most workers:** Sharanappa and Janah, "Microwork for Macro-gains."

81 **In exchange for lifting:** Ishaan Tharoor, "Is It Time for France to Pay Its Real Debt to Haiti?" *Washington Post*, May 13, 2015, https://www.washington post.com/news/worldviews/wp/2015/05/13/does-france-owe-haiti -reparations/?utm_term=.314f1ac6217f.

85 **Jason Atkins, founder and CEO:** Samasource, "360incentives Partners with Samasource," YouTube, November 5, 2013, https://www.youtube.com /watch?v=sqem1Phu4QYhttps://www.youtube.com/watch?v=sqem1Phu4QY.

86 **the United Nations High Commissioner for Refugees:** Krista Mahr, "Kenya Has Hosted Hundreds of Thousands of Refugees in the Past Two Decades. Now, It Wants Them Out," *Newsweek*, July 18, 2016, http://www .newsweek.com/2016/07/22/dadaab-closure-host-somalia-refugees-now -kenya-wants-them-out-481379.html.

86 **In May 2016:** Republic of Kenya Ministry of Interior and Coordination of National Government Facebook page, May 11, 2016, https://www.facebook .com/InteriorMinistryKenya/posts/1127943743935758.

87 **The ministry added:** Ibid.

87 **The following February:** Jeffrey Gettleman, "Kenyan Court Blocks Plan to Close Dadaab Refugee Camp," *New York Times*, February 9, 2017, https:// www.nytimes.com/2017/02/09/world/africa/kenyan-court-blocks-plan-to -close-dadaab-refugee-camp.html?_r=0.

87 **In an article for *Wired*:** Scott Carney, "An Economic Analysis of the Somali Pirate Business Model," *Wired*, July 13, 2009, http://www.wired.com /2009/07/ff-somali-pirates.

89 **As founder Hamdi Ulukaya:** World Economic Forum, "Davos 2016— Press Conference: The Refugee and Migration Crisis," YouTube, January 22, 2016, https://www.youtube.com/watch?v=dApJnaaNwQY.

89 **He has created:** Christian Harris, Mark Barbano, and Tammy Marino, "Popular Greek Yogurt Boosts State's Economy," *Employment in New York State,* New York State Department of Labor, June 2012, 3, https://www.labor .ny.gov/stats/PDFs/enys0612.pdf.

89 **the world's largest:** Chobani, "Chobani Celebrates Grand Opening of World's Largest Manufacturing Plant in Twin Falls, Idaho," December 17, 2012, http://www.chobanifoodservice.com/who-we-are/news-and-events /chobani-celebrates-grand-opening-of-worlds-largest-yogurt-manufacturing -plant-in-twin-falls-idaho.

89 **"I can tell from my experience":** World Economic Forum, January 2016, https://www.youtube.com/watch?v=dApJnaaNwQY.

90 **Beirut, which has more than 280,000:** UNHCR, "Syria Regional Refugee Response," http://data.unhcr.org/syrianrefugees/settlement.php?id=202& country=122&region=88 (last updated December 31, 2016).

CHAPTER THREE: THE CAPITAL OF HUSTLE

92 **displaced more than 1.8 million:** Internal Displacement Monitoring Center, "New Displacement in Uganda Continues Alongside Long-Term Recovery Needs," January 23, 2014, http://www.internal-displacement.org /sub-saharan-africa/uganda/2014/new-displacement-in-uganda-continues -alongside-long-term-recovery-needs.

92 **most of the internally displaced:** Ibid.

95 **In 2006, the government:** Pew Research Center, "Cell Phones in Africa: Communication Lifeline," Pew Research Center Global Attitudes and Trends, April 15, 2015, http://www.pewglobal.org/2015/04/15/cell-phones-in-africa -communication-lifeline.

95 **More than a third:** Tolu Oguniesi and Stephanie Busari, "Seven Ways Mobile Phones Have Changed Lives in Africa," CNN, September 14, 2012, http:// www.cnn.com/2012/09/13/world/africa/mobile-phones-change-africa/.

105 **"a dream deferred":** Langston Hughes, "Harlem," in *The Collected Works of Langston Hughes: The Poems: 1951–1967,* ed. Arnold Rampersad (Columbia: University of Missouri Press, 2001), 3:145. Originally published in *Selected Poems of Langston Hughes* (New York: Knopf, 1959).

113 **Vittana's idea was to bring:** Kate Cochran, "NexThought Monday—Why Did Vittana Close Down? The Real Question: Why Don't More Organizations Pull the Plug?" NextBillion, January 1, 2015, http://nextbillion.net /nexthought-monday-why-did-vittana-close-down.

114 **"[t]he donors who make the decision":** Ibid.

121 **television talk show host:** Stephanie Strom, "A Sweetheart Becomes Suspect; Looking Behind Those Kathie Lee Labels," *New York Times*, June 27, 1996, http://www.nytimes.com/1996/06/27/business/a-sweetheart-becomes -suspect-looking-behind-those-kathie-lee-labels.html?pagewanted=all.

129 **refugees are forbidden:** Ben Rawlence, "Story of Cities #44: Will Dadaab, the World's Largest Refugee Camp, Really Close?" *Guardian*, May 17, 2016, https://www.theguardian.com/cities/2016/may/17/story-of-cities-44-dadaab -kenya-worlds-largest-refugee-camp-closed.

133 **Mashable called it:** Ben Parr, "Social Good: iPhone App Lets You Give Work to Kenyan Refugees," Mashable, October 13, 2009, http://mashable .com/2009/10/13/give-work-iphone/#jgGtZ_OgWkqX.

133 **The terrorist organization:** Katherine Zimmerman, "Al Shabaab and the Challenges of Providing Humanitarian Assistance in Somalia," Critical Threats, September 8, 2011, http://www.criticalthreats.org/somalia /zimmerman-shabaab-challenges-humanitarian-assistance-somalia -september-8-2011.

133 **Then, on July 18:** KUNA, "Somalis Kidnap Kenyan Aid Workers," Kuwait News Agency, July 18, 2009, http://www.kuna.net.kw/ArticlePrintPage.aspx ?id=2014924&language=en.

135 **"Don't punk out and quit":** Ben Horowitz, "What's the Most Difficult CEO Skill? Managing Your Own Psychology," Andreessen Horowitz, March 31, 2011, http://www.bhorowitz.com/what_s_the_most_difficult_ ceo_skill_managing_your_own_psychology.

142 **It still affects approximately 2 million:** World Health Organization, "10 Facts on Obstetric Fistula," May 2014, http://www.who.int/features/factfiles /obstetric_fistula/en.

142 **the International Rescue Committee rape crisis center:** Nicholas Kristof, "In This Rape Center, the Patient Was 3," *New York Times*, October 8, 2011, http://www.nytimes.com/2011/10/09/opinion/sunday/kristof-In-This -Rape-Center-the-Patient-Was-3.html.

CHAPTER FOUR: HOME, AND THE FUTURE OF WORK

147 **Born and raised in the Mississippi River Delta:** Interview with Terrence Davenport, July 7, 2015.

150 **the world's fastest-growing crime:** State of California Department of Justice, "Human Trafficking," 2017, https://oag.ca.gov/human-trafficking.

152 **These companies have unprecedented revenue:** Rework America, *America's Moment: Creating Opportunity in the Connected Age* (New York: W. W. Norton & Company, 2015).

152 **globalization allows capital to move freely:** International Consortium of Investigative Journalists, "Giant Leak of Offshore Financial Records Exposes Global Array of Crime and Corruption," April 3, 2016, https://panamapapers .icij.org/20160403-panama-papers-global-overview.html.

152 **CEO pay, adjusted for inflation, went up:** Lawrence Mishel and Alyssa Davis, "Top CEOs Make 300 Times More Than Typical Workers," Economic Policy Institute, 2015, http://www.epi.org/publication/top-ceos-make-300 -times-more-than-workers-pay-growth-surpasses-market-gains-and-the -rest-of-the-0-1-percent/.

152 **Mississippi was the poorest state:** Catherine Rampell, "The Poorest States of America," *New York Times*, September 28, 2010, https://economix.blogs .nytimes.com/2010/09/28/the-poorest-states-of-america/?_r=0.

161 **stress in a pregnant woman:** Stephanie Pappas, "The Truth About How Mom's Stress Affects Baby's Brain," *LiveScience*, February 24, 2014, http:// www.livescience.com/43579-poverty-stress-infant-development.html.

161 **"'Free will' is the term":** Robert Sapolsky in conversation with Dacher Keltner, "Why and How We Act with Robert Sapolsky," City Arts & Lectures Conversations on Science Series, San Francisco, California, May 22, 2017.

162 **According to the Pew Research Center:** John B. Horrigan and Maeve Duggan, "Home Broadband 2015," Pew Research Center, December 21, 2015, http://www.pewInternet.org/2015/12/21/home-broadband-2015.

162 *Forbes* **named Merced:** Kurt Badenhausen, "America's Most Miserable Cities," *Forbes*, February 2, 2012, http://www.forbes.com/pictures/mli45h dlg/15-merced-calif/#1222800b7927.

162 **the most polluted city in the country:** Bryan Walsh, "The 10 Most Polluted Cities in America," *Time*, November 5, 2013, http://science.time.com /2013/11/05/the-10-most-polluted-cities-in-america/slide/1-merced-ca/.

163 **Rural Americans are more than twice:** Monica Anderson and Andrew Perrin, "13% of Americans Don't Use the Internet. Who Are They?" Pew Research Center, http://www.pewresearch.org/fact-tank/2016/09/07/some -americans-dont-use-the-internet-who-are-they/ (last updated September 7, 2016).

163 **More than thirty thousand people die:** Julia Franz, "In 2015 Alone,

33,000 Americans Died of an Opioid-Related Overdose. What's Fueling the Epidemic?," PRI, December 31, 2016, https://www.pri.org/stories/2016-12 -31/2015-alone-33000-americans-died-opioid-related-overdose-what -s-fueling-epidemic.

163 **The meagerly funded public schools:** Interview with Terrence Davenport, July 7, 2015.

164 **Due to the historically preferential bank loan practice:** Ibid.

166 **today there are public, private, and legislative:** Mark E. Myers, "Arkansas State Broadband Manager's Report," Arkansas Department of Information Systems, June 30, 2015, 11–15, http://www.arkleg.state.ar.us/assembly/2015 /Meeting%20Attachments/000/I14026/Exhibit%20H.19a%20-%20DIS%20 Semi-Annual%20Broadband%20Manager's%20Activities-Operations%20 Report%20ending%2006-30-15.pdf.

166 **the Federal Communications Commission:** Jake Williams, "FCC Grant Funds Rural Broadband in Arkansas and Beyond," *Statescoop*, September 3, 2015, http://statescoop.com/fcc-fund-helps-rural-arkansas-get-broadband.

166 **a revamped version:** Federal Communications Commission, "Connect America Fund (CAF)," last updated February 2, 2017, https://www.fcc.gov /general/connect-america-fund-caf.

166 **the carriers aren't expected:** "Windstream Gets Federal Funding to Expand Broadband in Rural Areas," *Arkansas News*, August 5, 2015, http:// www.arkansasnews.com/news/arkansas/windstream-gets-federal-funding -expand-broadband-rural-areas.

169 **the cost of center-based child care:** Child Care Aware of America, "Parents and the High Cost of Child Care: 2016—Arkansas," http://www.usa.child careaware.org/advocacy-public-policy/resources/reports-and-research /costofcare.

172 **Sara Blakely, the famous founder:** Robert Frank, "Billionaire Sara Blakely Says Secret to Success Is Failure," CNBC, October 16, 2013, http://www .cnbc.com/2013/10/16/billionaire-sara-blakely-says-secret-to-success-is -failure.html.

173 **Stanford biologist Robert Sapolsky:** Robert Sapolsky, *Behave: The Biology of Humans at Our Best and Worst* (New York: Penguin Press, 2017).

177 **Versions of this idea:** Ben Schiller, "Switzerland Will Hold the World's First Universal Basic Income Referendum," *Fast Company*, February 5, 2016, https://www.fastcoexist.com/3056339/switzerland-will-hold-the-worlds -first-universal-basic-income-referendum.

178 **School attendance goes up:** Give Directly, "Research on Cash Transfers," https://www.givedirectly.org/research-on-cash-transfers#cite16.

178 **Men's annual income:** Ibid.

CHAPTER FIVE: BEAUTY FOR HUMANITY: A NEW BUSINESS

182 **Using a combined:** Olivia Khalili, "Start with $10K, Grow the Pie, Sell to eBay—with Siddharth Sanghvi," Cause Capitalism, 2007, http://cause capitalism.com/world-of-good-sells-to-ebay/.

182 **"to demonstrate that you could":** R. P. Siegel, "eBay Acquisition: Has World of Good Sold Out?" Triple Pundit, March 8, 2010, http://www.triple pundit.com/2010/03/ebay-world-of-good.

182 **got into Whole Foods:** Ibid.

183 **hundreds of other companies:** Ibid.

185 **touted as a superfood:** John Colapinto, "Strange Fruit," *New Yorker,* May 30, 2011, http://www.newyorker.com/magazine/2011/05/30/strange-fruit -john-colapinto.

185 **triple bottom line:** Lianna Patch, "From Amazon Rainforest to California: How the Acai Got in the U.S.," *Brazil & US Biz,* April 2015, http:// brazilandusbiz.com/sambazon-acai-story.

186 **Luxury brand Chopard:** Eco-Age, "Chopard Launch the World's First Fairmined Watch," http://eco-age.com/chopard-launch-the-worlds-first -fairmined-watch.

186 **Missy and Scott Tannen:** Ellen Hoffman, "These Sheets Are One of the Biggest Viral-Marketing Successes of the Last Few Years—Here's Why," *Business Insider,* February 2, 2017, http://www.businessinsider.com/boll-and-branch -organic-cotton-fair-trade-bed-sheets-review-2016-10.

186 **Former U.S. presidents:** Kate Harrison, "The Secret to How This Company Is Getting Americans to Spend Millions on Fair Trade Luxury Bedding," *Forbes,* November 7, 2015, http://www.forbes.com/sites/kateharrison/2015 /11/07/the-secret-to-how-this-company-is-getting-americans-to-spend -millions-on-fair-trade-luxury-bedding/3/#4c83010a7d30.

186 **and Christina Aguilera:** Grant Cardone TV, "How Boll & Branch Is Disrupting a Sleepy Industry—Out Thinkers," YouTube, June 10, 2015, https:// www.youtube.com/watch?v=hUa1XC1KTm0.

186 **"It is not only":** Harrison, "The Secret."

187 **"If you really are serious":** Kevin Short, "Toms CEO Blake Mycoskie Offers Surprising Answer to His Critics," *Huffington Post,* November 11, 2013,

http://www.huffingtonpost.com/2013/11/14/toms-ceo-critics_n_4274637
.html.

188 **valued at $1.2 billion:** Douglas Macmillan, "Eyeglass Retailer Warby Parker
Is Valued at $1.2 Billion," *Wall Street Journal,* April 30, 2015, https://www
.wsj.com/articles/eyeglass-retailer-warby-parker-is-valued-at-1-2-billion
-1430444808.

188 **VisionSpring reports $280 million:** VisionSpring, "Our Impact," http://
visionspring.org.

188 **running ads that discourage:** Patagonia, "Don't Buy This Jacket, Black
Friday and the *New York Times,*" November 25, 2011, http://www.patagonia.
com/blog/2011/11/dont-buy-this-jacket-black-friday-and-the-new-york
-times/.

188 **paying workers an "additional premium":** Patagonia, "Patagonia and Social Responsibility in the Supply Chain: A History," http://www.patagonia
.com/corporate-responsibility-history.html.

188 **donating all $10 million:** Parija Kavilanz, "Patagonia's Black Friday Sales Hit
$10 Million—and Will Donate It All," *CNN Tech,* November 29, 2016, http://
money.cnn.com/2016/11/29/technology/patagonia-black-friday-donation-10
-million.

188 **"I've never respected the profession":** Yvon Chouinard, *Let My People Go
Surfing: The Education of a Reluctant Businessman* (New York: Penguin
Books, 2006), 1.

190 **"social and environmental performance":** B Corporation, "What Are B
Corps?," https://www.bcorporation.net/what-are-b-corps.

190 **"the world's largest multi-seller marketplace":** "World of Good Inc. Sells
Brand and Related Assets to eBay; Wholesale Division Acquired by Greater-
Good/Charity USA," *PR Newswire,* February 25, 2010, http://www.prnews
wire.com/news-releases/world-of-good-inc-sells-brand-and-related-assets
-to-ebay-wholesale-division-acquired-by-greatergoodcharity-usa-8533
4572.html.

190 **available to more than 84 million:** Richard Brewer-Hay, "Introducing
WorldofGood.com," eBay, September 3, 2008, https://www.ebayinc.com
/stories/news/introducing-worldofgoodcom.

191 **"A social business has":** Muhammad Yunus, *Building Social Business: The
New Kind of Capitalism That Serves Humanity's Most Pressing Needs* (New
York: Public Affairs, 2011), 121.

192 **in order to grow and scale:** Big Commerce, "Raven + Lily Triple Bottom Line Results," https://www.bigcommerce.com/case-study/raven-lily.

192 **Her partnerships with women:** Andrew Warner, "Raven + Lily, Turning Bullets into Jewelry," Mixergy, October 17, 2014, https://mixergy.com/interviews/kirsten-dickerson-raven-lily-interview.

199 **Before Hanli Prinsloo:** I AM WATER, "History," http://iamwaterfoundation.org/new-folder/history.

203 **Sephora has about twenty-three hundred stores:** Sephora, "About Us," http://www.sephora-me.com/en/sephora-saga/pid21.html.

204 **81.1 million by 2036:** Richard Fry, "Millennials Overtake Baby Boomers as America's Largest Generation," Pew Research Center, April 25, 2016, http://www.pewresearch.org/fact-tank/2016/04/25/millennials-overtake-baby-boomers.

205 **Consumers have indicated:** Elizabeth MacBride, "Jens Hainmueller: Will Consumers Actually Pay for Fair Trade?" Stanford Business, April 8, 2015, https://www.gsb.stanford.edu/insights/jens-hainmueller-will-consumers-actually-pay-fair-trade.

205 **When Walmart followed Yvon Chouinard's advice:** Seth Stevenson, "Patagonia's Founder Is America's Most Unlikely Business Guru," *WSJ Magazine,* http://www.wsj.com/articles/SB10001424052702303513404577352221465986612 (last updated April 26, 2012).

CHAPTER SIX: THE MOVEMENT IS NOW

208 **"Just as the commandment":** His Holiness Pope Francis, "Apostolic Exhortation *Evangelii Gaudium* of the Holy Father Francis to the Bishops, Clergy, Consecrated Persons and the Lay Faithful on the Proclamation of the Gospel in Today's World," Libreria Editrice Vaticana, 2013, http://w2.vatican.va/content/francesco/en/apost_exhortations/documents/papa-francesco_esortazione-ap_20131124_evangelii-gaudium.html.

210 **"Welfare projects, which meet":** Ibid.

211 **present to challenges:** Fortune + Time Global Forum, "Agenda Overview," http://www.fortuneconferences.com/global-forum-2016/agenda-overview.

212 **the recent controversy:** Negar Azimi, "The Gulf Art War," *New Yorker,* December 19 and 26, 2016, http://www.newyorker.com/magazine/2016/12/19/the-gulf-art-war.

212 **we are naturally empathetic:** Christopher Bergland, "The Neuroscience

of Empathizing with Another Person's Pain," *Psychology Today*, June 19, 2016, https://www.psychologytoday.com/blog/the-athletes-way/201606/the -neuroscience-empathizing-another-persons-pain.

216 **Bit Source in Kentucky:** Lauren Smiley, "Canary in the Code Mine," *Backchannel*, November 18, 2015, https://backchannel.com/canary-in-the-code -mine-903884eca853#.6lnh15jtb.

217 **Investigative journalist Seth Freed Wessler:** Interview with Seth Freed Wessler by Dave Davies, "Investigation into Private Prisons Reveals Crowding, Under-Staffing and Inmate Deaths," *Fresh Air*, NPR, August 25, 2016, http://www.npr.org/2016/08/25/491340335/investigation-into-private -prisons-reveals-crowding-under-staffing-and-inmate-de.

218 **the Justice Department announced:** Sally Q. Yates, "Reducing Our Use of Private Prisons" (U.S. Department of Justice memorandum, August 18, 2016), https://www.justice.gov/opa/file/886311/download.

218 **On the campaign trail:** George Joseph, "Why Private Prison Stocks Are Soaring," *CityLab*, November 14, 2016, http://www.citylab.com/crime/2016 /11/why-private-prison-stocks-are-soaring/507626.

218 **since the majority of prison inmates:** Christopher Petrella, "Ten Ways to Reduce the Prison Population in America," *Business Insider*, October 6, 2012, http://www.businessinsider.com/10-ways-to-reduce-us-prison-population -2012-10.

220 **about 672,768,000 for the average:** Walker Meade, "Every Breath You Take," *Herald-Tribune*, January 12, 2010, http://www.heraldtribune.com /news/20100112/every-breath-you-take.

222 **"The business of business":** Dan Pontefract, "Salesforce CEO Marc Benioff Says the Business of Business Is Improving the State of the World," *Forbes*, January 7, 2017, http://www.forbes.com/sites/danpontefract/2017/01/07/sales force-ceo-marc-benioff-says-the-business-of-business-is-improving-the -state-of-the-world/#13af8ad43180.

222 **"just 6% of consumers":** Cone Communications, "With CSR in Global Demand, Corporate Reputation Is at Stake, According to New Research from Cone Communications and Echo Research" (press release, May 22, 2013), http://www.conecomm.com/news-blog/2013-global-csr-study-release.

INDEX